LIVES *of the* TREES

ALSO BY DIANA WELLS

100 Flowers and How They Got Their Names
100 Birds and How They Got Their Names
My Therapist's Dog: Lessons in Unconditional Love

LIVES *of the* TREES

AN UNCOMMON HISTORY

DIANA WELLS

ILLUSTRATED BY HEATHER LOVETT

ALGONQUIN BOOKS OF CHAPEL HILL   2010

PUBLISHED BY

ALGONQUIN BOOKS OF CHAPEL HILL

POST OFFICE BOX 2225

CHAPEL HILL, NORTH CAROLINA 27515-2225

A DIVISION OF

WORKMAN PUBLISHING

225 VARICK STREET

NEW YORK, NEW YORK 10014

LIBRARY OF CONGRESS CATALOGING-IN-PUBLICATION DATA

WELLS, DIANA, [DATE]

LIVES OF THE TREES : AN UNCOMMON HISTORY /

DIANA WELLS ; ILLUSTRATED BY HEATHER LOVETT. — 1ST ED.

P. CM.

INCLUDES BIBLIOGRAPHICAL REFERENCES AND INDEX.

ISBN 978-1-56512-491-2

1. TREES — FOLKLORE.   2. TREES — MYTHOLOGY.   3. TREES — HISTORY.

I. LOVETT, HEATHER.   II. TITLE.

GR785.W45 2010

398.24'2 — DC22   2009031669

10 9 8 7 6 5 4 3 2 1

FIRST EDITION

In loving memory of

my father, Robert Coventry Grieg,

and my mother, Betty Burnford Brooke,

who loved, and planted, trees.

CONTENTS

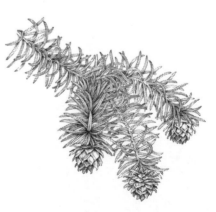

CONTENTS

Contents

ACKNOWLEDGMENTS

Once again I must thank the staff of the Krauskopf Memorial Library, particularly Janet Klaessig and Peter Kupersmith, for nearly a decade of professional assistance, enthusiasm, and friendship. For much-needed help in correcting mistakes, grateful thanks to Inea Bushnaq, Claire Wilson, and Vic Johnstone, who all did far more than should be expected from friends. As always, thanks to my lovely editor, Amy Gash; my publisher, Elisabeth Scharlatt, and my agent, Betsy Amster. Thanks above all, to my family — for all they do and all they are.

LIVES *of the* TREES

INTRODUCTION

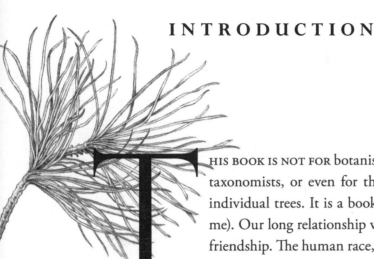

THIS BOOK IS NOT FOR botanists or dendrologists or taxonomists, or even for those want to identify individual trees. It is a book for nonexperts (like me). Our long relationship with trees is a story of friendship. The human race, we are told, emerged in the branches of trees and most of us have depended on them ever since, for food, shade, shelter, and fuel.

It's easy to find examples of humans revering trees. William Cowper marveled in 1786 about the Yardley Oak in an unfinished poem of the same name, calling the tree the "king of the woods":

> Thou wast a bauble once; a cup and ball,
> Which babes might play with . . .
>
> . . . .
>
> Time was, when settling on thy leaf a fly
> Could shake thee to the root, and time has been
> When tempests could not . . .

It's equally easy to find examples of humans destroying trees, although felling trees isn't necessarily merciless destruction. Agricultural and horticultural societies need cleared land to grow crops and make gardens. The kind of land on which flowers and vegetables grow best is often where trees also grow best. Even today, with all our technology, we not only need trees to counteract global warming but still rely on their products all the time. We seem to consume as much paper with our computer printouts as we did in our pre-"paperless" world. Anyone opening this book will be touching what was once a tree and very likely sitting on a wooden chair. Even "tree huggers" need their goods.

The conflict between use and reverence is not new. Because they are larger and older than we can ever hope to be, because they give shade, wood, food, and shelter, and because they stretch from earth to heaven, trees have been our gods since before recorded time. We know that ancient "pagan" people worshipped in sacred groves. That was why the Hebrew people were told (in Deuteronomy) that "thou shalt not plant thee a grove of any trees near unto the altar of the Lord thy God." In Judges, Gideon is ordered to destroy the altar of Baal "and cut down the grove that is by it." In *The Decline and Fall of the Roman Empire* (1787), Edward Gibbon described pre-Christian Germany where the "only temples . . . were dark and ancient groves," which, so he said, "impressed the mind with . . . a sense of religious horror."

In many cultures certain trees were selected as being especially holy and thought to have souls of their own, or souls of certain gods, or even of dead humans. In Greek mythology humans were quite often changed into trees to save them from a fate that the Victorians called "worse than death." The words "tree" and "truth" share the original Old English word root, *treow*. Trees are steadfast, linking the two realities of the dark earth and the bright sky.

The Tree of Life appears in cultures worldwide. Its roots were in the underworld and its branches supported the heavens, thus connecting death to salvation. The branches of the Tree of Life could be perches for the soul; sometimes the souls of children sat on them, waiting to be reborn. In Turkish lore, when a leaf dropped off the Tree of Life, it meant someone had died. The image of perching souls was used in the seventeenth century by Andrew Marvell, in his poem "The Garden":

> Casting the body's vest aside
> My soul into the boughs does glide;
> There like a bird it sits and sings
> Then wets and combs its silver wings.

In some cultures to cut down a sacred tree was even punishable by death. And felling a treasured tree was an irreversible way of hurting or insulting an enemy. In the biblical book of Deuteronomy, God's besieging armies are instructed to cut down the enemy's trees "if thou knowest that they be not for meat," sparing the fruit and nut trees because "the tree of the field is man's life." During the American Revolutionary War, the "Liberty Tree" in Newport, Rhode Island, was cut down by British troops as a gesture of dominance.

The most important trees in the Christian religion were those that had grown in the Garden of Eden. According to the Bible, every kind of fruit and nut tree was in the garden, as well as the famous Tree of Knowledge, the fruits of which were forbidden. The fruits of the Tree of Life, though, were not prohibited and eating them brought immortality, thus implying that the happiest state for humans would be perpetual life without "knowledge." Scholars, especially medieval scholars who worried about such things, could not decide how Adam and Eve could be "innocent" but also be truly man and wife, joined by God. In what sense were they connubial? One twelfth-century writer, Ernaldus of Bonneval, ingeniously suggested that there might have been *another* tree in the Garden of Eden "whose power could so temper man's nature that the genital organs would not more be moved to copulation than any other member." This interesting tree does not seem to have been identified as one we would recognize, although there were many nominations for the Tree of Knowledge (including the banana, apricot, and orange trees).

Fruit and nut trees have always yielded important food, but planting them was once considered a religious duty as well. In his *Spirituall Use of an Orchard* (1653), Ralph Austen wrote, "The World is a great Library and Fruit-trees are some of the Bookes wherein we may read and see plainly the Attributes of God." The trees themselves, he wrote, complained that people pluck their blossoms and fruit and then "go their waies; But speak never a word to us, neither do they understand what we say to them." Even if we don't believe we can talk to them (and lovers of trees have never excluded this possibility), trees in an orchard or garden have been tamed, brought in or planted to fit their environment. In Thailand spiritually unpredictable forest trees could not be transplanted into ordinary gardens because their unknown wild forces were feared. They could, however, be transplanted into temple or palace gardens, which were powerful enough to control them.

When settlers arrived in America, the endless forests both thrilled and frightened them. Much of Europe's trees had been used up, especially the largest trees needed for shipbuilding. But forests, as well as being valuable resources, were also scary wildernesses to be avoided. Indeed the word "forest" came from *foris* ("outside"), for they were places outside civilization where only outlaws lived. Trees were sent back to Britain by the shipload and the settlers cleared forests for farming, moving on when the soil was exhausted. Not everyone was blithe about this overuse. Colonel William Byrd, describing life in Virginia in the early eighteenth century, wrote a horrified account of a farmer casually hacking down a huge tree just so his cattle could graze on moss growing up the trunk.

Introduction

Even before the Revolution and the loss of American timber to Britain, John Evelyn had (in 1664) published *Sylva, or A Discourse of Forest-Trees and the Propagation of Timber in His Majesties Dominions,* in which he described all the trees he knew and the need to replant them. "Paradise itself," he wrote, was a "Sacred Grove planted by God himself and given to Man." He claimed that "nothing contributes more to Men's Long Lives than the planting of many trees," and that "you never shall know what he [a tree] is worth till he be dead." Evelyn successfully persuaded his contemporaries to plant thousands of saplings.

When William Penn founded Philadelphia he had specified that for every five acres of felled woodland, one should be left uncut. The city was to be a "greene country towne." This didn't happen. By the end of the eighteenth century, insurance companies were claiming that trees in front of houses were a fire risk and refusing to insure any house in Philadelphia with trees near it. In 1782 an article titled "The Oration of the Post" was published by Francis Hopkinson. The "post" was one of the tall wooden columns in the Senate building that (in the story) suddenly spoke out on behalf of the city's trees, claiming to be "a standing member" and one of the "principal supporters" of the House, with a right to voice opinions. "Trees as well as men are capable of enjoying the rights of citizenship and therefore ought to be protected in those rights." This oration had results: only two years later the Mutual Fire Insurance Company began accepting houses with trees in front of them, even adopting a tree as its symbol.

Trees, unlike many other staples of our lives, can be renewed. In medieval Europe trees were kept going for centuries by coppicing—that is, cutting them down and allowing harvestable shoots to grow up around the stumps. Not all trees can be treated this way. Big trees, however, were often depleted for defense purposes, to build fleets and make weapons. The eventual use of metal weapons didn't help much because charcoal was needed to smelt the metal. War, then as now, is a strain on the world's resources.

We are frequently reminded these days how important trees are to the health of our world. It's even suggested that that we might counteract the effect of carbon emissions by planting a tree, for example, whenever we take an airplane trip. It would require a lot of small saplings to counteract our very large global footprint, and too often we assume that a grid of conifers is a true replacement of an ancient wood we have destroyed. But planting a tree *is* a small way of saving a bit of our planet; it is also a kind of prayer. A famous saying of the first-century Jewish sage Rabban Yochanan ben Zakkai was, "If you should happen to be holding a sapling in your hand when they tell you that the Messiah has arrived, first plant the sapling and then go out and greet the Messiah."

Today, most of us are more aware of the importance of trees than we were in the past, but actually distinguishing individual trees isn't really essential to our lives. Trees are no longer intimate friends with their own names. It's no longer necessary to know which trees make the best firewood, yield good dye, provide nuts or fruit, or don't rot when used for building. Now we casually buy their products in supermarkets or lumberyards and heat our homes with fossil fuels. We can even live on a street named for a particular tree and not be able to identify the tree itself.

This once would have been unthinkable. When we read stories or poems from before our times, trees are called by their names, with the assumption that the reader will know exactly what is meant. Shakespeare's readers were familiar with the trees he frequently mentions, and so were Wordsworth's. Sometimes to recognize a tree could even be consequential. In the apocryphal book of Daniel two elders spy on the beautiful Susannah when she bathes in the fountain. These frustrated old men try to exact their revenge on Susannah for refusing to submit to them by claiming they had seen her making love with a young man under a tree in the garden. Susannah is condemned to die until Daniel questions the elders separately, and each describes a different tree under which the alleged seduction took place — one saying it was a "mastic tree," the other saying it was an "evergreen oak." It was assumed that had the tree actually existed, they would both have been able to name it correctly. In the end the elders, not Susannah, are executed. No judge these days would depend on a witness identifying the tree under which a crime took place!

One of the compensations of growing older is to look upward through the branches of a tree that we once planted as a tiny sapling. I have planted many trees around our house in Pennsylvania and still love each one of them. Some now as high as the house were unpacked from small boxes or even brought home from roadsides in the basket of my bicycle.

My husband continues to plant trees no higher than his own knee, and every time he does so I am reminded of a story about him as a very small boy, told to me, forty or so years ago, by my mother-in-law. He was, she said, in a school play, and she was to come and see him, but he did not tell her what part he was playing. She went. There he was, at the back of the stage dressed in green, waving his arms and smiling hugely. "He was so cute," chuckled his mother. "As proud as if he had the main part — and he was just a tree in the background." Cute, indeed, but maybe right, too? Perhaps he *was* playing the most important role on that stage — and on many other stages, as well.

ACACIA

Acacias are distinguished by their sharp thorns, and their name is derived from the Greek *akis*, "a sharp point." The thorns give them some protection from animals, but as we remember from *Winnie-the-Pooh*'s Eeyore munching on thistles, sharp points don't deter all browsers. The acacia's nutrious foliage and seedpods are eaten by camels, gazelles, and giraffes in the wild, as well as collected for feeding domestic animals. Acacias are legumes, or members of the pea family, and are widespread in desert regions of the Middle East, Africa, Australia, and South America. They can survive in very dry conditions because their roots have nitrogen-fixing nodules attached to them, enabling the trees to grow in poor soil (and even enrich it).

The largest trees of the biblical desert and Mount Sinai were acacias, and their wood was used to make the Ark of the Covenant on which incense was burned. The acacia, called *shittim* in Hebrew, is either the *Acacia nilotica* ("from the Nile"), or *A. seyal* (from the Arabic for "torrent"). Acacias often grow in *wadis* ("dry riverbeds"), which become torrents in the rainy season. The former are also called Babul trees (from the Sanskrit name) in Africa. These trees have paired spines that are one and a half inches long. Sometimes holes at the base of the thorns are enlarged by insects, leaving apertures through which the winds blow eerie music and giving them the name "whistling trees." Ants often live in acacia trees and suck their sap.

THE WOOD OF THE CATCLAW ACACIA IS SO HARD AND DENSE THAT NAILS WERE ONCE MADE OF IT TO HOLD SHIPS TOGETHER.

The Middle Eastern acacias are frequent hosts for the parasitic mistletoe *Loranthus acaciae*, which has brilliant flame-colored flowers. Some scholars think this was the biblical "flame of fire" rising out of a thorn-bush but not consuming it that convinced Moses he was standing on "holy ground" in the presence of God (Exodus 3). Others prefer a less botanical explanation. Whatever one believes, acacias were widely used in biblical times, for their dense, hard wood, their leaves and pods, and a gum that exuded from their bark. This was called gum arabic and was popular as a medicine. When dissolved in water it makes a mucilaginous substance thought to be soothing to inflamed organs. Until quite recently the U.S. postal service used gum arabic on the back of stamps.

Acacias grow in southwestern America and Mexico. The catclaw acacia, whose thorns are just like sharp extended cat's claws, has the botanical name *A. greggi*, derived from the nineteenth-century explorer and botanist Josiah

Gregg, who died after being lost in the woods. The wood of the catclaw acacia is so hard and dense that nails were once made of it to hold ships together.

The sweet acacia, *A. farnesiana*, is another American acacia. It was sent home to Europe in the seventeenth century by Spanish missionary priests and was grown in the garden of Cardinal Odoardo Farnese (who gave it his name). In his *Sylva, or A Discourse of Forest-Trees* (1664) the Englishman John Evelyn wrote that "the French have lately brought in the *Virginian Acacia* which exceedingly adorns their *Walks*." Soon the acacia's intensely fragrant flowers were being used to make perfume and, even today, "cassie" is a basic ingredient of French perfumes.

Acacias grow abundantly in Australia where they are called mimosas (or wattles), because of their foliage, which resembles the foliage of a plant from the Barbados, the *Mimosa pudica*, or sensitive plant (which isn't a tree). This name, meaning "shy mimic," comes from the Greek *mimos* ("mimic") and refers to the way the sensitive plant's leaves shrink when touched. The leaves of acacia trees are less sensitive, though they do droop at night or in wet weather. The leaves of the pseudoacacias, or "false acacias" (*see* Locust), are similar in form and habit. The silk tree (*Albizia*) has similar flowers and foliage and is also called a mimosa. Its botanical name is for the Italian Filippo degli Albizzi, who introduced the tree from Africa in 1749.

Early Australian settlers used acacia trees to make fences and walls. The wood is tough and pliable and resists insects. They called the trees wattle trees after the woven wattle fences of Britain. A wattle is something twisted together like a fence or basket and it came to mean a bag as well. This in turn was applied to the baglike growth under a turkey's neck! The word "wallet" is similarily derived, with the "l" reversed with the "t."

Wattles are important Australian trees. The bark is used for tanning and the wood is excellent for building. They are also very beautiful. Because sheep prefer to graze on other plants, mimosas have become too abundant in some parts of Australia. The gold wattle, *A. pycnantha* ("densely flowered"), is named for its myriad golden flowers. These are like pom-poms, composed of tufts of sepals. The gold wattle is the official floral emblem of Australia. Standing beneath the millions of sweet-smelling golden powder puffs in spring is a heady experience. It couldn't take much more to convince you that you were standing on holy ground.

ALDER

When the pale bark of the alder is cut the sap turns blood red. This, unsurprisingly, has given the tree a special place in human imagination. It may also have been partly because of where alders could live that sinister powers were attributed to them in times past. A copse of alders, called a carr (from the Old Norse *kjarr*), can grow where other trees can't: in boggy soil that is low in oxygen. They have nodules on their roots containing a nitrogen-fixing bacterium called *Frankia alni* (*alnus* is the Latin name for "alder"). These alni nodules are similar to the nitrogen-fixing nodules in the legume family but technically aren't related. Alders not only live where other trees can't but, like legumes, they enrich the soil. They help reduce pollution because they are able to absorb metals into their leaves. The wind-pollinated catkins reproduce abundantly. The female flowers become conelike and remain on the tree all winter. The seeds can float.

Boggy marshes swirl with misty miasmas that can be very suggestive. In Goethe's famous 1780 ballad, the *Erlkonig*, or "Alder King," a young child rides with his father through swampy woods and hears the Alder King trying to lure him away. But his father, saying the boy hears only the rustling of leaves and sees only the moonlight on the pale tree trunks, does not listen to his son's fears. When they get to their destination, however, he finds with horror that *In seinen Armen das Kind war tot*, "the child in his arms is dead." The Alder King has got him. There were also legends of alder women—beautiful young women who lured and trapped men, then turned into gnarled old hags. These reflected the alder tree itself, which when young has smooth pale bark that becomes black and fissured with age.

The European or black alder, inspiring these Germanic legends, is *Alnus glutinosa*, for its "sticky" young leaves, which were once used to sweep out houses in spring. Fleas, it was hoped, would be trapped onto the sticky surfaces. In Old High German the tree was *elo*, or *elawer*, which can mean "reddish yellow" and refers to the strange coloration of the sap. In Anglo-Saxon the alder was *alor*; the letter "d" was added later. Although the European alder is a northern tree, some cultures believed, because of its bloodlike sap, that it was the "crucifixion tree" from which Christ's cross was made. Other trees, for a variety of reasons, were thought to share this curse and, like the alder, were not always native to the Middle East!

SOME CULTURES BELIEVED, BECAUSE OF ITS BLOODLIKE SAP, THAT IT WAS THE "CRUCIFIXION TREE" FROM WHICH CHRIST'S CROSS WAS MADE.

The wood, the bark, and the leaves of the alder tree were all at different times and places thought to have healing properties. Peter Kalm, sent by Carl Linnaeus in 1747 to explore North America and look for plants that might be useful to send back to Sweden, published an account of his experiences called *Travels in North America*. In it he wrote, "A Swedish inhabitant of America told me that he had cut his leg to the very bone . . . he had been advised to boil the alder bark and wash the wound often with the water . . . and had soon got his leg healed, though it had been very dangerous at first."

Alder wood is rich in protein and very attractive to woodworms, so it's not much good for ordinary building. But it is the best possible wood for *underwater* construction because it doesn't rot in water. Much of Venice still stands on pilings of alder wood. The wood was also used for clogs. Like willow and birch, alder wood makes charcoal that is especially useful for manufacturing gunpowder. Alder groves were sometimes planted near gunpowder factories and coppiced, or cut to a stump to allow harvestable shoots to grow up again.

The largest American alder is the red alder, or *A. rubra.* Alders also grow in Central and South America as well as Asia, Siberia, and northern Africa. They can be large trees or shrubby bushes. Sometimes the American winterberry is called a black alder although it is really a deciduous holly. It has wonderful red berries in winter. Another garden shrub, *Clethra alnifolia,* commonly called sweet pepper bush, isn't an alder either, though *Klethra* is the Greek for "alder;" this plant has "leaves like an alder." In the 1730s John Bartram sent species of both these "alders" to his friend and correspondent Peter Collinson in London (*see* Bald Cypress). Collinson complained that "to my great loss some prying, knowing people looked into the cases, and took . . . the *Spirea Alni folio."* That's what *he* thought. Perhaps they were spirited away by the *Erlkonig?* Alders are powerful and even "alder-leaved" plants might perhaps have a bit of magic of their own.

ALMOND

"My tears would be enough to water this dry land," wrote the eleventh-century Arab king al-Mu'tamid, "but they are dyed with blood." This poet-king had been ousted from the Caliphate of Córdoba by Berber conquerors and exiled with his wife to Morocco, where he died. The court at Córdoba had been one of the last glories of Moorish Spain, full of poetry, feasting, and flowers. Al-Mu'tamid first spotted his wife, I'timad al-Rumaykiyah, washing clothes in a stream. The king indulged her every whim. One day he found her weeping with disappointment because a few snowflakes had fallen around Córdoba and then melted. The king immediately promised Rumaykiyah snow every winter. He had all the hills around the city planted with almond trees, whose snowy blossoms appear in earliest spring on the bare branches. So, until the couple was sent to Morocco, Rumaykiyah had "snow" every winter. In the deserts of

Morocco she had to earn money for her family by spinning. No wonder al-Mu'tamid wept floods of tears at the memory of the hills of almond trees under the new rulers.

Almond trees are closely related to peach trees and share a common ancestor, but peaches bear edible fruit while almonds don't. The early spring almond blossom is easily killed by frost; peaches bloom later and we eat their juicy fruit. The almond "nut" is actually the kernel of the hard, green (and undigestable) almond fruit.

Almond kernels are of two kinds, from different trees. There are sweet almonds (*Prunus amygdalis dulcis*) and bitter almonds (*P. amygdalis amara*). *Prunus* means "plum." Both contain almond oil with varying amounts of amygdalin. Amygdalin breaks down in water to form hydrocyanic (cyanide), also called prussic, acid. The oil of bitter almonds contains large amounts of amygdalin, which also dissolves in saliva, with deadly consequences if ingested. That's why detectives in fiction smell the nostrils of corpses to detect the scent of almonds and, if it's present, deduce that the victim was poisoned with cyanide. Bitter almonds aren't served salted at cocktails (even by would-be murderers) because they are unpalatable anyway. We do use their oil, though, for cosmetics and flavoring essence, after it's been separated from the amygdalin.

Humans must have sorted out almonds early on because they were being eaten in the Bronze Age. They probably originated in Persia. We know they were enjoyed in ancient Greece, where they got their name *amygdale*. Some etymologists say the Sumerian *ama ga* ("great mother") was the origin of the name and that the tree was correspondingly sacred. The Romans called almonds Greek nuts. The English name comes from the French *amande*.

In medieval Britain almonds were used a great deal, even though the fruits don't ripen there. As it was a nonmeat product, the monks could drink almond "milk" (made from powdered almonds in water) on fast days. There was also a tradition that a few almonds taken before drinking would prevent drunkenness. The oil was used medicinally. Gerard's *Herball* of 1597, revised by Thomas Johnson in 1633 (*see* Banana) claimed that almond oil is good for urinary complaints and that it "slackens the passages of the urine and maketh them glib and and slipperie . . . especially if a few scorpions be drowned and steeped therein."

The thirteenth-century abbot of Cirencester, Alexander Neckham, called almonds *Noyz de l'almande, nux Phyllidis.* In this Greek legend Phyllis mourned her lover, Demophon, who hadn't come home from the war, fearing he had been killed or had deserted her. She died of grief, and the gods, in pity, turned her into a tree. Then Demophon returned, too late, only to find a tree instead of his beloved. He flung his arms around the tree trunk and its naked branches burst into flower. It was the first almond tree.

This and other legends gave the tree an association with rebirth. Naked almond twigs put into warm water will burst into blossom with astonishing rapidity. That's what must have happened when Aaron's rod, put on the Tabernacle of the Lord with the other eleven tribal rods, "brought forth buds, and bloomed blossoms, and yielded almonds." So Aaron became "head of the house of their fathers" (Numbers, 17). The biblical name for the almond was *shaked,* or "awake tree," because the tree wakes up so early, promising spring in January in the Middle East.

Most of our almonds are grown in California these days. Popular varieties include Nonpareil (meaning "without equal") and Jordan almonds. Jordan almonds don't come from Jordan; the name comes from the French *jardin,* or "garden," where almonds grow. The Italian name for almond is *mandorla,* and this is also the name of the almond-shaped border around religious paintings—especially depictions of the Ascension of the Virgin Mary, the almonds being a symbol of hope.

APPLE

The Adam's apple is a part of the male anatomy that was supposed to have been created when Adam bit the apple offered him by Eve and a piece stuck in his throat forevermore—a perpetual reminder of his wife's (and his) wrongdoing.

Apples are not native to the Middle East, and anyway the juicy tempting fruit we know now did not exist in Old Testament times, not to mention Edenic times. The "fruit" mentioned in the Bible was *tappuach* in Hebrew, not any specific fruit but called an apple by Western translators because apples were common by then.

Our domestic apples are probably crosses between crab apples and wild apples from an area near the Caucasian mountains, brought west by traders or animals. Crab apples, widespread in Europe, Asia, and America, have been eaten since ancient times. Crab apples, or scrab apples (an Old English name for them), are extremely sour and can only be consumed cooked or fermented.

A crabby person is sour and bad tempered. "Apple" comes from the Old Icelandic *epli*, later the Gaelic *ubhal*. The European crab apple is *Malus sylvestris* ("wild").

Our domestic apple is *M. domestica*. By classical times eating-apples were well known. Pliny the Elder described about two dozen varieties. The Latin for "fruit" was *pomum* and the Roman goddess Pomona was responsible for looking after the fruits of the earth. The French for "apple" is *pomme*. *Malus* also means "evil," and a popular medieval pun combined both meanings to tell the story of Adam and Eve's "evil apple." Apple seeds contain poisonous cyanide. Poisonous mistletoe, which from ancient times had sinister associations, grows readily on apple trees and was sometimes associated with them. During the ancient ritual of wassailing, which took place at Christmastime, apple trees were sprinkled with cider and cakes were left as offerings to protect the trees from harm.

By the time the Romans left Britain, the domestic apple was well established. Most early Christian monasteries had their own orchard where apples were grown for eating, medicine, and cider. A healing ointment made of apples, rose water, and pig fat was called a *pomatum*, and we still use the word "pomade" for oil used to slick down the hair — not fashionable these days but once used by most smart gentlemen.

Early apples grown from seed, or pips, were called pippins, and the seedling was unpredictable. To ensure the same apple as the parent, the tree has to be grafted. The Etruscans practiced grafting, although not all cultures accepted the technique. The Jewish religion forbade it, but the Christian church encouraged grafting because it symbolized attaching new members of the church onto the Tree of Christ. Meddling with God's design by hybridization, though, was the subject of theological debate in Britain until almost the nineteenth century.

Apple

Named apples, particularly *patented* named apples, didn't have any importance in the past, and consequently there were literally hundreds of varieties grown by individuals. In 1629 the English botanist John Parkinson wrote *Paradisi in Sole Paradisus Terrestris* (*Paradisi in Sole*, or "Park in Sun," forms a pun on his own name). In it he wrote, "The sorts of Apples are so many, and infinite almost as I may say, that I cannot give you the names of all." Certain apples, however, gained a particularly favorable reputation and were sometimes named for the place where they grew or for the grower. The earliest record of this seems to have been the Roman 'Sceptian' apple, named for a freed slave who grew it. By the Middle Ages popular apples in Britain included the 'Pearmain' (shaped like a pear), and the head-shaped 'Costard' apple, which got the name from the medieval slang for head, *coster*.

Parkinson also mentioned a "yellowish green" apple called 'Flower of Kent.' This was said to have grown in the garden of Isaac Newton's mother in Lincolnshire, whence Newton fled to avoid the plague of 1666. Apparently he really did sit under an apple tree, and an apple dropping from the tree started Newton thinking about the force of gravity. There does not seem to be a record of the apple actually falling onto his head.

When settlers went to North America they took apple seeds with them. The Spaniards had not established apples in the New World because it was generally too warm where they settled. Apples need a cold period to set fruit. The first known orchard in North America was planted in 1623, by William Blackstone, or Blaxton, on Beacon Hill in Boston. He was an Episcopalian and he didn't stay long, because first his followers went back to Europe and then a Puritan settlement made him feel unwelcome. So he moved to Rhode Island, but the 'Blaxton Yellow Sweeting' remained in the Beacon Hill orchard, doing even better when honeybees were imported shortly afterward to aid pollination. The honeybees spread rapidly across the continent and were known by the Indians as white man's flies.

Apples flourished in America, hybridizing with native crab apples to make many new varieties. The famous Johnny Appleseed (or Chapman) carried seeds as far west as Illinois. He thought grafting "cruel" to the trees and collected leftover seeds from cider presses. Apple cider was widely drunk and most farms had a press.

🍃 THE "FRUIT" MENTIONED IN THE BIBLE WAS *TAPPUACH* IN HEBREW, NOT ANY SPECIFIC FRUIT BUT CALLED AN APPLE BY WESTERN TRANSLATORS BECAUSE APPLES WERE COMMON BY THEN.

In the nineteenth century the naming of apples began to be taken seriously. In about 1811, John McIntosh discovered a chance seedling in Ontario and made grafts from it. The 'Red Delicious' was found on the farm of Jess Hiatt in Iowa in about 1872. He called it Hiatt's Hawkeye until it was bought by the Stark Brothers nursery and remarketed as the Delicious. The 'Golden Delicious' was another chance seedling from Virginia. Stark Brothers named it not because it was related but because 'Red Delicious' was so popular.

The word "apple" has entered our language in many ways. We give an apple to the teacher if we want to make a good impression, but stupid people are "apple-knockers" (someone who knocks apples off a tree). A "rotten apple" can destroy a whole barrelful of good ones, just as one person "good to the core" can save a situation. "Core" comes from the French *coeur*, or "heart." The "apple of our eye" is someone we treasure and love.

The biblical fruit, described as "good for food" and "pleasant to the eyes," certainly applies to apples. Scholars have endeavored to discover what the Edenic fruit really was, if the garden was in another location (where apples grow better) or if it existed at all. Apples are tasty, beautiful, and good for you, too—that's surely enough to make them special, whether or not they once grew in Paradise.

APRICOT

The apricot's botanical name is *Prunus armeniaca*, which means "plum from Armenia," but apricots originated in China, where they were cultivated from ancient times for their blossoms, fruits, and kernels. They most likely traveled to the Middle East, along with other Chinese commodities such as silk (*see* Mulberry), and Alexander the Great might have brought them home.

The ancient world was familiar with apricots; their common name probably comes from the Arabic *al-barquq*. When they were grown in Spain by the Moors their Spanish name became *albaricoque*. But apricots ripen early, and some etymologists suggest that their name perhaps comes from the Latin *praecox* ("early") and *apricus* ("ripe").

Apricot trees need a temperate climate, with a cool winter to set the fruit but no early frosts that kill the blossoms. They grow well in the Middle East and were widespread in the biblical land of Palestine. Some scholars propose that the apple of the Bible was actually an apricot, which would be more likely found in the Garden of Eden than an apple (*see* Apple).

The Old English name *apricock* might have had a connection with the part of his anatomy that Adam discovered (or was shown by Eve). In *A Midsummer*

Night's Dream, Titania bids her fairies feed Bottom with "Apricocks and dewberries," perhaps emphasizing for Shakespeare's bawdy audiences some of the difficulties of a love affair between a fairy and a donkey.

Apricots were introduced to Britain from Italy by Henry VIII, but even if the king himself was lusty, the trees did not flourish. They don't thrive on the East Coast of North America either. But in California, where they were brought by missionaries, they are an important crop. Like other soft fruits, they don't travel well and are mostly canned or dried. Dried Hunza apricots are a staple food of the Hunza people of mountainous northern Pakistan, whose exceptional longevity is sometimes attributed to apricots, which contain a hundred times more vitamin A than any other fruit. Some cultures extract oil from the kernels presumably with caution for they contain toxic prussic acid (*see* Almond).

THE OLD ENGLISH NAME *APRICOCK* MIGHT HAVE HAD A CONNECTION WITH THE PART OF HIS ANATOMY THAT ADAM DISCOVERED (OR WAS SHOWN BY EVE).

The Confucian "ideal" garden included an apricot orchard of cultivated trees. Wild apricot trees no longer grow in China. In the nineteenth century, however, the Lazarist monk, Abbé Armand David (*see* Handkerchief Tree) was able to collect apricot seeds from the Peking Mountains and send them back to the Jardin des Plantes in Paris, where they grew. At first the trees were called after him, *Armeniaca davidiana.* Abbé David, who traveled throughout China, was the first Westerner to describe the panda. The Chinese, he wrote, called it "'child of the mountains' because its voice imitates that of a child." David did much for botany but it is sad to read about his little panda. Its stomach, he wrote in his diary, "was full of leaves." Of course there is only one way he could have discovered that.

The Japanese "umeboshi plum," available in American health food stores as well as being popular in Japan, is believed to promote a long and healthy life. It is really an apricot, dried and salted, and has, appropriately, a shelf life of a hundred years or more.

ASH

The wood of ash trees is tough and pliable but also splinters when it breaks. Sometimes the ash tree was called the widow-maker, from the way the tree could suddenly shatter unexpectedly when cut and kill the woodcutter. The botanical name *Fraxinus* is from its Latin name. Some etymologists think this derives from *frango* ("I break") because of the way the wood breaks.

The Anglo-Saxon name *aesc* referred to both the tree and a spear made from it. The Danish was *ask* and the Dutch and German *Esche*. Where strong, pliable staves were needed, ash wood was used. Virgil wrote that the Amazon warriors used ash wood spears. In *Coriolanus*, Shakespeare (as usual) described ash staves with more economy, accuracy, and beauty than any of us could: "My grain'd Ash an hundred times hath broke / And starr'd the moon with splinters."

Ash trees are common in both the Old and New Worlds. Many place names, such as Ashdown or Ashwood, reflect the presence of ash trees. Ashes grow quickly but can halt growth until light is available to them. They can live hundreds of years or indefinitely if coppiced (*see* Alder), as they often were to make ash poles. The mature trees, with their long pinnate leaves, cast only a light shade. The leaflets forming the long, feathery leaf are uneven and it was supposed to be "lucky" to find an ash leaf with its leaflets opposite and even.

Ash is easily bent when steamed. American Indians made splint baskets out of ash, and ash walking sticks with bent handles are still popular. The wood is excellent firewood, too, burning well even when green. In 1664 John Evelyn published *Sylva, or A Discourse of Forest-Trees* as part of an effort to manage Britain's dwindling forests. He wrote that ash logs were particularly "fitted" for warming "Ladies chambers."

The ash tree's single-bladed seed, known as a samara (*see* Maple) was called an *avis-lingua* ("bird's tongue") by the Romans because of its shape. The seed is edible but not, as far as we know, a Roman delicacy, like the lark's tongue or the tongues of other small birds.

Perhaps because they grow so high and their roots grow down so deep, ash trees were often sacred trees in the past. The Norse Tree of Life, or Yggdrasil, was traditionally an ash tree. Its top touched heaven and its roots penetrated the underworld — and a squirrel ran up and down it to report on how things were going in the two worlds. The Norse god Odin created the first man, Ask, from an ash. (The first woman was created from an elm.) Ash trees are members of the olive family (along with privet and lilac).

The magic properties attributed to ash trees persisted until the nineteenth century. They were supposed to repel snakes. In his 1577 *Gardener's Labyrinth*, Thomas Hyll wrote that snakes "are mightily displeased and sorest hate the Ash-tree, insomuch the serpents neither to the morning nor the longest evening shadows of it will draw near, but rather shun the same and flie far off." He described an experiment conducted by Pliny the Elder whereby a snake was enclosed in a circle of ash leaves and a fire was also lit in the center of the circle. The snake, it was reported, rather than crossing the ash leaf barrier crept to the fire "where she perished." Not surprisingly ash leaves were used to cure snakebites: they were to be mixed with a "pleasant white wine," which would achieve a "happy success."

Long after Hyll's time, parents were still curing children with "ruptures" (or hernias) by "passing" them through a cleft ash tree. The ash tree was split and held open with wedges and the child was passed through the cleft several times. Afterward the tree was bound together, and if the cleft fused properly, it was thought the child would also be cured. In *Letters from Selbourne*, Gilbert White described this procedure, in a letter dated January 8, 1776, adding, "We have several persons, now living in this village who, in their childhood, were supposed to be healed by this superstitious ceremony." Superstition or not, the nineteenth-century writer Reverend Hilaric Friend gravely told his readers that a child whose "parents were intelligent, respectable people" was "passed through" a cleft ash on January 18, 1876, and they were "perfectly satisfied that a cure had been wrought."

The European, or common, ash is *Fraxinus excelsior*, or "taller." (*Celsus* means "lofty.") The most widespread American ash is the white ash, or *F. americana*. Mark Catesby sent a white ash back to England. Catesby is best known for his drawings, predominantly of birds, which he then engraved and published in the *Natural History of Carolina, Georgia, Florida and the Bahama Islands*. (To celebrate the publication he got married, in 1747, when he was sixty-five years old.) Other American ash trees include the *F. pennsylvanica*, or green ash (for its bright green shoots), and *F. nigris*, or black ash (which like the European common ash has black leaf buds). The prickly ash, sometimes called the toothache tree, isn't an ash but a kind of citrus (the fruits of which were once chewed to alleviate toothache).

🌿 ITS TOP TOUCHED HEAVEN AND ITS ROOTS PENETRATED THE UNDERWORLD—AND A SQUIRREL RAN UP AND DOWN IT TO REPORT ON HOW THINGS WERE GOING IN THE TWO WORLDS.

In China the native ash, called by us the Chinese ash, was known as the Bailashu, or white wax tree. It was cultivated for the production of a white wax with which insects coated the leaves. A seventeenth-century Jesuit priest, Father Gabriel de Magalhães, traveled in China and described this wax as "the most beautiful, the clearest and the whitest that ever was seen."

Gilbert White mentioned another ash, which he called the shrew ash. This wasn't a different species but a common ash that had had a hole bored into it, into which was closed up, alive, a "poor devoted shrew." The tree was then used to make poultices, which were applied to the legs of cattle, supposedly paralyzed from a shrew mouse running up them. Presumably this must have worked *sometimes* or else it wouldn't have been done.

From spears to baseball bats, from snakes to shrews, from heaven to hell, the ash tree has been with us a long time. We don't use it, or believe in it in all the ways we once did, but when all is said we are probably going to agree with Gilbert White. After dismissing the "superstitions" connected with the tree, he concluded that ash trees "are pleasing objects." They certainly are that.

ASPEN

S haking and quaking in trees, as in religious sects, is not necessarily a sign of weakness. Aspens, with their tremulous fluttering leaves, are some of the toughest trees on earth. Indeed, the very trembling of their leaves is a strategy to avoid damage from gusty winds in the exposed places where aspens so often grow. Aspens can live in barren, mountainous regions, as well as many other places. Their heart-shaped leaves are borne at the end of long, flattened stalks so that instead of resisting breezes and breaking, they bend with them.

In autumn the aspen's leaves turn golden yellow and fall to the ground, exposing the delicate branches. If the parent tree is destroyed during the winter, its extensive root system can put up new suckers as soon as conditions are favorable again. Unless the roots themselves are damaged, aspens can survive fire, ice storms, or mutilation. The root system often extends many yards beyond the parent tree, putting out new suckers that in turn grow more roots. Aspen groves of genetically identical trees beg the question of whether such clumps are really "one" tree. Sometimes they cover acres of ground and if they are considered to be a single tree, that would make them the largest living organisms we know—and probably some of the oldest, too.

Aspens are a kind of poplar, their botanical name being *Populus tremula* (the European aspen), or *P. tremuloides* (the American aspen). The Chinese aspen is *P. adenopoda* ("gland footed"). Ironically the "trembling poplars," so tough and widespread, were associated with timidity—and sometimes with shame. Even though the trees were surely trembling long before the birth of Christ, Christian legend said that the aspen was a proud, sturdy tree that grew on the road to Calvary. When the crucifixion procession passed by, it refused to bow down and was punished by having to tremble in shame thereafter. There is an almost identical North American Indian legend, which describes the tree being punished for refusing to bow down to the Great Spirit.

The American Indians called the aspen noisy leaf. The fluttering, rustling leaves can be heard distinctly from quite a way off. Even though aspen trees are either male or female, an old European name for the tree was woman's tongue. Gerard's revised *Herball* (*see* Banana) explained, "Poets and some others report" that the leaves are like "woomens tongs . . . which seldom cease wagging." Both men and women afflicted with "palsy" would hang snippets of their hair on the branches and ask the tree to take over their own "trembling."

Aspen wood was sometimes used for arrows and in 1416 the English parliament passed a strange law forbidding the use of "asp" wood, except for making arrows, and imposed a fine of a hundred shillings if it was used for clogs. The law was repealed in 1464 because "very much Asp Timber there is." The name asp, used by these fifteenth-century lawmakers, was the name of the tree, deriving from *ösp* in Icelandic and *aespe* in Anglo-Saxon; the adjective aspen described the tree or its properties. In George Chapman's play *Caesar and Pompey* (1631), Cato describes a fearful man saying "what an aspen soul hath such a creature! / How dangerous to his soul is such a fear." By Tennyson's time, in the nineteenth century, aspen was no longer an adjective but the name of the tree itself. The message of fear, however, remained in *The Lady of Shalott*: "Willows whiten, aspens quiver / Little breezes dusk and shiver." The Lady of Shalott can see the quaking aspens, symbols themselves of a cursed existence, in her mirror. When the handsome Sir Lancelot appears,

IRONICALLY THE "TREMBLING POPLARS," SO TOUGH AND WIDESPREAD, WERE ASSOCIATED WITH TIMIDITY — AND SOMETIMES WITH SHAME.

she cannot be content with seeing only his image and she leans out of her window to look properly at him. The mirror, reflecting the trembling aspens, shatters. The curse is fulfilled and her doom is complete.

AVOCADO

In *A New Voyage Round the World* (1697), William Dampier described the "Avogata pear-tree." It is "commonly pretty high," he wrote, and the fruit makes "an excellent dish." He added, "It is reported that this fruit provokes to lust, and therefore is said to be much esteemed by the Spaniards."

Dampier did not elaborate on whether the avocados he found lived up to their reputation. Perhaps he only dared to taste them because he and his pirate companions spent most of their time at sea where they took care not even to *think* about women. His ship, which had been seized from Dutch slave traders, was renamed by the buccaneers *Bachelor's Delight*. Almost at once they sold off the sixty slave women in the hold. The ship's navigator, whose name was William Ambrosia Cowley, recounted that on Valentine's Day 1684 the crew had begun "discoursing the intrigues of women," whereupon a storm arose, "so that we concluded the discoursing of women at sea was very unlucky, and occasioned the storm." Even so, enough sailors considered avocados such a welcome meal that another name for them was "midshipman's butter."

The Aztec name for the fruit was *ahuacatl*, which in Spanish became "avocado." English variations of this included "avigato," which may have been the origin of the name "alligator pear." This might also have been due to the rough skin of some avocados found, like alligators, only in the New World. The Incas told the Spanish conquistadores that their name meant "testicles." The hanging fruit does look a bit like these organs. Years later, the aging Louis XIV in faraway France got hold of *la bonne poire* ("good pear"), hoping its encouraging attributes would be useful to him.

Avocados were probably first eaten and spread by large prehistoric creatures. The big seeds wouldn't easily pass through the digestive tract of most modern browsers, although some smaller wild avocados are eaten whole by the quetzal bird of Costa Rica. These birds (about the size of a large crow) manage to ingest the whole fruit and then regurgitate the stone after digesting the pulp. They often nest near avocado trees because the nutritious flesh helps the females to produce eggs. The male quetzal, too, if the avocado's reputation is correct, no doubt benefits from such a diet.

The avocado tree itself has curious reproductive habits. The small, greenish flowers, which have no petals, are hermaphrodite. Each flower opens twice, once in the morning and once in the afternoon. To ensure cross-fertilization each tree bears flowers that are female or male receptive *either* in the morning or the afternoon, and vice versa. That means that different trees have to be pollinated from another tree on the opposite time schedule. Avocado growers had to be sure to plant both kinds of tree—until modern manipulation reduced the need for such an ingenious system.

Before the Ice Age, avocados grew in North America and Europe. They are thought to have survived in Mexico and spread from there. They have been cultivated in Mexico since about 8000 BC. Now they are grown commercially wherever it's warm enough—particularly in Israel for the European market and in Florida and California for the North American market.

The famous Hass avocado, which dominated the North American market for a long time and is self-fertilizing, was actually an example of *failed* manipulation. It was accidentally created by a Californian mail carrier Rudolph Hass, who (in 1926) tried to create a hybrid avocado by making a graft onto a seedling grown from a pit. The graft didn't take, but the seedling used for rootstock produced fruit that Hass's children claimed was the best they had ever tasted, so their father raised some more trees. With its dark skin (which hides bruises) and long shelf life, the Haas avocado immediately became popular with vendors.

Before modern hybridization there were three kinds of avocado. The Mexican avocado could be grown in California because it tolerates cold better than the West Indian avocado, which only grows in tropical climates and has a smooth green skin. The Guatamalan avocado is largest, with a rough skin that can be black, purple, or green. Avocados are members of the laurel family, many of which have aromatic leaves, and the Mexican avocado tree's leaves smell of anise. Avocados are mostly evergreen, sometimes losing leaves for a short period.

The avocado's Latin name is now *Persea americana*. Some etymologists say it was once thought to come from Persia (hence *Persea*), and that *americana* was added to correct the error. The name *Persea* more probably comes from the Greek name for a different tree: an Egyptian laurel. For a while the avocado was called *P. gratissima*, meaning "very acceptable." Avocados are the most nutritious fruit known, high in protein and vitamins and containing heart-friendly oil. They might even enhance sentiments of the heart. They taste delicious. *Gratissima* seems to have been a very good name to call them—even if it is no longer used.

BALD CYPRESS

In 1791 William Bartram published an account of his *Travels* around the state of Florida. His father, the famous farmer and botanist John Bartram, had worried frequently about "Billy." "Botany and drawing are his delight," wrote John, "but I'm afraid won't get him his living." John died more than a decade before his son's *Travels* was published, and it's sad he never knew the brilliance of this book, which influenced so many people, including the poets Coleridge and Wordsworth (*see* Franklin Tree).

When we read his narrative we could be right next to William. He comes upon a stand of bald cypresses and writes about the tree: "Its majestic stature is surprising and in approaching it we are struck with a kind of awe, at beholding the stateliness of the trunk, lifting its cumbrous top towards the skies, and casting a wide shade upon the ground, as a dark intervening cloud, which, for a time, excludes the rays of the sun." He goes on to describe eagles and storks perched on the flat tops of the trees. Some of the trunks, he tells us, are twelve feet in diameter. The base of the bald cypress trunk is enlarged and deeply furrowed-looking, as Bartram wrote, as if supported by "prodigious buttresses." Above these the main trunk could rise for another ninety feet.

His description is still with us, but few, if any, trees as grand as the ones he saw remain. The bald cypress grows in swampy land and its wood is wonderfully resistant to rot and insects. Settlers took advantage of it—the bigger the tree, the more useful it was, with no thought of tomorrow.

There are still bald cypress groves in southern wetlands. They are called domes because the trees grow in circular groups in and around ponds and swamps. The highest trees tend to be in the middle, gradually diminishing in height as they reach the edges of the swamp, presumably because the peaty soil in the center suits them best.

THERE IS A HUGE AND FAMOUS SPECIMEN, THOUGHT TO BE BETWEEN TWO THOUSAND AND FOUR THOUSAND YEARS OLD, NEAR OAXACA IN MEXICO.

The bald cypress's botanical name is *Taxodium distichum*. The taxodiums are (for now) part of the Cypress family. Another taxodium is the Montezuma cypress, or *T. mucronatum*. *Taxodium* means "like a yew," and these trees do have flat, pointed leaves similar to those of the yew tree (*mucronatum* means "pointed"). The leaves are in pairs along the branchlets, hence the name *distichum* ("in pairs"). The pond cypress is *T. ascendens* ("growing up") and there is a "nodding" variety (var. *nutans*) with shoots pointing downward. The bald cypress loses its leaves in autumn and becomes bald.

Bald cypresses grow in stagnant water, although their seeds need a dry spot to germinate. They are often surrounded by pneumatophores, perpendicular root growths which resemble and are called "knees." Some botanists think they help aerate the roots (*see* Mangrove). William Bartram thought old hollow knees "serve very well for beehives."

Although bald cypresses seem to have evolved to grow in swamps and are often found there, they can also grow well on drier land and in gardens. The Montezuma cypress grows on drier land, too, and botanists think that its presence in Mexico indicates that this country was once much wetter than it is now. The Montezuma cypress, which gets its name from the last Aztec emperor (1466–1520), is evergreen, only losing its leaves if it grows in a colder climate. There is a huge and famous specimen, thought to be between two thousand and four thousand years old, near Oaxaca in Mexico. It is called El Tule, from the Nahuatl name for an aquatic plant, although its location now is quite dry. The Aztec religion respected a Tree of Life, which joined the water on earth to the sun in the sky—and these cypresses often touch the water as well as growing to immense heights—so they were probably sacred trees. According to the nineteenth-century Harvard historian William Prescott, the whole of Mexico "was well covered" with woods before the Spanish conquest, and he quotes Aztec law that administered severe penalties for cutting down trees.

Nowadays many bald cypress groves are protected from logging. And El Tule is watered with underground pipes to preserve it. The original swampy land where these trees flourish, though, is becoming scarce as our population increases and we tap underground aquifers for our water. Bald cypresses can adapt to having less water, but we don't know the consequences of eliminating the swamps where they live. Water may be getting scarcer for trees—and for humans—but so far we haven't adapted to using less. Indeed we pour it away as if there really were no tomorrow.

BAMBOO

If it's safe to say that you can't have a forest without trees, bamboos (although technically grasses) are certainly trees. In forests, bamboos can grow to over one hundred feet tall, with stems as thick as any tree trunk. In the thirteenth century Marco Polo described bamboos, or "canes," in his *Travels*. "You must know," he wrote, "that these canes are more than three palms in girth and from ten to fifteen paces long." He reported many uses for them, including the construction of the "Great Khan's" palace and for fires, which "make such loud reports that . . . the wild beasts are greatly frightened and make off as fast as possible."

In Asia, where they originate, bamboos are so important that a Chinese poet, Su Tung-po, commented that it would be better to have "food without pork than life without bamboos." Used in making rope, building materials, paper, water pipes, sleeping mats, baskets, thatch, and chopsticks, bamboos also provided shade and beauty in gardens. They should be planted, said the seventeenth-century writer Ji-Cheng in the *Craft of Gardens*, "where the moonlight is dim and faint . . . In this way you can increase the mystery of the place and engulf yourself in an even deeper emotion." He recommended that four-fifths of every garden be planted with bamboo.

Bamboo came to Europe in about the seventeenth century, and there were specimens in the Oxford botanical garden in 1645. But they were greenhouse exotics and weren't really grown in gardens until the nineteenth century. There are many kinds of bamboo, some hardy in northern climates and some tender. There are bamboos that spread *rapidly* by underground rhizomes and clumping bamboos (which clump!). Gardeners might want to establish which kind they are planting according to their intent.

The name "bamboo" comes from the Dutch *bamboes*, adapted from the Malayan name *mambu*. The genus is *Bambusa*. The many varieties include the *B. phyllostachys* (with "leaf," *phyllo*, like "corn," *stachys*) and the giant *B. dendrocalamus* (from *dendron*, "tree," and *calamus*, "reed). The *B. arundinaria* comes from the Latin *arundus* ("a reed") and includes the "cane," which grows wild in the southern states, forming canebrakes, once used to shelter runaway slaves. Sugarcane is also a kind of grass.

Bamboos have feathery waterproof leaves and plumed flowers. But many bamboos only flower once every ten to eighty years and then die immediately afterward. An Asian saying describes an old man as someone who has seen the bamboo "flower twice." Some species of bamboo will flower simultaneously wherever they are growing. This still has no satisfactory scientific explanation. It means, though, that pandas, who depend on bamboo for food and shelter, might suddenly find themselves in a dying forest.

Bamboo shoots are good food for humans, too. A Chinese legend told about a woman who was dying and begged her son for a bowl of bamboo shoot soup. Unfortunately it was in the middle of winter and no shoots had yet emerged. But her devoted son wept warm tears onto the earth so copiously that shoots sprang up to provide his mother with her last meal. These days, what with freezers, canned vegetables, and nursing homes, comparable filial devotion might be less easy to find.

Although it doesn't produce shoots until spring, bamboo was called, in China, one of the Three Friends of Winter (along with the apricot and the pine). Bamboo is evergreen and very pliant, so it bends rather than breaking in winter storms. This was considered by the Chinese to be exemplary of true gentlemanly behavior, and bamboo was often the subject of poems and paintings. There was even a school of bamboo artists. The easy grace of the bamboo was akin to the fluidity of calligraphy. An eleventh-century bamboo artist instructed his pupils to "realize" the whole plant, rather than diddling with details and to "move the brush . . . as the buzzard swoops when the hare jumps out."

CHINESE POET SU TUNG-PO COMMENTED THAT IT WOULD BE BETTER TO HAVE "FOOD WITHOUT PORK THAN LIFE WITHOUT BAMBOOS."

"Heavenly" or "sacred" bamboo is an unrelated shrub. It looks like bamboo and is called Nandina bamboo, from its Japanese name *nanten*. In Japan it is an important garden plant because, it is said, if you have a bad nightmare you can tell it to the *nanten* in the morning and none of the evils you dreamed of will come to pass.

In spite of the fact that a nineteenth-century Scottish gardener, Mairi Sawyer, planted a grove of bamboos that she called bamboozlem to confuse her friends, "bamboozling" doesn't seem to be etymologically connected with this curious plant. But if ever a plant was connected with human life it must be the bamboo. Wrote T. S. Eliot in *Sweeney Agonistes*:

Under the bamboo
Bamboo bamboo
Under the bamboo tree
Two live as one
One live as two
Two live as three
Under the bam
Under the boo
Under the bamboo tree.

It's no accident that a group of third-century Chinese poets called themselves the Seven Sages of the Bamboo Grove. One of them took care to be accompanied always by his servant carrying a shovel, so if he happened to die suddenly he could be buried at once—in the bamboo grove.

BANANA

Mostly we associate the banana tree with its easy-to-eat nutritious fruit. In Chinese gardens, even where it's too cold for bananas to yield fruit, they are often planted for their huge leaves. Listening to the evening rain on the banana leaves was a pleasure planned by Chinese gardeners, and bananas were planted close to houses or pagodas for just this purpose.

Although they grow as high as many small trees, botanically bananas aren't trees but giant herbs. What we think of as their trunk is really fibrous fleshy leaves tightly whorled together. The true stem is short and underground and comes out of a tuberous rhizome, or underground storage chamber. After producing fruit, the main stem dies down and new shoots sprout around it.

Modern cultivated bananas are triploids, with three sets of chromosomes. The flower of these bananas looks like a huge heart emerging from the furled leaves. It doesn't get pollinated and the tiny banana seeds are sterile. We do not know how far back wild bananas were, accidentally or purposely, hybridized to obtain a plant, the fruits of which formed an important part of the human diet. Probably this occurred in Southeast Asia.

The earliest Western record we have of bananas is that Alexander the Great found them in India. Arab traders slowly brought them to the Mediterranean regions. In the sixteenth century European travelers and explorers began describing bananas they had seen and tasted. Before the end of the nineteenth century bananas were still hardly known except where they grew, because they don't travel well. It wasn't until refrigerated "banana boats" could bring them rapidly to European and American markets that they became more than a curiosity. Indeed, in the Philadelphia Centennial Exposition of 1876, bananas were still being sold (at ten cents apiece) as a "curiosity of the Indies."

The first bananas were seen in Britain, it is thought, in 1633, when the apothecary Thomas Johnson hung a bunch brought from Bermuda in his shop window. Johnson, a botanist as well as a loyal Royalist, was killed in battle, but he did have time to revise John Gerard's *Herball* of 1597, which when reprinted in 1636 included the banana. He described the leaves being "of bignesse sufficient to wrap a childe in of two yeeres old" and called the plant the Adam's apple tree. Jews, Christians, and Muslims considered the likelihood that the banana was the Tree of Knowledge described in Genesis (*see* Apple). The shape of the fruit was suggestive of carnal knowledge. Also, as Johnson pointed out, bananas could be connected with Christianity because when the fruit is cut crosswise the center, where the remains of the small seeds are clustered, "may be seene [to be in] the shape and forme of a crosse."

In the eighteenth century Carl Linnaeus classified all known plants, giving

them two names. Linnaeus was also the first European to persuade a cultivated banana plant to bear fruit. He named the sweet banana *Musa sapientum*
("of the wise"), referring to Alexander the Great's report that the wise men,
or Brahmins, in India were to be found sitting under banana trees. Even so,
Alexander apparently didn't let his troops taste the fruit. Pliny the Elder in
his *Natural History* repeated this story, writing that bananas *were* eaten by
these wise men. Bananas contain serotonin, a substance that we associate with
our own well-being. Even if eating them doesn't help
ease the brain (always an aspiration of the wise), they
are very nourishing. Linnaeus's name was also honoring Antonius Musa, who was physician to the Roman
emperor Augustus. Musa pulled Augustus through several serious illnesses and a statue of him was erected in
Rome (next to that of Asclepius, god of healing).

THE MAIN
COMEDIAN WAS CALLED
THE TOP BANANA, OWING
TO THE LONG RUBBER
BAT RESEMBLING A
BANANA WITH WHICH
HE PLAYFULLY HIT THE
OTHER COMEDIANS.

Plantains are botanically the same as sweet bananas
but must be cooked before being eaten. Linnaeus distinguished between the two kinds, naming the plantain
M. paradisiaca (a name later applied to sweet bananas
as well). Linnaeus thought that bananas grew in the
Garden of Eden, and, as he wrote to the Royal Swedish Bible Commission,
their leaves were used for Adam and Eve's "aprons," because the "*fikon löf*
(fig leaf)" would not have provided adequate coverage.

Curiously, the Arabic for "tip of the finger" is *al-bahanah*, and some have
made a connection between this word and the fingerlike fruits of the banana.
The Arabic name for the fruit is *moz*, not *bahanah*. Even so, a bunch of bananas is known in the trade as a "hand." Many languages, for obvious reasons,
use "banana" to refer not to a finger but to the male anatomy, and the fruits
have consequently been thought to be aphrodisiac. The name "banana" probably comes from a West African name.

Banana

In burlesque shows of the early twentieth century the main comedian was called the top banana owing to the long rubber bat resembling a banana with which he playfully hit the other comedians—all a bit crazy. Love can make you a little crazy, too, and people in love are sometimes described as being "bananas" about each other.

Because they are propagated from suckers (with identical clones) and grown in such huge quantities, cultivated bananas could be in danger of being wiped out by diseases to which they are not resistant. In their native countries bananas are eaten widely, and the plants are also used for thatch, umbrellas, and fibers for weaving cloth and rope. Perhaps the saddest use of a banana was described in a UNICEF report of January 30, 2006. In the Democratic Republic of Congo yet another child was killed during violent upheaval. The baby was laid to rest in a shallow grave, on top of a banana leaf. A banana leaf is just big enough, as we are reminded, to wrap around a "childe . . . of two yeeres old."

BAOBAB

I f you attend to a baobab too late you can never get rid of it
again. It overgrows the whole planet. Its roots pierce right
through. And if the planet is too small, and if there are too
many baobabs, they make it burst into pieces," wrote Antoine de Saint-
Exupéry in *The Little Prince*, shortly before his death in the spring of 1943 when
his plane was shot down in the Mediterranean. In the story, too, a pilot has
crashed his plane. The Little Prince appears and the two learn about each
other's worlds. The Little Prince asks the pilot for a sheep to eat the baobabs
that are engulfing his tiny planet.

The baobab tree grows in the African desert, over which Saint-Exupéry pi-
loted mail planes, and it is as strange a tree as anything imagined on an alien

planet. Africans call it the upside-down tree, because the sparse branches (leafless for much of the year) look like roots. There are several legends explaining why God became angry with the tree and tuned it upside down.

Baobabs have the capacity to store large amounts of water in their soft, spongy trunks. The trees are massive and their thick trunks can swell or contract according to the amount of water they contain. The Kalahari Bushmen learned how to pierce the tree with hollow straws and suck out the liquid. The baobab was sometimes called the Tree of Life, because it contained life-giving water.

All parts of the baobab are valued in Africa. The fruits, seeds, and leaves are edible and rich in vitamin C. They are a favorite food of baboons, giving the tree another name: the monkey-bread tree. Elephants eat the bark (which contains tartaric acid), and unlike most trees, even if the bark is stripped off it can grow back again and the tree will not die (*see* Cork). Humans strip baobab bark, too, using it to make strong string or rope. "As secure as an elephant bound with baobab rope," goes one Swahili saying. Baobab flowers, which can be seven inches across, are white. They are pollinated by nocturnal creatures, including bats, perhaps adding to the baobab's reputation as a fearsome tree, growing at the entrance to the dark world of spirits. Baobabs can live for thousands of years.

In 1592 Prospero Alpini, an Italian botanist, first described what he called the *bahobab*, in his *Plants of Egypt* (though the tree isn't native to Egypt). There are several species of baobab in Africa, and Madagascar, and there is one in Australia. The most common African baobab is the *Adansonia digitata*, named for Michel Adanson, who renounced the priesthood to become a botanist. He joined the French Campagne des Indes

(India Company) and went to Africa, where he explored the treacherous Senegal River. He found baobab trees that were a hundred feet tall and described them in his *Natural History of Senegal* (published in 1757). Carl Linnaeus honored him by naming the tree *A. digitata* (*digitata* for "fingerlike" leaves). Adanson was a staunch supporter of the African culture he encountered, learning the Senegalese language and firmly opposing slavery. In spite of Linnaeus's compliment, Adanson always refused to call this African tree by its botanical name.

AFRICANS CALL IT THE UPSIDE-DOWN TREE, BECAUSE THE SPARSE BRANCHES (LEAFLESS FOR MUCH OF THE YEAR) LOOK LIKE ROOTS.

Some African legends say that baobab trees fall, fully grown, from heaven. In some places local people leave offerings at the foot of a baobab tree to ask for protection. Traditionally villagers meet under a baobab tree to make important decisions. When baobabs die they collapse into a powdery mass, soon dispersed by the desert winds, as if they had magically disappeared. These trees are, rightly, treasured and revered by the African people, and in spite of the Little Prince's fears, baobabs aren't at all invasive.

BEECH

Fond lovers, cruel as their flame,
Cut in these trees their mistress' name.
Little, alas, they know or heed,
How far these beauties hers exceed!

So wrote Andrew Marvell in 1681 in *The Garden*. Lovers, before and since, have not been able to resist carving their sentiments into the smooth gray bark of beech trees. The inscriptions, as the tree grows, get bigger with time. *Crescunt illae; crescent amores*. "As these (letters) grow, so does our love," Roman sweethearts believed (or hoped).

Beech bark is very thin and its elasticity allows it to expand as the tree grows. Other trees have different ways of adjusting the growth of the tree to the outer bark, sometimes splitting and becoming fissured or flaking off to accommodate the expansion beneath it. Their smooth, silvery bark makes beech trees instantly recognizable.

In several languages the name beech is similar to the word for "book." In Anglo-Saxon, the tree was *boc*, and *bec* meant "book." In German, the tree is *Boche*, and *Buch* means "book." As well as inviting inscriptions on the actual tree, slabs of beech bark were used from early times to write on, and sometimes they were tied together to make the first books.

The Latin name for the beech tree is *Fagus*, which comes from the Greek *phagein*, "to eat." Beechnuts, although small, are very nourishing for humans and livestock. Like acorns (*see* Oak) they were known as mast and particularly used to fatten pigs in autumn.

The European beech is *Fagus sylvatica* ("growing in woods"), and the American beech, similar in almost every way, is *F. grandifolia* ("big leaved"). European settlers in America cut down whole beech forests because they knew that beech trees like fertile limey soil, which is also the best for farming. The American beech forests also provided the staple diet of passenger pigeons. John Audubon described the pigeons "arriving by the thousands" to eat the beechnuts. Under the great trees hunters were waiting, along with hundreds of hogs "to be fattened on the pigeons which were to be slaughtered." Passenger pigeons did not survive this kind of massacre and the felling of their principal source of their food.

Beech wood doesn't contain tannin or resins, so it's not as durable for building as other hardwoods. Because it gives off no aromatic oils, it has always been used to make bowls and utensils. If John Gerard's 1597 *Herball* is to be trusted, beech shouldn't be used for firewood because when it is brought indoors "there followes hard travell of childe and miserable deaths." But the water from the "hollownesse" of beech could, he said, cure "naughty scurfe, tetters and scabs of men, horses, kine and sheepe." Then and later, beech leaves were used to make mattresses. In the seventeenth-century John Evelyn wrote in his *Sylva, or A Discourse of Forest-Trees* (*see* Ash) that beech leaf mattresses "continue sweet for seven or eight years," unlike straw ones which soon become "musty and hard." He does not mention "memory foam" properties, so dear to modern mattress companies.

Beech leaves might have memories, albeit of a different kind, because they stay on the tree well into winter. Often beeches are used to make hedges, which change from green to rusty brown during the cold weather. The curled up new leaf buds are long and pointed, as sharp as pins, and were once used as toothpicks. In spring the emerging green "glistering" leaves make a "noble shade," wrote Evelyn. Their dense shade is enjoyable to humans but also helps protect the pale, delicate bark from sun exposure.

The first copper beeches were apparently noticed near Zurich, Switzerland, in about 1680. Here a group of them was said to have sprung up in a place where five brothers had murdered one another. Their spilled blood colored the leaves red. Copper beeches weren't brought into English gardens until the eighteenth century. According to Canon Ellacombe (who wrote *In a Gloucester Garden* in 1895), the poet William Wordsworth complained that "there were only two blots in his beautiful Vale, a copper beech and Miss Martineau" (the latter was a writer and traveler who built a house near Lake Windermere where Wordsworth lived). Some modern gardeners also dislike copper beeches, saying that if you have one the best place to look at the view is standing right beside it—so it isn't included. These trees can grow huge and not much grows in the shade beneath them. But standing beneath a mature copper beech is, for some, like being in a huge rose-tinted cathedral. Even ordinary beeches have branches that bend down toward the ground, making a pale-green cave beneath them.

In spite of their shallow roots, beech trees sometimes endure for a very long time. In Carrol Creek, Tennessee, a large beech tree finally died in 1916. Until 1880 an inscription was clearly legible carved in its bark. It read:

> *D. Boone*
> *Cilled A Bar*
> *On Tree*
> *In Year 1760.*

BIRCH

Shadows of the silver birk
Sweep the green that folds thy grave
Let them rave.

S ilver birch, our name for the European birch, *Betula pendula* ("drooping birch"), is thought to date from this 1830 *Dirge* by Alfred, Lord Tennyson. Tennyson's "birk" was the Scottish name for the tree, and the many British place-names with the "birk" prefix shows how widespread the birch tree was and still is.

Birches grow in northern Europe, Russia, Asia, North America, Iceland, and Greenland. They were probably the first trees to restore the bare scraped land left by the glaciers of the Ice Age. They don't live for long (about eighty years), but they multiply prolifically by suckers and by seed. Indeed, a single birch catkin contains about five and a half *million* grains of pollen. Birch trees can live in the bleakest conditions—on tundra and moor and bare mountainsides—as long as they have enough light.

Birches themselves are full of light, with airy leaves and pale bark. Their Sanskrit name *bhrag* meant "shining." Most birches have light, smooth bark that contains betulin, a crystalline substance making it pale as well as waterproof. Because the bark also invites inscription and often flakes off in papery curls, some say that another origin of their name is the Sanskrit *bhurg*, meaning "a tree for writing upon." President Jefferson wrote to Meriwether Lewis recommending birch bark paper for copying field notes, because "paper of the birch [is] . . . less liable to injury from damp than common paper."

Humans used birch trees long before writing was invented. The Gallic for the tree was *beith* (pronounced "bey"). The Anglo-Saxon name was *birce*. Birch bark made shelter and clothes. The buds and leaves as well as the bark could be eaten, and the sap yielded a kind of beer. The rolled-paper bark strips became torches. Most of all, the waterproof bark was used for canoes:

> "Give me of your bark, O Birch-tree!
>
> . . . .
>
> I a light canoe will build me
>   Lay aside your cloak, O Birch Tree!
> Lay aside your white-skin wrapper!
>
> . . . .
>
>   And the tree with all its branches
> Rustled in the breeze of morning,
> Saying, with a sigh of patience,
> "Take my cloak, O Hiawatha!"

North American Indians, such as Longfellow's Hiawatha, built strong, light canoes out of the bark of the paper or canoe birch, *B. papyrifera*. A canoe was like "a yellow water-lily," noted Longfellow in *The Song of Hiawatha*, with the silver outer bark inside and the yellow inner bark outside. The pieces were sewn together with fibrous roots (*see* Larch).

In both the Old World and the New, babies' cradles were often fashioned out of birch bark, not only because it was light and waterproof but also because birch trees were magical and would help protect the infant. Some of these children might well have been conceived in the dappled shade of a birch wood, especially in Scotland where birches were common. On Beltane, or May Day, couples would habitually go off together into the woods. The church frowned on this but endorsed another May Day custom of bringing young birches into villages to make maypoles. On New Year's Eve the old, bad year was often swept out with a besom, or broom, made of birch twigs. In between times witches were thought to ride through the skies on such brooms.

Birches are very flexible and can bend against the gusty winds in the bleak places where they grow. These pliant branches were uses in bundles for whipping those who seemed to need punishment. The Latin for birch was *betula* (hence our botanical name), and the Romans carried birch bundles, or *fasces*, in magisterial processions to show who was in charge. "Fascists" thereafter have whipped the noncompliant into shape, if they can. But even loving parents "birched" their little boys. The sixteenth-century herbalist William Turner (*see* Larch) wrote of the birch that "it serveth for many good uses, and for none better than for betynge of stubborn boys, that either lye or will not learn." Turner himself complained of being "pened up in a chamber" with his large family of children and not being able to write because of their "noyse."

🌿 THEY WERE PROBABLY THE FIRST TREES TO RESTORE THE BARE SCRAPED LAND LEFT BY THE GLACIERS OF THE ICE AGE.

Luckily for the world, children (even when it is considered acceptable to beat them) know how to play. The young trees have lent their springy branches to children for what the poet Robert Frost called swinging—climbing a birch until it arches over and springs back up when you jump. When children swing on birches they whip back afterward, but if held down too long by crueler ice storms the young trees remain bent. Frost described young birches permanently bent over on their "hands and knees," like young girls with their hair thrown over their heads "to dry in the sun."

Birch trees are beautiful to see—and to touch. Helen Keller described stroking "the smooth skin" of birch trees when she blindly walked through silent woods. There are numerous kinds of *Betula*, including the yellow, white, silver, downy, river, water, and Asian birches, and many of our parks and gardens are ornamented with birch trees. "One could do worse than be a swinger of birches," wrote Frost. Indeed one could.

BOX

The Greeks made small boxes out of the dense wood of the boxwood tree to hold ointments and such things. They called them *pyxides*, from *pyknos*, "dense," and in the Catholic Church the sacred host is still kept in a *pyx*. The Romans changed the Greek name to *buxus*, meaning both "a box" and the tree. Our botanical name for this small tree is *Buxus sempervirens* ("evergreen"). Box leaves contain a substance we call buxine, and most animals, including deer, won't eat them.

The evergreen box is associated with funerals and hopes for eternal life. The poet William Wordsworth referred to a custom of placing a basin of box sprigs next to the church door, so that after a funeral those attending could each take a piece to cast into the new grave. Box was also used to replace Christmas holly in preparation of the Easter Resurrection ahead. "Instead of Holly now upraise / The Greener Box for show," wrote the seventeenth-century poet Robert Herrick.

Some people find the scent of box oppressive. The herbalist John Gerard, writing at the end of the sixteenth century, stated that box leaves "are of an evill and lothsome smell." Some even said they smelled of death. The British queen Anne, who succeeded to the throne in 1702, disliked the smell so much she had the box planted by her Dutch predecessors, William and Mary, removed from the formal gardens at Hampton Court and Kensington Palace.

Box has been used from Roman times to make clipped edgings and topiary. It grows slowly and can be formed into whatever shape one wishes. Some scholars think that the Romans brought the box tree to Britain. Other scholars say it's native to Britain. The Romans had plenty of clipped box in their gardens and remains of box clippings are still to be found on archeological sites of Roman villas in Britain. A landscape gardener, or *topiaries*, gave us the term *topiary*. Pliny the Elder described his garden in loving detail, including box "clipped into innumerable shapes, some forming letters spelling the gardener's name, or his master's." One wonders just when the name of the gardener or the "master" took precedence. There were also, scattered around, "small obelisks" and "different animals" of clipped box.

When formal gardens were popular in Britain they were most often edged or made into "knots" or elaborate patterns with clipped box. When topiary was going out of fashion in the eighteenth century, Alexander Pope satirically referred to "St. George in box, his arm scarce long enough, but / will be in a condition to stick the dragon by next April." Left alone, the box will become a small tree with a trunk "the bignesse of a man's thigh," as John Parkinson wrote in his garden book of 1629 (*see* Apple). He dismissed any medical properties it might have except as a vermifuge for horses.

Box is not native to America but was brought over by those who wanted grand gardens in the English style. William Penn used box in his Pennsbury Manor garden, and it flourished in the mild climate of many southern plantations. In the mid-nineteenth century a hardier Japanese box was introduced.

Boxwood has always been highly prized and not only for boxes. Box roots, called dudgeons, were often used to fashion dagger handles. Macbeth described "gouts of blood" on "thy blade and dudgeon." Being "in high dudgeon" isn't apparently etymologically connected with dagger handles, but it seems as though it should be. These dudgeon handles might be intricately engraved, and one of the most common uses of boxwood was (and is) for making wood engravings. Thomas Bewick (1753–1828) is credited with making boxwood engravings an important art form. Bewick was from Newcastle-on-Tyne and was apprenticed to a metal engraver there. At that time metal engravings were considered artistically superior to wood engravings, which were used for letters and illustrations of children's books and given to the apprentices to make. But in his spare time Bewick made and published two books of wood engravings, one on quadrupeds and one of birds, and they immediately sold widely.

Wood engravings became popular, especially as paper could now be made fine and smooth enough to take the delicate lines, and until the mid-nineteenth century they were often used to illustrate books. Sometimes photographs were copied onto the wood blocks and then engraved. Boxwood, often imported from Turkey, was in great demand. Wood engraving is done on the end-grain of a block, so when wider images were wanted the blocks would have to be glued together.

The American box elder is neither a box tree nor an elder. It is a short-lived

> BOX ROOTS, CALLED DUDGEONS, WERE OFTEN USED TO FASHION DAGGER HANDLES.

and quick-growing tree, useful for fast shade. It gets its common name because its pale wood can be used for making boxes. It is sometimes called an ashleaf maple, and its botanical name is *Acer* ("maple") *negundo*. *Negundo* is from the Benghali name for the chaste tree, *Vitex negundo*, which has similar leaves. The Greek chaste tree (*V. agnus-castus*) was important in harvest festivals, during which participating women had to abstain from sex. Pliny said that they made mattresses of the chaste tree leaves "to cool the heat of lust and keep themselves chaste." From sacred boxes to daggers, from funeral rites to chastity, truly ingenious are the ways we humans use and name the trees.

BREADFRUIT

On August 26, 1768, a small British ship left Plymouth harbor bound for Otaheiti (Tahiti). It was sent by the Royal Society of London so that astronomers on board could observe the transit of Venus over the sun (an event not predicted to recur for more than a century). The *Endeavour* was commanded by James Cook, who kept a journal of all he saw. This included an account of a native Tahitian (who had stolen a musket) being shot by one of the sailors. Cook attended the funeral and observed a sack of breadfruit lying near the body—presumably to provide sustenance into the next world.

The breadfruit was a staple of the islanders' diet. To procure it, wrote Cook, "costs them [the Tahitians] no trouble or labour but climbing a tree. The tree which produces it does not indeed shoot up spontaneously; but if a man plants ten of them in his life-time, which he may do in about an hour, he will . . . completely fulfil his duty to his own and future generations."

Breadfruit

The breadfruit tree is *Artocarpus altilis*, from the Greek *artos* ("bread"), *karpos* ("fruit"), and *altilis* ("well fed"). It grows to about one hundred feet, producing large fruits about the size of a melon or (as Gauguin painted it) a luxurious bosom. It has few or no seeds. The tree is from the Pacific Islands, where it was cultivated so far back that, as Cook wrote, it no longer grew spontaneously but had to be propagated by cuttings. The fruit was usually roasted, often pounded into a paste.

Cook's description immediately interested West Indian plantation owners searching for a cheap and abundant food to feed the many slaves used in the profitable sugar cane industry. In 1778 George III "bountifully" sponsored the *Bounty*, under the command of Lieutenant William Bligh, to take cuttings of breadfruit trees from Tahiti to the West Indies. Over eight hundred saplings (set in special slotted benches) were given the state cabin. The gardener "may never be refused the quantity of water he may have occasion to demand," ordered Bligh. All rats (that might gnaw the saplings) were to be poisoned, and "the crew must not complain if some of them who may die in the ceiling make an unpleasant smell."

Captain Bligh, who gave these and other orders, was said to be fussy and overbearing, and (as every schoolchild knows) not long after leaving Tahiti the crew mutinied. They threw the breadfruit plants overboard and abandoned Bligh and a few others in a small open boat. After a seven-week journey of over three thousand miles Bligh and his men reached Timor. Bligh went on to London and in 1793 successfully took another cargo of one hundred breadfruit trees to Saint Vincent, where they prospered. The slaves refused to eat the fruit, though, so it was used to feed hogs and chickens.

"IF A MAN PLANTS TEN OF THEM IN HIS LIFE-TIME, WHICH HE MAY DO IN ABOUT AN HOUR, HE WILL . . . COMPLETELY FULFIL HIS DUTY TO HIS OWN AND FUTURE GENERATIONS."

Bligh himself had another tree named for him, the ackee, or *Blighia sapida* (*sapida*, "pleasant to taste"), which he sent from Jamaica to London. The ackee fruit looks like a peach and has the texture of scrambled eggs, but only the *ripe* outer cover, or aril, of the akee is safe to eat; the rest is very poisonous. Perhaps that's appropriate for a fruit named after a man of volatile temperament. Eighteen of his crew respected and liked Bligh well enough to volunteer being cast adrift in an open boat rather than desert him. But the rest of his crew so hated him that they had to "disappear" from the known world: they settled on Pitcairn Island, where they fought among themselves but left survivors whose descendants live there still and still don't always get along!

CACAO

The names cacao and chocolate, the product of this tree, come from the Aztec name *tchocoatl*, which in turn probably came from the Mayan *cacahauchtl*. In both cultures a beverage made from seeds of the cacao tree was drunk by the elite and offered to the gods: the Mayans drank chocolate before going into battle; the Aztec god Quetzalcoatl (for whose return the people were waiting when Europeans arrived) was said to have tended a cacao tree.

When the Swedish botanist Carl Linnaeus classified all the plants known at his time, he called the cacao tree *Theobroma cacao* from the Greek *theos* ("a god"), and *broma* ("food"). Linnaeus knew that chocolate was a sacred drink, but maybe he also thought it tasted divine. Many of us think so, too. To the Aztecs the seeds of the cacao fruit, which we call beans, were so valuable they were used as money. When the Spanish conqueror Hernando Cortés arrived in the Aztec capital he was welcomed and offered chocolate to drink. When he asked for gold he was given cacao seeds. In 1523 a Spanish missionary Father Petrus de Angleria pointed out that it was a good kind of money "which permits no speculation, since it cannot be kept very long." But even though limited for long-term capital investment, beans were useful currency. The Spanish navigator Fernández de Oviedo noted that a rabbit could be purchased for ten beans, a mule for fifty, a prostitute's services for ten—and a good slave for a hundred.

These beans, or seeds, are very acrid, but the pulp surrounding them is sweet. Monkeys and probably early humans learned to open the cacao pods, eat the pulp, and spit out the seeds. The pods require such human or simian intervention because they can't drop from the tree or open by themselves. There are about a hundred seeds in each pod.

At some point in history humans discovered that if the pulp isn't eaten but left to ferment, the seeds inside the fruit change and develop a "chocolatey" flavor. The Aztecs dried and crushed the beans, mixing them with water, and then added powdered chili peppers to make a hearty brew that was poured from one vessel into another until it became a thick froth, served in special cups. Cortés was offered this concoction from gold cups served by naked virgins— if it had seemed somewhat unpalatable it would certainly have been enhanced by its presentation. Spanish conquerors took chocolate back to Spain.

Instead of pepper, the Spanish mixed chocolate with sugar, and sometimes vanilla, making a drink that immediately became wildly popular. It wasn't long before Spanish ladies were accused of drinking chocolate in church, and the clergy debated whether it could be consumed on "fast" day, since it was, after all, only a liquid. In 1636 the pamphlet *Question moral si el chocolate quebrante el ayuno ecclesiastico* strived to resolve, among other dilemmas, whether a priest could have a cup of chocolate before celebrating Mass.

Chocolate drinking spread throughout Europe, often served in special houses (*see* Coffee). Samuel Pepys wrote in his diary that he was going to drink "jocolatte," which he found "very good." By this time milk was often added to the mix (slab chocolate was not made until the nineteenth century). Once Europeans had discovered the delectability of chocolate, the cultivation of cacao trees spread. Early plantations were on the Caribbean island of Martinique and in the Philippines. By the end of the eighteenth century cacao was cultivated in Trinidad and Brazil.

The original tree from Central America is the *criollo* (or "native") cacao. Criollo beans can make a palatable drink with much less fermentation than *forastero* (or "foreign") beans from trees native to South America. But *criollo* cacao is more susceptible to fungus and diseases. So-called Trinidad cacao is a *forastero* hybrid. All cacao trees, which are small evergreens, need shade (and a tropical climate) to prosper.

Creamy pink cacao flowers bloom directly out of the tree's trunk and branches, looking like paper ornaments nailed to the bark. The flowers (pollinated by midges) are replaced by large round pods, also attached to the trunk, making the tree look like an illustration from a fairy tale. Even the diseases of cacao trees sound slightly out of this world. A dangerous fungus they are susceptible to is called witches' broom and it makes new shoots look like ragged broomsticks. Black pod, mealy pod, and swollen shoot are other ailments of this curious tree. When grown in plantations close together the trees are much more apt to get diseases than when clustered in tropical forests.

TO THE AZTECS THE SEEDS OF THE CACAO FRUIT, WHICH WE CALL BEANS, WERE SO VALUABLE THEY WERE USED AS MONEY.

Our love of chocolate seems to increase. At one time it was thought to be bad for you, even if pleasantly sinful. Recent studies, however, suggest that chocolate can reduce heart disease and there are even suggestions that chocolate contains antidepressant substances. Chocolate lovers, sometimes called choca-holics, can indulge with a clear conscience. However, raising chocolate can be exploitive of workers and ecologically unsound.

Scientists are still trying to explain exactly why chocolate can make you feel so very good, transporting you to magical delight. Once it was thought to be real magic. In the court of Louis XIV, Madame de Sévigné wrote to her daughter telling her about a young marquise who was served chocolate daily by a handsome slave. The next year "because she drank so much chocolate when she was expecting," thought Madame de Sévigné, the marquise gave birth to a little black baby (who died).

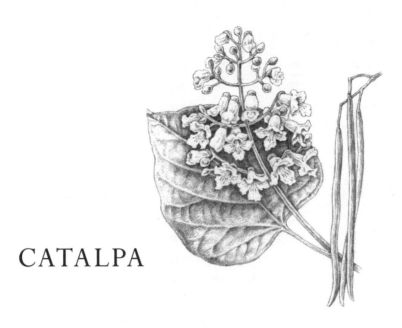

CATALPA

And tho' the inhabitants [of Carolina] are little curious in Gard'ning, yet the uncommon Beauty of the Tree has induc'd them to propagate it; and 'tis become an Ornamental to many of their Gardens, and probably will be the same to ours in *England*" wrote Mark Catesby, in his *Natural History of Carolina, Florida and the Bahama Islands*, which he published in ten sections between 1731 and 1743.

Catesby first went to America to visit his sister, and then returned in 1722 to find new plants, which were often of more interest to British gardeners and collectors than to the settlers themselves (who were too busy farming and surviving to have much interest in "Gard'ning"). Catesby, as he recounted, brought wild specimens of the catalpa first to Americans and then to English gardeners. Seeds were planted in Britain in the 1720s.

The tree, although not much used by native inhabitants, had a Cherokee

Indian name, *kutuhlpa*, and this became "catalpa." It was also called the Indian bean tree, on account of its long, brown, beanlike seed pods, which hang from the branches for most of the winter. Another name, cigar tree, was both for the shape of the seeds and the (erroneous) belief that Indians smoked them. In the South it is sometimes called the fish bait tree, since it is the preferred food of the catawba worms, three-inch-long caterpillars of the catalpa sphinx moth, which fishermen collect for bait. The tree that Catesby found was the southern catalpa. The northern catalpa is less floriferous, larger leaved, and hardier. The leaves of the southern catalpa emit an unpleasant smell when crushed.

> ANOTHER NAME, CIGAR TREE, WAS BOTH FOR THE SHAPE OF THE SEEDS AND THE (ERRONEOUS) BELIEF THAT INDIANS SMOKED THEM.

The catalpa's botanical name is *Catalpa bignonioides*. It was at first classed with the trumpet vine, once *Bignonia radicans*. The trumpet vine and the catalpa don't look very akin to us, although the flowers were once thought similar (and later the climbing bignonias were reclassified as campsis, from the Greek *kampsis*, "bending"). Joseph de Tournefort named the bignonia to express his "Esteem and Veneration" for Abbé Bignon, who was Louis XIV's librarian. Tournefort, whom Bignon had nominated to the French Royal Academy of Science, botanized in Europe and the Middle East and, in 1694, published *Elémens de botanique*. He was killed in Paris when a passing carriage crushed him against a wall, and he bequeathed his own books to Bignon.

The Bignonia family includes not only the catalpa but the South American jacaranda, our name deriving from its Brazilian name. Jacarandas don't grow in cooler climates but are abundant now in South Africa and Australia. In Australia, when the jacaranda blooms, in midsummer, "Christmas time is near." It is also a sign that end-of-year examinations are approaching, and it may even be too late to start studying for them by the time the trees have flowered. Down under, it is sometimes called the exam tree.

As often occurs in the plant world, there are Asian as well as American catalpas. The Chinese catalpa is called *quishu* in Mandarin, and the flowers are pink, spotted with brown, purple, and yellow. The American catalpa's flowers are white, spotted with purple and yellow. In China a later flowering catalpa, or *Zishu*, was used for coffins, and this catalpa was often planted around houses along with mulberry trees (to provide food for silkworms). Thus the living and the dead were provided for, and the word *Sangzi* (a combination of mulberry and catalpa) means "home."

Catalpas aren't long-lived trees, but they grow fast, up to one hundred feet high. Catesby was right, and catalpas did do well in Britain, but they did even better after the northern catalpa was sent from America. Sometimes American and Chinese catalpas are hybridized. Not all the plants sent from abroad have been as successful as catalpas. In the 1770s plant imports were increasing rapidly, and William Chambers (who introduced the concept of the "Chinese garden") suggested that gardeners "avoid all the exotics that vegetate with difficulty in our climate, for though they may be rare, they cannot be beautiful, being always in a sickly state." This is still very good advice to gardeners.

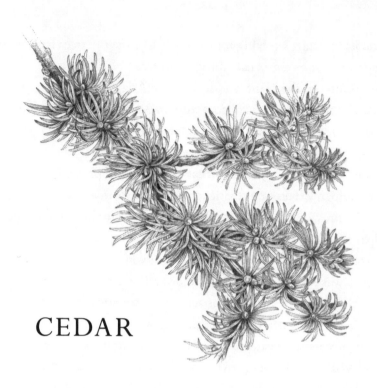

CEDAR

There are no true cedars native to America or Europe, although the name has been given to other trees, especially those with aromatic wood. Indeed, the cedar waxwing, which feeds upon the berries of the so-called red cedar (really a juniper), should logically be called a juniper waxwing.

There are only a few true cedars worldwide, and these are native to Asia Minor, the Himalayas, Cyprus, and northern Africa. The biblical "cedar of the Lord" is the *Cedrus libani* ("cedar of Lebanon") treasured from ancient times for its aromatic wood. Solomon used this cedar wood to build the Temple of Jerusalem, and also his house of cedar. He had to get the wood from Lebanon, and arranged with King Hiram to send "fourscore thousand hewers" to the mountains to help cut the trees down. The temple beams were huge trunks of cedar trees and the walls were paneled with cedar planks "so no stone could be seen."

The Hebrew name for the cedar, *erez* or *ahrahzim*, means a "strong firmly rooted tree." The English name cedar comes from the French *cèdre*, deriving from the Greek *kedros*. The Indo-European root *ked* ("to smoke") and the Hebrew word *qatar* ("to smudge") are probably connected to this tree because cedar wood was once burned at sacrificial offerings. Native Americans, too, used aromatic wood in "smudging" ceremonies, where chips were smouldered in an abalone shell to purify dwellings. They might have used the so-called red cedar or the incense cedar (*Calocedrus decurrens*) or other fragrant conifers.

The cedar of Lebanon grows in European and American parks and gardens more abundantly than in its native land. Even in the sixteenth century the explorer Leonard Rauwolf (*see* Coffee) went to the Middle East (in search of the original crown of thorns) and, when he was invited to Mount Lebanon, said he could only find twenty-six big cedars and no young ones. The large trees had been logged to near extinction, the young ones eaten by goats. There are few stands left these days, although efforts have been made to save them. When Queen Victoria heard of the plight of the biblical cedars she paid for a protective wall to be built around one of the groves.

The cedar of Lebanon may have been brought to Europe by crusaders, but it is not recorded growing in England until the end of the seventeenth century. It was still rare enough in Europe in 1729 for Antoine de Jussieu of the Jardin des Plantes in Paris to claim that he had smuggled two seedlings back to France in his hat, using his own drinking water to keep them alive. There is a similar tale about the coffee tree, both of the stories at least showing the value of these two plants.

The *Cedrus brevifolia* ("short leaved") is native only to the island of Cyprus. The Atlas cedar (*C. atlantica*) originated in North Africa and North America. The blue Atlas cedar is like the Atlas cedar, with egg-shaped cones sitting upright on the flat horizontal branches, but has smoky gray-blue foliage. Particularly fine specimens of cedars of Lebanon or Atlas cedars are often chosen as a background for wedding ceremonies. That's appropriate because these trees can live for thousands of years, as well as having ancient spiritual associations.

THE HEBREW NAME FOR THE CEDAR, *EREZ* OR *AHRAHZIM*, MEANS A "STRONG FIRMLY ROOTED TREE."

The name of the deodar cedar actually means "tree of the gods," from the Sanskrit *devadaru*. Deodars grow in the Himalayan Mountains. Rudyard Kipling's tales of India frequently mention the fragrant deodar logs floated down the rivers from the mountains. In *The Miracle of Purun Bhagat*, Kipling wrote not of the logs but of the "dense dark" deodar forest: "Under the shadow of the deodars stood a deserted shrine to Kali . . . who is sometimes worshipped against the smallpox." One supposes the shrine was "deserted" because the British had introduced the smallpox vaccine, along with much more efficient methods of logging the cedars.

CHERRY

America's favorite cherry, the darkly sweet Bing, owes its name to the Chinese foreman who worked in the Lewelling orchards in Milwaukie, Oregon. We don't know much about Mr. Ah Bing except that in 1889, after working for thirty-five years in the orchard, he visited China and was not permitted to reenter America. Poor thanks for his delicious legacy.

We cultivate three kinds of cherry: the sweet, the sour, and the flowering. Sour cherries grow wild worldwide and were known to the Greeks and Romans. The Latin name for cherry, *cerasus*, is said to come from Kerasus, a Greek settlement on the shores of the Black Sea. The Romans said cherries were brought home by Lucullus, a Roman general known for his lavish banquets. More probably Lysimachos, a Greek general in Alexander the Great's army, brought them back from Asia Minor. Anyway, the word *cerasus* became *cerise* in French, which changed to "cherries" in English. At first "cherries" meant *one* cherry, until the plural-forming "s" was dropped and we had a "cherrie," or cherry, for a single fruit. It is seldom that one eats just one cherry, so the change was perhaps not necessary.

From early on cherries were associated with seductive beauty. Chinese and European poets wrote of "cherry lips," and "cherry ripe" meant much more than an edible fruit ready to pick. As well as a symbol of earthly delight they could also be a heavenly delight, and in religious paintings the Christ child is sometimes shown holding a bunch of cherries. The old folk song "Cherry Tree Carol" demonstrates the cherry's sensuality, as well as its place in heaven. On the midwinter trip to Bethlehem, Mary, pregnant with Jesus, spots a cherry tree laden with ripe fruit and begs Joseph to pick her a bunch. He angrily tells her to "let the father of thy baby gather cherries for thee." Miraculously, the tree "bowed down, bowed / low down to the ground," allowing Mary to take some fruit, and revealing that God was the child's father.

Sweet cherries are a fragile crop, and many more sour cherries than sweet are grown commercially to be used for jam, jelly, and cherry pie. Cherry pie, too, can be a part of love: "Can she bake a cherry pie, Billy Boy, Billy Boy?" No one, after all, sings love songs about pumpkin or mince pies. Heliotrope, the flower affectionately called cherry pie, symbolizes eternal love in the language of flowers.

European settlers found wild cherries, which the North American Indians dried and put in pemmican. Like all wild cherries, they were small and sour. One settler called them "red Bullies . . . as wilde as the Indians." Sweet cherries were soon imported from Europe and often hybridized with wild ones. By George Washington's time, as every schoolchild knows, cherry trees were valued in American gardens. The story of cutting down the cherry tree was almost certainly fabricated by Mason Locke Weems, who wrote a nineteenth-century biography of Washington. But it does carry two important messages: first, that American presidents are not thought to tell lies; and second, that cherry trees shouldn't be hewn down irresponsibly. The latter sentiment still holds good—at least for lovers of trees.

The city of Washington is famous for actual cherry trees as well as presidents. The original exquisitely beautiful flowering cherry trees were a gift made to the city by the mayor of Tokyo in 1910.

In Japan cherry trees were particularly valued for their blossom, rather than their fruit. It is said that this dates back to the fifth century when the emperor Richu was offered rice wine at a banquet and a cherry blossom fell into his cup, captivating him with its beauty. Cherry trees were planted in the imperial gardens and ladies of the court would wear pink kimonos in springtime to match the cloudy pink blossoms covering the leafless branches.

Flowering cherries have been planted all over Japan. When they flower everyone takes time off to enjoy them, sometimes staying up all night to get every moment of their bloom. The show doesn't last long, the petals falling, say the Japanese, "when they must," just as we, too, die when our time has come.

Life, as we know, is short—especially if we measure it in the number of times we can experience the blossoming of spring. As Alfred Edward Housman versified in "Loveliest of Trees":

> Now, of my threescore years and ten,
> Twenty will not come again,
>
> . . . .
>
> And since to look at things in bloom
> Fifty springs are little room
> About the woodlands I will go
> To see the cherry hung with snow.

The "Shropshire Lad" was only twenty years old—what a wondrous gift indeed *fifty* more springs would be to some of us.

CHESTNUT

A sailor's wife had chestnuts in her lap,
And mounch'd, and mounch'd, and mounch'd.
"Give me," quoth I:
"Aroint thee witch!" the rump-fed ronyon cries.

The disappointed first of *Macbeth*'s three witches avenges the "sailor's wife" for refusing to share her chestnuts by creating a storm, which delays the husband "seven-nights nine times nine." In spite of Shakespeare's story, John Evelyn in his 1664 *Sylva, or A Discourse of the Forest-Trees* (*see* Ash) complained that chestnuts, "delicacies for princes," were only fed to pigs in Britain. But, he wrote, they were a "lusty and masculine food . . . [that] makes Women well complexion'd." Perhaps the witch wanted to look as pretty as possible!

We often call the chestnut a sweet chestnut to differentiate it from another tree, the horse chestnut (*see* Horse Chestnut). Sweet chestnuts came from

Persia, where, it was said, they were fed to children to make them fat and healthy. The Romans called the tree *arbor panis*, or "bread tree," because sweet chestnut flour was a staple food where the tree was abundant and cereals were hard to grow. The sweet chestnut is 23 percent protein but also has more starch than other nuts (or nutlike seeds) so it's very filling. Although chestnut flour contains no gluten (like cereal flours) it was used to make a kind of bread, the original "polenta" of northern Italy. Before wheat was common and potatoes came to Europe, chestnut bread kept many poor people alive.

The Greeks introduced chestnuts to the ancient world. The Romans imported them to Britain, where they did so well they were presumed to be native there. Chestnuts also flourished in Italy, France, and Spain. The nutritious fruits were dried and ground, and sometimes stored in a drawer—giving rise to the French expression "living out of a drawer" (or being poor). Another French expression, *lits de parlement*, or "talking beds," referred to using chestnut leaves for mattresses, which rustled when the sleeper turned over. In Spain dancers twirled to the rhythm of castanets, or *castañetas* (the diminutive of *castañas*, or "chestnut," in Spanish), once two dried chestnuts tied together and clicked against each other.

The Old English name *chesteyne* came from the Old French *chastaigne*, in Latin *castanea*. It's generally supposed that this came from the Greek city of Kastane where the trees grew. Early on the tree was (in English) a *chesten* and the nut a *chesten-nut*. Later the tree itself was called a "chestnut."

The beautiful color of the nuts, and especially their sheen, was used to describe shiny hair of a particular reddish hue (less common in the days before hair dyes). In France the best and largest chestnuts were called *marrons*. These were the fruits with a single seed inside the burr; consequently, they were larger than the *chataigne*, which consisted of several seeds inside each burr. The poorer people and animals ate the *chataignes*. The rich might also enjoy *marrons glacées*, a confection that is achieved in sixteen separate stages. *Marron* also described a color and became "maroon" in English. It also meant a noisy firework (from the explosion of the nuts as they roasted). A fugitive slave who hid in the (often chestnut) woods was a *nègre marron*, and from this we get our word for those who are stranded in wild surroundings, or "marooned."

Chestnuts are native to parts of Asia and America, too. The Chinese chestnut is *C. mollissima* ("very soft"), and the Japanese one is *C. crenata* ("scalloped"). Wherever chestnuts grew, their seeds were eaten and their fine timber (which is almost indistinguishable from oak wood) was used. When Europeans came to North America the predominant forest tree was the American chestnut. Settlers employed it with abandon, cutting thousands of trees to build houses and fences. Chestnuts, however, can regenerate from the roots if the stumps are left, and the American chestnut continued to be a common tree until the beginning of the twentieth century.

IN SPAIN DANCERS TWIRLED TO THE RHYTHM OF CASTANETS, OR CASTAÑETAS (THE DIMINUTIVE OF CASTAÑAS, OR "CHESTNUT," IN SPANISH), ONCE TWO DRIED CHESTNUTS TIED TOGETHER AND CLICKED AGAINST EACH OTHER.

About 1904 the first cases of chestnut blight were noticed on trees in the New York Botanical Gardens. This blight is caused by a fungus that had arrived with imported Chinese chestnuts resistant to it. In spite of new legislation to control imported plant diseases (passed in 1912 and 1919) it was too late for American chestnuts, and the disease spread rapidly. The blighted chestnut "keeps smoldering at the roots / and sending up new shoots," noted Robert Frost, but these shoots die, too, as soon as they reach a certain size. In *Evil Tendencies Cancel*, Frost made the optimistic suggestion that "another parasite / shall come to end the blight," but sadly this has not yet happened. Attempts to create disease-resistant hybrids have not as yet restored to us these magnificent trees. A smaller American chestnut, the chinquapin, is resistant to chestnut blight, but does not have the magnificence of the sweet chestnuts we have lost, and its nuts are very small.

The European or "Spanish" chestnut is *Castanea sativa* (meaning "cultivated"). It isn't wholly resistant to blight but is cultivated in Spain and Italy, from where our sweet chestnuts now come. They aren't as large or sweet as the fabled nuts of the American chestnut, *C. dentata* (for its "toothed" leaves), but remain a part of our Christmas tradition and memories.

CHINA FIR

The China fir, or *Cunninghamia lanceolata* ("spear-shaped" leaves), was described by James Cuninghame in 1702 but did not make its way to Europe until the mid-nineteenth century. Robert Fortune sent it, and many other new plants, back to Britain when he explored China, in 1842, disguised as a "Chinaman" wearing a false "pigtail." The Chinese were discouraging to foreigners and Fortune carried a stick loaded with lead, a gun, and a Chinese dictionary. To avoid arousing suspicions since he was not adept at using chopsticks, he did not eat at inns. He also took along three of the recently invented "Wardian cases." Nathaniel Ward accidentally discovered that plants would survive in a closed glass container when he hatched a chrysalis in a sealed bottle containing earth and later found a small fern thriving. This revolutionized plant transportation.

We know rather little about James Cuninghame (or Cunningham) for whom the tree was given its botanical name. But what we do know is quite dramatic. He was a Scot who went to Chusan Island (off the coast of Shanghai) as a surgeon employed by the East India Company. In 1703 Cuninghame was on another island when its settlement was attacked by Macassan rebels; everyone except Cuninghame himself was massacred. He was wounded, though, and then imprisoned, but finally in 1709 he started back home to Britain. He apparently died at sea on the voyage home.

During his time in China, Cuninghame managed to send home descriptions of many plants and some actual specimens, including a camellia. He also detailed, for the first time, how tea was cultivated in China. The *Cunninghamia* was at first called *Pinus lanceolata* but was renamed in honor of the surgeon. An evergreen tree with very shiny spiked needles, the China fir can reach eighty feet high or more. It bears cones and is a conifer, but in spite of its common name, it isn't a fir but a kind of swamp cypress. There are only two species of the *Cunninghamia*, and it is a rare tree in gardens. In southern and central China it can form thick forests. The Chinese call it *shanmu* and consider it an important timber tree.

> IT BEARS CONES AND IS A CONIFER, BUT IN SPITE OF ITS COMMON NAME, IT ISN'T A FIR BUT A KIND OF SWAMP CYPRESS.

The Victorians loved new exotic plants. Monkey-puzzle trees and China firs, which have similarities, were planted enthusiastically, but the former is hardier and did better in England (*see* Monkey-puzzle). William Robinson, the iconoclast of Victorian garden fashion, hated both trees. The *Cunninghamia*, he wrote, is a "tree of the pine tribe, and perhaps the most miserable-looking ever introduced; something like an Araucaria [monkey-puzzle] it is usually full of dead twigs." He was wrong about the "pine family" and only right about the "dead twigs" because China firs are marginally hardy in Britain and much of North America. Where it belongs, it is a magnificent tree. If it looks homesick that's surely not the tree's fault, but our own.

CINCHONA

When Linnaeus named this tree *Cinchona*, he was honoring the countess of Chinchon, wife of the Spanish Viceroy to Lima. It was said that the countess was dying from ague (or malaria) and was given the powdered bark of the tree, which immediately alleviated her fever and saved her life. She, so the story goes, was so grateful that she obtained a supply of this miraculous bark, took it home to Spain, and distributed it to the poor who were suffering from malaria. Her name will not be forgotten (even though Linnaeus omitted the first "h" in it), but the story, scholars have decided, is unlikely to be true. What *is* true is that the bark of this tree (related to the coffee tree) mitigates and controls malaria, and that using it had a tremendous impact on human history. Incidentally, it's a very pretty tree with evergreen leaves and pinkish lilaclike flowers. It can reach about eighty feet high.

In South America, where the cinchona tree is native, the bark was used medicinally, principally as a febrifuge, long before European explorers introduced malaria. About the time of the countess's story (she died in 1641), the bark was taken to Europe and given to malaria sufferers, with miraculous results. Most likely Peruvian converts first shared it with Jesuit missionaries, who started collecting it and sending it to Europe. The ground bark was called contessa's bark or Jesuits' bark. No one knew how or why it relieved the tertian ague (so called for its regularly repeated fevers) — but it did.

The sales of bark and its medicinal success benefited the Jesuit order and the Catholic Church. Protestants hotly denied these curative properties and stuck to the old system of medicine, which prescribed keeping the body's humors balanced by "bleeding," for fevers (and other ills). Oliver Cromwell probably died of malaria because he flatly refused to take "powder of the devil."

Charles II also had malaria, and after being bled almost to death by his physicians, a Dr. Robert Talbor was allowed to give him a dose of "secret" medicine and cured him. Talbor then went to France where he cured the dauphin. Louis XIV bought the secret of the remedy (rose leaves, lemon juice, and ground cinchona bark), but Talbor did not live long enough to enjoy his reward, dying the very next year.

Malaria was (and for that matter still is) widespread. It was thought that the disease had some connection with swampy places having *mal'aria* ("bad air"), but it wasn't associated with mosquitoes until the end of the nineteenth century. Insect bites were considered a part of life, and many a traveler complained of them. Peter Kalm, in his *Travels*, published in English in 1770 (*see*

Alder), described how "when they [mosquitoes] stung me here at night, my face was so disfigured by little red spots and blisters that I was almost ashamed to show myself." Although we are told that Cleopatra made love to Antony under a net, nobody thought of netting actually saving lives. When the Panama Canal was being made, those who went to hospital for any reason probably caught malaria or yellow fever, even if they did not have either disease when they went in. The nuns put saucers of water around the legs of hospital beds (to prevent ants crawling up) and sometimes decorated the (unnetted) windows with flowers in vases of water, thus unwittingly creating perfect breeding grounds for mosquitoes, which carried both diseases.

THE BARK OF THIS TREE MITIGATES AND CONTROLS MALARIA, AND USING IT HAD A TREMENDOUS IMPACT ON HUMAN HISTORY.

Cinchona bark was in much demand as Europeans went farther into tropical countries. The Jesuits had recommended planting five trees (for the five wounds of Christ) for every tree stripped of its bark and killed. As profits grew, fewer trees remained or were replanted. Meanwhile malaria was spreading. In the southern United States the disease took an enormous summer toll. The only safe people were those of West African descent whose hereditary sickle-cell anemia protected them (the malaria parasite can't take advantage of that shape blood cell). Window screens were still rare. The rich fled to cool summer homes; the poor died. Worst hit were armies.

In 1820 two French scientists isolated quinine, the alkaloid that controls malaria, from cinchona bark. They named the substance from *quinquona*, the South American native word for the bark of this tree. Cinchona bark, however, was becoming scarcer and European colonial powers decided that their sources of quinine should be safeguarded and accessible. Several expeditions were sent to South America to procure seeds or plants of the cinchona tree. At the time it was not known that the potency of the bark varied with trees from different places and of different species. Several attempts to establish quinine plantations failed, either because the seeds didn't germinate or because the trees were low in quinine.

The most successful introduction was of seeds collected by Charles Ledger, an English alpaca trader. These seeds, which grew into trees whose bark was exceptionally high in quinine, were actually found by Ledger's Bolivian assistant—who was killed by his countrymen shortly afterward for giving valuable seeds to a European. In 1865 Ledger sent the seeds home, but the British government wasn't interested. So he offered them to the Dutch, who raised them on Java and soon had a world monopoly of quinine. The new cinchona tree was called *C. ledgeriana* (now *C. officinalis* 'Ledgeriana'). Part of the Dutch success was owing to new methods of harvesting the bark, either by coppicing (cutting the main stem and letting shoots grow up), or "mossing" (covering the stripped areas of the trunk with protective moss).

Once quinine was available and relatively cheap, Europeans could live in places that had previously been "the white man's grave." They could also dose their workers and exploit places that had been inaccessible. It is safe to say that quinine was responsible for the boast that "the sun never sets on the British Empire." Who knows how history would have differed without quinine, dutifully drunk each evening in tonic (mixed with gin) as the sun set around the world: a sure example of a medicinal cocktail.

It wasn't until 1897 that Dr. Ronald Ross reported in the *British Medical Journal* that he had finally seen malarial cells in the stomachs of female anopheles mosquitoes that had fed on the blood of malaria patients, confirming that malaria was carried by these insects ingesting blood before laying their eggs. The male mosquito, by the way, is blameless—he feeds on nectar. Ross wrote a short poem to celebrate his discovery:

I know this little thing
A myriad men will save.
O Death, where is thy sting?
Thy Victory, O Grave?

It was a tremendous discovery, but sadly, millions of people, mostly children, still die of malaria. Synthetic quinine, to which some mosquitoes are now resistant, is a less reliable cure than the bark of the miraculous cinchona tree.

CINNAMON

Nowadays we think of cinnamon as an ingredient of comforting foods: sticky, sinful buns; warm apple pie on a chilly November Thanksgiving; cinnamon toast dripping with butter; creamy soothing rice pudding. What has this to do with a turbulent history and bark ripped from a tree?

The ancients used cinnamon as well as cassia, and brought both to Egypt. Maybe to justify their high prices, Arab traders encouraged a belief that these spices were collected by them at considerable risk, and they were mysterious about the spices' origins. The Greek historian Herodotus wrote that collectors had to cover their eyes to protect themselves from "creatures like bats" and described huge cinnamon nests built onto high precipices "which no one can climb." He told how Arabian traders would leave large chunks of donkey or ox meat in the valley below these nests. While the men watched "from a safe distance," the winged creatures collected the meat and carried it up to their nests. The chunks were so heavy that they broke the nests, which then fell to the ground. The traders picked up the shattered nests (or cinnamon sticks). As late as the twelfth century a medieval bestiary described the "cinomolgus" birds whose "nests sell for very high prices."

Mostly the ancients didn't use cinnamon in food as we do, although they did flavor wine with spices. Cinnamon was used medicinally, and oil of cinnamon does have therapeutic properties. It was also used to embalm the dead and burn at funerals. The bully emperor Nero kicked his pregnant wife, Poppaea, in the stomach so hard she died. Somewhat tardily, he tried to make amends by burning at her funeral all the cinnamon to be found in Rome—a full year's supply.

Like many rare commodities, cinnamon was used as an aphrodisiac. The Old Testament book of Proverbs warns young men about the kind of woman "whose feet abide not in her house." Instead, she waits "at every corner," telling her victim that she has perfumed her bed with cinnamon, and inviting him to "take our fill of love until the morning." The warning concludes that "many strong men" have succumbed to this spicy approach.

At the end of the fifteenth century Portuguese traders discovered the true source of cinnamon on the island of Ceylon (Sri Lanka). The botanical name of the cinnamon tree is *Cinnamomum zeylanicum. Zeylanicum* means "from Ceylon." *Kinnamomon* was the Greek word for "cinnamon" and may come from a Semitic root *Kin*, meaning "China." Cassia, often substituted for cinnamon, does in fact come from China. There are other cinnamon trees, but the variety from Sri Lanka is considered superior by gourmets.

The Portuguese lost no time in exploiting the wild cinnamon trees they found. These trees are evergreen, with pinkish red young leaves that turn to shiny green. The bark is peeled from young shoots during the rainy season when it is most pliable. It is scraped and then dried in the sun until it curls to make "cinnamon sticks." When in 1636 the Dutch took over the island, cinnamon had always been collected from wild trees, but colonists started propagating the trees in groves. There were still heavy penalties protecting the trade, including death for possessing a single illicit cinnamon stick. It wasn't until the nineteenth century that cinnamon was propagated more widely. The French introduced it to the Seychelle Islands. The cassia grown in Egypt is said to have originated from two cuttings originally smuggled to the famous Jardin des Plantes in Paris by the intrepid Pierre Poivre (*see* Clove).

THERE WERE STILL HEAVY PENALTIES PROTECTING THE TRADE, INCLUDING DEATH FOR POSSESSING A SINGLE ILLICIT CINNAMON STICK.

The cinnamon tree was placed in the Laureacae, or laurel, family by Linnaeus. The story of its naming is that Linnaeus was visiting another young botanist in Amsterdam, Johannes Burman. Burman tested his rival by giving Linnaeus the leaf of a "rare" plant to classify. Linnaeus put the leaf into his mouth and pronounced it to be laurel. Burman, who was working on his *Thesaurus Zeylanicus* ("Flora of Ceylon"), said triumphantly that the plant wasn't a laurel, whereupon Linnaeus replied that it was of course cinnamon but should be in the laurel family. A botanical pecking order having been established, Burman then promptly invited Linnaeus to stay with him and help him with his book.

The French call both cinnamon and cassia *canelle* and most of the "cinnamon" used by us is really from the cassia tree (*C. aromataicum*), which is not in the Laurel family. Its bark is coarser and cheaper than that of cinnamon. Taoists believed that cassia was the food of gods, originally brought down to earth from heaven by a hare, the sacred inhabitant of the moon.

Columbus hoped to find valuable spices when he traveled to America, and he believed he had at least discovered cinnamon when he found the *Canella winterana*, a tree native to Florida and the West Indies. Its aromatic bark is used in scented sachets. It could presumably be used to scent the sheets of the lascivious—but it isn't cinnamon. In 1540 Gonzalo Pizarro (brother of the conqueror of the Incas) led an expedition to search for cinnamon in Peru. The expedition to La Canela was a complete disaster. Only eighty men of the two thousand who set out came back, without cinnamon.

Cinnamon powder often was, and still can be, adulterated. So those who want the true spice need to get their own sticks and grind them. This is hard work, because they are tough, as most dried bark would be. For us they are cheap and readily available, probably too cheap for the countries that provide them.

CLOVE

Cloves look like little brown nails, and their name comes from the French *clou*, "nail" (from the Latin *clavus*). The Persian *Neckhak* and the German *Nagelchen* also mean "little nail." In spite of their utilitarian appearance, cloves are actually the unopened, dried buds of the clove tree flower. If left unpicked these buds develop into small flowers that in turn produce a seed. The tree grows to about thirty feet and is evergreen with very shiny leaves that are rosy pink when they emerge.

Cloves are native to the Moluccan, or Spice Islands, in the East Indian archipelago. We don't know how long ago their aromatic properties were discovered and used, but by the Han Dynasty (200 BC to AD 220) they had been imported to China and were prevalent in the imperial court. Before being allowed to approach the emperor, courtiers were handed a clove to suck, to be sure their breath would not be offensive to him.

Arab traders brought cloves and other spices west, and a Greek name for them was *caryophyllum* (meaning "nut leaf").The Arabic was *qarumfel*, which eventually became *girofre* in French and "gillyflower" in English. Carnations were also called gillyflowers because they smelled like cloves. Often in paintings depicting the life of Jesus there are carnations symbolizing the "nails" (or cloves) that will be used for the crucifixion. Sometimes the Christ child will be depicted holding a carnation, seemingly because it's pretty but really because it predicts the grim future.

The earliest accounts of the clove trade described Arab traders leaving goods on mats on the beach, returning to their ships, and the next day finding a payment of cloves on the mats. The natives (probably very wisely) did not show themselves and were thought by some to be genies. Cloves have accounted for many a violent death. The Portuguese forcibly established themselves on the Spice Islands, staying for about a hundred years until the Dutch drove them out in 1605 and took over the spice trade. The Dutch protected their monopoly by eradicating all the clove trees except those on the island of Amboine. This seriously violated a native custom of planting a clove tree for the birth of a new baby. Under the Dutch there was a death penalty for anyone taking clove seeds or seedlings off the island.

> BEFORE BEING ALLOWED TO APPROACH THE EMPEROR, COURTIERS WERE HANDED A CLOVE TO SUCK, TO BE SURE THEIR BREATH WOULD NOT BE OFFENSIVE TO HIM.

Peter Poivre ("Pepper") started his career as a French missionary. He lost his right arm to a British cannonball off the island of Sumatra, but he continued sailing the dangerous seas in search of spices. In 1745 he managed to steal seedlings of the clove tree from the Dutch and send them back to France, so breaking the Dutch monopoly. Eventually Madagascar and Zanzibar became important centers for raising cloves. A huge market for them is still in Indonesia where clove cigarettes (called *Kretek*) are widely smoked. Harvesting cloves is labor intensive because the fragile buds have to be carefully picked and sorted before being dried in the sun.

The botanical name of the clove used to be *Eugenia caryophyllus* or *E. aromatica*, after Prince Eugène, Duke of Savoy, who was born in Paris in 1663 but fought for the Austrian emperor Leopold. Prince Eugene was a soldier for thirty-nine years and was wounded thirteen times. He defended Vienna from the Turks and was at Blenheim with the Duke of Marlborough. In between all this he acquired an estate at Belvedere in Vienna but never lived there (presumably he was too busy fighting). However, the gardens became famous, and when he died in 1736 (he never married) the imperial family took over his estate. The large *Eugenia* genus was named for him, but the clove tree was more recently moved into the Myrtaceae, or myrtle, family and given the name *Syzygium aromaticum*, from the Greek *syzygos*, "joined," or ""yoked" (referring to the configuration of the leaves).

Cloves are still used to alleviate toothache and help control bad breath. Some historians say they were once popular aphrodisiacs on account of their shape — in spite of their rather diminutive size! Oil of cloves is still an important ingredient of seductive perfumes, and warm apple pie, with cloves, can cure a lot of ills and bring comfort to most of us.

COCONUT

I f you imagine that the three indentations at the base of a coconut (*Cocos nucifera*) look a bit like two eyes and a screwed up little mouth you are not the first to think so. In fact the name coco comes from a Portuguese or Spanish slang word meaning "a little monkeylike face." *Nucifera* means "nut bearing." The three holes, or indentations, are scars where the coconut was attached to its stem before it fell (or was knocked) to the ground.

These holes have to be absolutely waterproof and provide an exit for the new shoot when the time comes. It takes the nut a year to mature, and the young nuts are full of liquid, which gradually turns into "meat." Coconuts are so impenetrable they can bob around in the ocean for months, retaining their ability to germinate, floating from island to island, shore to shore, until they land on some beach and sprout. If the nut hasn't been opened and eaten, an applelike growth forms within it, out of which a delicate stem sprouts, unerringly pointing toward one of the three soft spots in the thick shell.

William Dampier (*see* Avocado) circumnavigated the globe three times, took part in mutinies and piracy, and thought nothing of dunking sailors on a ship's bowsprit until they drowned. He found coconuts, describing with wonder how "Nature hath so contrived" this ability of the tender shoot to emerge. He called coconuts, of all plants, "the most generally serviceable to the Conveniences as well as the Necessities of humane life."

It's most likely that coconut palms originated in Southeast Asia and then traveled across the Pacific to the Americas. Neither Christopher Columbus nor other New World explorers mentioned finding coconuts on the East Coast of America or the West Indies. They were not known to the classical world either. On the Pacific Coast, however, pre-Columbian pottery depicts coconuts. The Egyptians may have obtained them from Arab traders in about the sixth century AD. When Marco Polo encountered coconuts at the end of the thirteenth century, he called them pharoah's nuts. He wrote that "from one nut a man can have his fill of meat and drink."

Spanish explorers carried coconuts to South America and established them there, but even where they could have flourished, coconuts didn't immediately spread farther north. These days it's hard to imagine any Florida beaches without coconut palms, but it wasn't until the end of the nineteenth century that coconuts dramatically increased along the coastline. The story is that a ship, the *Providencia*, was carrying a cargo of coconuts from Havana to Barcelona when, on January 9, 1878, it was wrecked off the Florida coast. The coconuts

floated ashore out of the wreckage, soon sprouted, and colonized rapidly. Some of the shipwrecked sailors swam ashore, settled, and called their new town Palm Beach.

Apart from being eaten widely, coconuts are still used in countless other ways. Their fibrous husks, called coir, make rope and mats. The oil, pressed from copra, or dried coconut meat, is used, among other things, for soaps, creams, lipsticks, and margarine. Coconut "milk" from pounded coconut meat is important in much Eastern cuisine. Less obvious uses include making synthetic rubber, brake fluid, detergents, and plastics. In Thailand a baby's first taste of solid food used to be a spoonful of soft, immature coconut meat, administered by a priest. In our culture coconuts are ingredients of cakes and candy, or prizes at fun fairs. In other cultures the coconut was a sacred tree.

THE NAME COCO COMES FROM A PORTUGUESE OR SPANISH SLANG WORD MEANING "A LITTLE MONKEYLIKE FACE."

Strictly speaking, the coconut palm isn't a tree at all, although almost all of us think of it as one. Botanically it is a stemmed plant, more akin to grasses than trees. It doesn't have bark like most other trees, but the sap rises through the whole stem, or "trunk." Coconuts have no taproots and they spread their dense shallow roots outward for long distances. They grow in sandy soil, often right at the edge of the sea, and their very flexible trunks can bend against ocean winds. As the tree grows, the lower leaves fall off, leaving a characteristic scarred surface, and since there is no "bark" the scars don't heal, as on true trees. Even though they look as if they grow on completely arid sandy beaches, washed constantly by tides, coconuts do need fresh water and often take advantage of freshwater pools near the sea.

The massive eruption of the volcano Krakatoa in 1883 completely destroyed the nearby islands. Only eighteen months later coconuts were found germinating on the ashy beaches on the island of Lang. The coconut is a tree of life. It also has a life span oddly comparable to a human's. It takes about a year for the new shoot to emerge from the nut. At twelve to fourteen years it can reproduce and continues to do so for about sixty years. It lives to about eighty years. In a plant so close to us in so many ways, if we fancy that we see a small human face in each of its nuts, perhaps it's not so very surprising.

COFFEE

The Arabs called the coffee fruit *bunn* and the coffee brew *qahwa*. Coffee "beans" are the seeds of the beautiful coffee tree, a shiny-leaved evergreen that can grow more than ten feet high. The flowers are white and scented and the berries bright red. Each drupe (a fruit whose seed is protected by a hard casing) contains two seeds rich in caffeine.

Coffee trees probably originated in Ethiopia. The discovery of the properties of coffee goes back farther than dependable history. A popular legend is of a first-century Ethiopian goatherd called Kaldi, who noticed his goats dancing and prancing after feeding on coffee trees (the leaves contain caffeine, too, although not as much as the seeds). Kaldi tried chewing some berries himself and greatly enjoyed the sensation they produced. In one version of the story he told his father about them. In another version, popular in the West, he brought some berries to a nearby monastery. There were Orthodox Christian communities in Ethiopia at the time, and he gave them to the abbot, who impatiently tossed them into the fire. The heavenly aroma of the beans roasting immediately caught the abbot's attention. From then on, coffee kept the monks awake during their night vigils. In another story, circulated in the East, Kaldi took the beans to a mosque. We know that one way or another coffee spread through the Arab world and that the Sufi sect in Yemen drank coffee to stay awake during their nocturnal rituals. Coffee was known as the beverage of the friends of God.

In the sixteenth century "wine of Araby" began to be discovered by Westerners. In 1573 Leonard Rauwolf, a German botanist and explorer, described sampling a drink called *chaube*, which made him feel "curiously animated." The Turks, he said, drank it "in public without fear of being seen." This wasn't always so, for coffee drinking was banned at different times both in the East and West by Muslims and Christians. At one time in Constantinople, illicit coffee drinkers could be punished by being sewn into a sack and tossed into the sea. Even so, some people evidently couldn't give it up.

The chief trading port for coffee was at Mocha, where coffee was brought down from the mountains of Yemen to be exported. That is where we get the name for our mocha lattes. Extras like vanilla and raspberry are a modern refinement, although cardamon was added to coffee by the Arabs early on.

By the end of the seventeenth century, Europeans were enthusiastically drinking coffee. Clement VIII, who died in 1605, was said to have tasted coffee and decided that it was "a pity to let the infidels have exclusive use of it" and that it should be a "Christian Beverage." Coffee houses became popular.

Here men met and exchanged ideas. Women were excluded. In London, coffee houses were sometimes called penny universities, because in them one could receive an education. They were not without critics. Some women objected to losing their men to hours of drinking coffee and, in 1674, published a *Petition against Coffee*, claiming that it "Eunucht our husbands." A counter-pamphlet said that, on the contrary, coffee "adds spiritualescency to the Sperme."

Pamphlets notwithstanding, little seems to have had much impact on coffee drinking or the popularity of coffee houses, which were sometimes suspected to be centers for antigovernment groups. In 1675 Charles II tried to abolish coffee houses but had to withdraw the edict because of popular protest. The American Revolution was supposed to have been plotted in Boston coffee houses, and drinking coffee became a patriotic symbol—whereas drinking tea was considered pro-English. John Adams wrote to his wife that he was trying to "wean" himself from drinking tea. In Napoleonic France, Napoléon Bonaparte (who drank quantities of coffee himself and whose wife Joséphine came from a coffee plantation in Martinique) tried to reduce coffee consumption in France to make the country more independent. This may have been when the French started adding chicory to coffee, a custom that is still preferred in New Orleans. The French continued to enjoy coffee, the empire was lost, and poor Napoléon on his deathbed begged for a just a "teaspoonful" of coffee, which his doctor was afraid to allow him.

There have always been claims that coffee is harmful to health. The human liver tries to eliminate caffeine from our bodies (that's why coffee is a diuretic), but some remains to affect our brains, and we're still arguing about whether this is dangerous or merely pleasant. Linnaeus (who also drank coffee) said that he knew of "three distinguished persons who from over-indulgence in coffee could scarcely get their hands to their mouths," adding ominously that all three were "now dead!"

Producing *Coffea arabica* could not remain a monopoly of the Arab world. By the end of the eighteenth century the Dutch, French, and British were growing coffee in their own foreign plantations, often using slave labor. A coffee plant from the Jardin de Plantes in Paris was supposedly taken to the island of Martinique to start plantations there. The story (probably legendary) was that Mathieu de Clieu carried the first plant there and shared his water ration on the voyage with his valuable seedling (*see* Cedar).

C. arabica is not the only plant containing caffeine. Indeed, weight for weight tea leaves contain more caffeine than coffee leaves. There are many other plants that contain caffeine, a substance that is thought to be present in order to deter insects—one could call caffeine a kind of insecticide!

C. canephora, or robusta coffee, grows in Africa and can stand a wider range of conditions than *C. arabica*. It produces berries more quickly than *C. arabica* trees, and these contain much more caffeine. Robusta coffee is often mixed with arabica coffee, although coffee connoisseurs scorn the flavor. There is a kind of coffee called *Kopi luaka*, which is brewed from beans that have been eaten and then excreted by civet cats in Sumatra. Some people are willing to pay astronomical prices for a brew of these beans, which, after being separated, cleaned, and roasted, are said to contain an extra something.

At one time in Constantinople, illicit coffee drinkers could be punished by being sewn into a sack and tossed into the sea.

When coffee is hard to get or thought harmful, other substitutes and additives are tried. In times of scarcity "coffee" has been made from acorns and dandelions. When settlers went to Kentucky they were delighted to find a tree with long brown pods that could be roasted and used to make a coffeelike drink. The Kentucky coffee tree *Gymnocladus dioica* is so called from *gymnos*, "naked," and *klados*, "branch," because its leaves emerge late and fall early. These trees are dioecious, with the male and female reproductive organs borne on different trees. The Kentucky coffee tree is a very handsome deciduous tree but contains no caffeine. The name coffee tree stuck, but the use of its beans as a pick-me-up did not.

It's technically possible to poison oneself by drinking too much coffee—but how much is too much? The French writer Honoré de Balzac apparently drank sixty cups of coffee every night, and he claimed that his ideas then came marching into his mind "like battalions." Ludwig van Beethoven brewed his coffee using sixty beans per cup. The results in both cases seem to have been nothing but good.

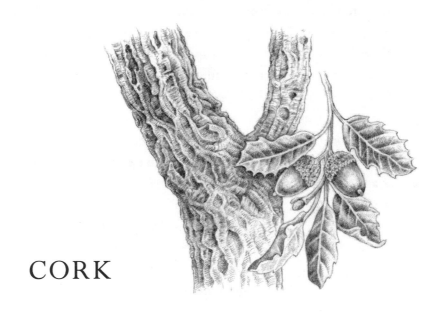

CORK

At the beginning of *Remembrance of Things Past*, Marcel Proust describes being a child in bed, falling into sleep like a "dark tunnel," and waking in the night disoriented from an "abyss of not-being." While writing this and other memories, Proust himself spent most of his time in bed, in a dark shuttered room, completely lined with cork.

Cork comes from the cork tree, a kind of oak. Its outer bark, which can be several inches thick, is composed of dead cells lined with a waxy substance. The gaps between the cells are filled with air, making the bark both waterproof and very light. The trapped air also makes cork a poor conductor of sound—so allowing Proust thirteen years of silence while he wrote his famous novel. Not everybody afterward has had an equally long cork-lined seclusion to *read* the book in its entirety.

Soundproofing was only one of the many uses for the bark of this extraordinary tree. It grows in Mediterranean regions, particularly Spain and Portugal, and its properties seem to have been appreciated from ancient times. Cork bark was used for shoes and floating fishing nets by both the Greeks and Romans. The Greek word for "cork" is *phellos*, and the outer bark of trees, called the phellem, has two layers under it, the phellogen and the phelloderm. The cork oak differs from other trees in that its corky layer of bark is very thick, and the air-filled cells can be compressed but will swell up again. When a cork is eased out of a bottle there is a loud "pop," and that is how our sodas (once sealed with real corks) got their name "soda pop."

Even these days, fine wines are often sealed with real cork, which is cut so the air ducts (or lenticels) lie transversely and the cork won't leak (you can see these lines by cutting a cork vertically). An extra wine charge in a restaurant is called a corkage fee. Presumably wines with screw tops or in cardboard boxes can't be damned by wine snobs as "corked" (meaning the cork hasn't done its job properly), although they might be damned for other reasons. The *real* cognoscenti, however, can still impress their dinner companions by complaining a wine is "suberous," which is another word for "corky." The Latin *suber* ("cork") gave the tree its botanical name *Quercus suber* (*Quercus* means "oak"). The waxy substance in the cell walls is called *suberin*.

Since it's so light and waterproof, cork has been used since ancient times for the soles of shoes or sandals. John Evelyn in his 1664 *Sylva, or A Discourse of Forest-Trees* (*see* Ash) told about "the Grecian Ladies" in cork sandals "whence they were called light-footed." He goes on to describe what must have been the earliest platform shoes: "*Venetian* Dames took it [cork] up for their monstrous *Chopines*; affecting or usurping an artificial eminency above *Men*, which *Nature* has denied them." The "Ladies" might have answered that elevated soles protected their feet from muddy streets. Our name cork came via its use for shoes. In Spain a cork shoe was *al-corque* (*al* is the Arabic definite article; *corque* probably came from the Latin *cortex*, "bark").

Cork was such a valuable commodity it was natural to want to spread the trees. In 1813 Thomas Jefferson wrote that he hoped to import cork oaks to America. The acorns he planted failed to "vegetate" and the young trees died. Corks still mostly come from Spain and Portugal. It is thought that the hot desert winds, or siroccos, encourage the tree to make its thick protective bark (often impregnated with sand). The rough "virgin bark" is carefully cut and pared off before commercial bark replaces it. Unless the underbark is damaged, the tree will continue to live and make new outer bark every few years. Cork oaks are evergreen and can live for hundreds of years.

No other tree provides commercial bark, but there are other "corkwoods" not related to the cork oak. The southern corkwood (a kind of poplar) has extremely buoyant wood and grows in swamps. Its botanical name is *Leitneria floridana*, for Edward F. Leitner, a German doctor who, while botanizing in Florida, was killed on March 10, 1838, by Seminole Indians. Another "corkwood" is a tree native to New Zealand, also with very light wood, used by Maoris to make canoes. In Asia the *Phellodendron* (*phellos* "cork," *dendron* "tree") is called the Amur cork tree.

These days natural cork is mostly replaced by synthetic substances. Our sodas come in cans or bottles with twist-off caps. Huge fishing nets scour our ocean floors rather than bobbing on cork floats over the waves. We don't use real cork for flooring or soundproofing walls.

In Spain the cork orchards, or *dehesas*, were sustainable for generations. The oak bark was harvested in continual cycles, and around the trees pigs grazed on the fallen acorns. These small cork farms are labor intensive and can't compete with factories. Paradoxically, the future of cork trees is uncertain, because we no longer need their bark as once we did.

COTTONWOOD

The cottonwood gets its common name from its fluffy white seeds that look like cotton balls. According to Carl Linnaeus's pupil, Peter Kalm, French explorers first called the tree *le cotonnier*. At that time (1747), the cotton plant, grown for its fibers, had not yet been imported to North America, even though it gave its name to this native tree.

The eastern cottonwood's botanical name is *Populus deltoides*, *deltoides* for its heart-shaped leaf, the shape of the letter *delta* (or "d") in the Greek alphabet. Cottonwoods are a kind of poplar. The black cottonwood is *P. trichocarpa* ("with hairy fruits").

Native Americans, of course, were familiar with cottonwoods and used their wood, buds, and bark. One name for the tree was *canyáhu*, meaning "peel-off wood." The bark peels off easily from the tree, and the substance under it was sometimes pounded and eaten. Buds were used medicinally, and large cotton-wood tree trunks made dug-out canoes. The triangular leaves could be folded and fastened with a thorn to make tiny toy tepees, and some Indian legends even said that children playing this way actually invented the tepee. Children, believed the Sioux holy man Black Elk (1863–1950), are "pure and therefore the Great Spirit . . . may show them many things which are not revealed to older people." A young cottonwood was also used for the traditional sun dance ceremony. It was chosen the year before it was cut and, during the year, was visited and prayed to. The U.S. government discouraged the sun dance until the Vietnam War, when tribal elders insisted their young men should be al-lowed time to dance it before leaving to fight.

Settlers in America had little reverence for the cottonwood tree. Its wood is light and soft, and it was mainly used for nondurable projects, including coffins. Later it was popular for making crates and cigar boxes. Cottonwoods are not long lived (about a hundred years), but they are fast growing. Like other poplars (*see* Poplar), they often grow near water or where water can be found. They can reach nearly two hundred feet high and six feet in diameter and provide welcome shade in hot climates. They were often the biggest trees around in southern states. Because of this, and their horizontal branches, they were used as "gallows trees" for hanging criminals (or those thought to be criminals).

The "cotton" from which the tree gets its name has no relation to it, and it isn't even a tree but a shrub. Cotton was known to the ancient world but did not take the place of wool and linen for a long time. Herodotus, writing in about 445 BC, described trees that "produce a kind of wool better in quality and more beautiful than sheep's wool." The Greek name for this plant was *gos-sipium* (now botanically *gossypium*). When the Arabs began growing it, around the tenth century AD, they called it *qutun*, which is how we got "cotton."

When cotton became an important southern crop, harvesting it was very labor intensive, requiring many hands, and its production was an excuse for slave labor. In Mark Twain's *Huckleberry Finn*, published in 1884, a boy and his companion, the runaway slave Jim, take refuge on a raft and float together down the Mississippi River. Huck is constantly surprised at the sensitivity and integrity of his companion. They float during the night and "at the first streak of day . . . we tied up to a towhead in a big bend [of the river] and hacked off cottonwood branches with the hatchet and covered up the raft with them." A "towhead," he explains, "is a sand-bar that has cottonwoods on it as thick as harrow-teeth." The boy and the slave huddle together under the sheltering cottonwoods, and Huck Finn slowly learns that he respects, and loves, Jim. Here at least "cotton" and slavery are friends.

ONE NAME FOR THE TREE WAS *CANYÁHU*, MEANING "PEEL-OFF WOOD."

CYPRESS

The cypress is named for Kyparissos, a boy whom the Greek god Apollo loved. Apollo pursued young boys and young women with equal ardor. He was particularly fond of Kyparissos, though, and gave him a pet stag, which the boy accidentally killed. Kyparissos was so overcome with remorse that he would not be comforted, begging the god to let him perpetually mourn. So Apollo turned Kyparissos into a cypress tree.

Cypresses were often planted near tombs. Because they will not, like some other trees, regenerate if they are cut down, they symbolized death. They are evergreen, pointing toward heaven, also suggesting a possibility of eternal life. In the Middle East they were planted in gardens, too. Islamic gardens, places for contemplation as well as pleasure, were full of religious symbolism such as sacred life-giving water channels dividing them into four (the cosmos). Cypresses alternating with fruit trees, especially oranges, symbolized the connection of life with death (*see* Orange).

The Mediterranean cypress is *Cupressus sempervirens*, or "evergreen." Cypresses last a long time, both before and after they die. The aromatic wood was used by the Egyptians to make coffins, still in our museums. The cypress-wood doors of Saint Peter's in Rome lasted for about a thousand years before being replaced. No one has yet found the remains of Noah's ark (though some still look for them) but, if it existed, it was built of long-lasting *gopher* wood, translated as "wood from Cyprus." The island of Cyprus gets its name from the tree. The sixteenth-century herbalist John Gerard wrote of cypress wood that it is "not hurt by rotting, cobwebs, nor any infirmities or corruption."

It's hard to imagine southern France, Spain, or Italy without Italian cypresses (*C. sempervirens* 'Stricta') dotting the hot, dry landscape. Their thin columns are like straight black exclamation points, although poor Vincent Van Gogh, when he painted them at San Remy shortly before he killed himself, saw them differently, undulating torturously toward the heavens.

The name cypress is confusing, because not all trees called cypresses are cypresses, and some trees not named cypress *are* cypresses. This is because many conifers look alike. Taxonomists and botanists are still spending (one presumes) hardworking mornings trying to sort them all out. DNA testing is helping to clarify true cypresses, false cypresses, and hybrid cypresses—and there are literally hundreds of them altogether.

The *C. sempervirens* of the Middle East is a true cypress but not the only one. Another is the Patagonia cypress of South America with the botanical name *Fitzroya cupressoides*, the only member of its subfamily. It gets its name from Captain Robert Fitzroy, commander of the *Beagle*. Fitzroy was a Christian who could not accept Darwin's theories. Years after the voyage was completed and the *Origin of Species* had been published, he still raged against Darwin. He ended up cutting his own throat. The tree named for him grows luxuriantly in Chile and Argentina, where it can live up to three thousand years. Its leaves are arranged in groups of three, with a distinctive white base. One hopes that at least the irascible Fitzroy liked the tree.

Another true cypress is the Mexican cypress, usually called cedar of Goa. It was once mistakenly thought to have originated in Portugal, which had a colony in Goa, on the west coast of India—such are the ways names are given! The Monterey cypress, *C. macrocarpa* ("large fruited"), was named by a German botanist employed by the London Horticultural Society to collect plants in California. When Karl Theodore Hartweg found the Monterey cypress in 1846, he said it "closely resembled" the cedar of Lebanon, but he didn't call it a cedar. The Monterey cypress grows larger outside its natural habitat in California. It is thought to have been stranded after the Ice Age in a less lush habitat than it originally had, and prefers.

California's incense cedar is a true cypress whose botanical name, *Calocedrus decurrens*, comes from the Greek *kalos*, "beautiful." "Decurrent" means the leaf base forms a wing merging with the stalk beneath it. All this beauty has been of doubtful assistance to the tree, because its wood makes pencils and (in spite of computers) we still use a great many pencils. Those of us (like this writer) who love trees but still prefer writing with pencils face a dilemma here. All cypresses these days are also threatened with cypress canker, a worldwide destructive blight.

The botanical name for false cypresses is *Chamaecyparis*. This comes from the Greek *chamai*, meaning "creeping" or "lowly."

The *Chamaecyparis* group includes huge trees, not "lowly" at all. The majestic southern white cedar, a false cypress, is *C. thyoides*. Its wood was used by the earliest settlers to make beams and roof shingles because it doesn't rot. When supplies of large trees became scarce it was discovered that huge old trees could be harvested from under peaty swamps and the timber would still be good. *Thyoides* means "like a thuja" (*see* Juniper).

The best-known false cypress is *C. lawsoniana*, first sent to Scotland in 1854 by William Murray, who was gathering material for his "Notes on Californian Trees." He sent seeds to his colleague Charles Lawson who had a successful nursery garden near Edinburgh. Murray's seeds grew into trees which have been a part of British gardens ever since. Charles Lawson wrote *Pinetum Britannicum, A Descriptive Account of All Hardy Trees of the Pine Tribe Cultivated in Great Britain*, illustrated with beautiful colored lithographs. It would be a much stouter volume if compiled now, partly because the many cultivars of the Lawson cypress form a tribe of their own, ranging from erect to pendulant, gold to blue.

THE CYPRESS WOOD DOORS OF SAINT PETER'S IN ROME LASTED FOR ABOUT A THOUSAND YEARS BEFORE BEING REPLACED.

In the coldest regions of northwestern America grows the *C. nootkatensis*, a false cypress from the Nootka Sound in British Columbia. Sometimes it is called the stinking cypress, since its leaves when crushed give off a catty odor. The Nootka cypress was one of the parents of the famous and widespread Leyland cypress. The other parent was the Monterey cypress. Leyland cypresses come from a chance hybrid found in 1888 at Leighton Hall in Shropshire, near Wales. Nootka cypresses were being raised from seed and a Monterey cypress grew in the same garden. By the beginning of the twentieth century Leyland cypresses became widely popular because they grow so fast and can form a dense hedge almost instantly. They are often the cause of disputes between neighbors—they can grow very high if not rigorously pruned—and apparently high fences can make bad neighbors, who complain that their sunshine has been preempted. There are also many, many hybrids of the Leyland cypress. Its botanical name is × *Cupressocyparis leylandii*, which means "hybrid Cypress cypress of Leyland." The reiteration of "cypress" is exceedingly apt—as these trees are repeated over and over again, edging the crisp lawns of millions of gardens.

DATE

The Koran devotes a *sura*, "chapter," to Mariam (Mary, mother of Jesus) who gave birth to her son under a palm tree. In some Christian legends Mary gave birth to Jesus under a palm tree, which also offered her its fruit, the date. Maybe this is why old herbalists instructed women to eat three dates after giving birth. In Gerard's revised *Herball* of 1633 (*see* Banana) dates were said to be good for "wambling of womens stomackes that are with childe."

By the twelfth century the word "date" was in the English language, but the fruits weren't common much before Tudor times. By Shakespeare's era dates were used in cooking and his allusion (in *Troilus and Cressida*) to a man "baked with no Date in the pye" was culinarily familiar enough to make a good risqué joke.

From prehistory a difference between male and female date trees was recognized. Assyrian carvings show winged figures pollinating the female date palm by hand — as was the custom from whenever dates were first cultivated, so far back we have no records. Since they are not attractive to insects, wild dates would have had to rely on sporadic pollination by the wind until someone discovered that tying a bunch of male flowers near the female flowers guaranteed a fine crop. Because it was known to have two sexes (centuries before the sexuality of plants was accepted), the date was a symbol of fertility and considered especially akin to humans. Mohammed pointed out that besides their sexuality, date palms, like people, irrevocably die if their heads are cut off.

Date palms probably originated and spread from the Euphrates valley (thought by some to be the original site of the Garden of Eden). Palms will grow in Europe, but do not ripen fruit, except in southern Spain. The Romans and Greeks grew date palms and ate dates but imported the fruit. The best dates came from Jericho.

The Arab people not only ate dates but relied on them generally. There were, said an Arab proverb, as many uses for the date as there were days in the year. The prophet Mohammed instructed his followers to honor the date palm for "she is your aunt . . . made of the same stuff as Adam." The fast of Ramadan is still traditionally broken by eating a date. The less sweet dates were made into "bread." The sweeter ones were crushed or dried to be carried across the desert — often the only food except for milk. Even the camels were fed crushed date stones. The leaves made shade and thatch. The fibers made ropes. The Hebrews condemned *shekar*, or date wine, but Marco Polo wrote that date wine "makes a man drunk sooner that grape wine," adding, "And very good it is."

The scientific name for the date palm, given by Linnaeus, is *Phoenix dactyl-ifera*, from the Greek *dactylos*, meaning "finger." Fingers have three sections, as does the group of poetic syllables also called a dactyl. Date fruits resemble stubby, unjointed fingers (but not syllables). The Greeks may have imported dates from Phoenicia, because they called the date palm Phoeni-cian. When Linnaeus named the date palm *Phoenix* he was also alluding to the mythical bird, which died and rose again from burned ashes. The date palm was also symbolic life and of rebirth, not only in Christian countries but also Arab ones. Sometimes sacred date palms were hung with offerings, including clothes and weapons. In Islamic gardens the stems of date palms were sometimes sheathed in precious metals.

꙰ UNLIKE OTHER TREES (AND MANY HUMANS) A DATE PALM DOESN'T INCREASE IN GIRTH WITH AGE.

The date palm was one of several candidates for the Tree of Life in the Garden of Eden. In some legends Adam was allowed to take three plants from Eden and he chose dates, wheat, and myrtle — the first two useful food staples, and the latter a symbol of love (another staple).

Dates are palms, and palms aren't like most trees (*see* Coconut). They are monocotyledons — that is, their seeds put out just one sprout rather than the paired leaves familiar to gardeners who sow seeds. The tree "trunk" isn't of heartwood surrounded by layers of cambium (or bark) as in most trees, and palms can't be dated by counting growth rings. Unlike other trees (and many humans) a date palm doesn't increase in girth with age. It grows upward, often to a hundred feet high, but not outward, retaining its youthful waistline. Young palms seem short and stubby. They have no branches, only a crown of feathery leaves on top. After about five years the lower leaves die, leaving a characteristically scarred tree stem. The fruits, which a date palm can produce for about eighty years, are in huge pendulous clusters hanging from the top of the tree. Since they have to be pollinated by humans, date growers prefer younger, shorter trees.

Date groves, called gardens in the Middle East, consist of about fifty female trees to every male tree—a haremlike arrangement that echoes some cultures. Male pollen could even be traded in Eastern markets, often marked as being from particularly virile trees. The palms are generally propagated by suckers rather than by seeds. When all the suckers have been cut from a date palm it won't produce new ones.

Date palms were probably spread by travelers carrying suckers. The Arabs took them to Spain. An eighth-century Arab poet, Abd al-Rahkman, in the city of Córdoba, compared his homesickness to that of a date palm in his garden: "You have sprung from soil in which you are a stranger, and I like you am far from home." He prays for the comfort of rain, "streaming from Heaven in a grateful downpour." Actually dates cannot tolerate water from the atmosphere (even from heaven). Their tops have to be quite dry and their roots wet for them to ripen fruit, which is why they flourish in desert oases with underground water.

The Spanish took date palms to the New World, but they weren't grown commercially in America until the early twentieth century, when the irrigated desert was found to suit them admirably. The American center of date commerce is, appropriately, in Mecca (California). The most common date established commercially in the United States was the semidry 'Deglet Noir', a name from the Arabic *daglet el nour*, or date "of light." Some Arabic names are less ethereal, such as "bride's fingers," or "mule's testicles." There are many differently shaped dates. The Portuguese name for the fruit is *tâmara*, from the Arabic *tamr*. Tamar is still a popular Hebrew name for girls, graceful as date palms. The biblical Absolom's "fair sister" was called Tamar—and her tragic story is sordid as any "news" we read today (the curious can see Samuel 2: 14).

Biblical place-names often reflect widespread cultivation of dates. Bethany means "the house of dates." Another name, *hazazon-tamar* (*chatz'tzon tamar* in Hebrew), means "felling of the palm," an important reminder that cutting down date trees was one of the best ways of hurting an enemy. Not only was a staple food plant removed, but a symbol of grace and of rebirth was also destroyed.

EBONY

Long before Paul McCartney's duet with Stevie Wonder, ebony, the darkest of woods, was often paired with pale ivory. Both these substances have given their name to a color, and it is possible that the two names themselves share the common root *ebu*, "elephant." Ebony is not only black but extremely hard, as is ivory. The Greek name was *ebenos*.

Because of its blackness, the throne of Pluto (king of the underworld) was said to have been made of ebony. Certainly ebony wood was used in Egyptian tombs. Among the offerings made to Tyrus, in the book of Ezekiel, were "horns of ivory and ebony." Marco Polo (who explored Asia from 1271 to 1295) wrote of other uses. He had seen trees with "wood called ebony, which is very black and is used for making chess-men and pen-cases."

Ebony wood has always been a luxury. Only the heartwood is used and the trees (which come from East Africa, India, and Sri Lanka) don't get massive. Their timber has to be harvested in short lengths. The so-called true ebony is *Diospyros ebenum*, also called Ceylon ebony. It grows to about sixty feet and the heartwood is a uniform jet black. Ebony wood is so dense that you can't put a nail into it. It's hard to carve but can be polished to a smooth gloss that doesn't even look like wood, especially evident in piano keys and musical instruments like clarinets. An "ebonist" is one who works or trades in ebony and "to ebonize" is to make other wood look like ebony.

Diospyros means "divine grain" or "food of god" and more appropriately applies to the persimmon. Ebony *is* a kind of persimmon (*see* Persimmon) bearing fruit that is edible (if not palatable). In spite of this, the darkness of ebony was once associated with death and the tree was believed to be poisonous. In Shakespeare's *Hamlet*, the ghost of Hamlet's father reveals that he was murdered with "cursed Hebenon" poured into "the porches of my ear." "Hebenon" is assumed by most scholars to mean ebony, and Marlowe, too, alluded to the assumed poisonous "juice of Hebon." But even its associations with death didn't preclude the beauty of ebony: "Is ebony like her? O wood divine! / A wife of such wood were felicity," declares Lord Berowne in *Love's Labour's Lost*.

"Is ebony like her? O wood divine! / A wife of such wood were felicity."

In our days, black is not automatically associated with death and evil. Widows no longer shroud themselves in ebon clothing, a color more often favored by hip urban executives. Black is smart, and black is beautiful. When *Ebony* magazine was launched in 1945, it was meant to attract, and did, millions of intelligent young Americans.

But even if they "live together in perfect harmony" on a singer's piano keyboard and are breathtakingly beautiful, real ivory from elephant tusks and real ebony are best avoided by those who care about saving our animals and our trees.

ELDER

Carl Linnaeus dedicated his *Genera Plantarum* to his eighteenth-century contemporary and patron, the great Dr. Herman Boerhaave. It was said that Boerhaave refused to receive Voltaire because he would not honor someone who did not honor God. But it was also said that whenever Boerhaave passed an elder tree he respectfully doffed his hat to it.

In 1664 John Evelyn (*see* Ash) said of the elder tree that it was "a catholicum against all infirmities whatever." Long before his time, all parts of it were used medicinally. Berries and flowers were used to make healing concoctions. Both elder flower water (for the skin) and elderberry wine (for the spirit) are still popular today. The Old English name for the common elder (*Sambucus nigra*) was *ellern*, possibly associated with *aeld* ("fire"). The hollow stems might have been used to blow into fires to get them going. The stems of elder branches are filled with soft pith that is easily removed to leave a hollow pipe. In Scotland the tree was called "bore tree" because one could bore through the stems.

The botanical name *Sambucus* is thought to be associated with the Greek for a musical instrument, a *sambuke*, which was usually a stringed instrument, but the word may have been applied to musical instruments in general. The Roman naturalist Pliny the Elder said that "It is a belief among the shepherds that if they cut a horn or trumpet from the wood of this tree it will give all the louder a sound if cut in a spot . . . out of hearing of the crowing of the cock."

The elder tree was associated with all kinds of magic, good and bad. The common elder is a small tree about twenty feet high and was often planted by doorways to keep out witches. A sprig of elder was sometimes put into a coffin to protect the spirit of the dead. Until well into the nineteenth century the driver of horse-drawn hearses always carried a whip with an elder wood handle. As well as repelling bad spirits, elder leaves repelled flies, and branches of elder were attached to horses' heads.

There was also bad magic connected with the tree. In Germany, Frau Holle, or "Mistress Elder" (from *Hollunder*, "elder"), had to give permission before any part of the tree was used. If a cradle were to be fashioned from elder wood she might harm or steal the baby. After permission had been sought the heartwood of elder could be used to make it, because unlike the pithy new branches, the heartwood and roots of this tree are very hard and solid.

Even though it is a small tree, not native to Palestine, it was once thought that Judas Iscariot hanged himself from an elder. In the fourteenth-century *Piers Ploughman*, we read that "Judas he iaped with unwen siluer [Judas fooled with Jewish silver] / And sithen in an eller honged him after." A fungus that looks a little like an ear and grows on elders and elms was given the unpleasant name of *Auricularia auricula-judae*, or "ear of Judas." Another name for the elder was devil's tree, or stink tree (for the musky smell of the flowers).

The *S. nigra* ("black") is found all over Europe and now naturalized in North America, too. Elderberries found in America include the naturalized red elderberry (*S. racemosa*, "with bunched flowers"), the native *S. caerulea* ("blue"), the Mexican elder (*S. mexicana*), and the Canadian elder (*S. canadensis*). Not all parts of all elder trees are edible. Even the common European elderberry was said to be deadly poisonous to turkeys and peacocks, and elderberries should not be eaten raw.

Elder trees grow wild but have been cultivated for a very long time. These days there are many hybrids available for gardeners. In the past they were used for hedges. Gerard's *Herball* (*see* Banana) described the elder, or "Arn," as being "the bignesse of a meane tree" on which the "floures grow on spokie rundles." He said elders were "planted about conie-burrowes for the shadow of the Conies" (rabbits). At that time (the end of the sixteenth century), rabbits, introduced by the Normans, were not wild but kept for their meat and fur in protected warrens.

A SPRIG OF ELDER WAS SOMETIMES PUT INTO A COFFIN TO PROTECT THE SPIRIT OF THE DEAD.

The sixteenth-century poet Edward Dyer said that it was time to shear sheep when the ". . . verdant elder spreads / Her silver flowers . . ." But perhaps the nicest tribute was from William Cobbett, best known for his *Rural Rides* (1830). A cup of elder wine, he said, just before bedtime on a cold winter evening, is "a thing to be run for." One can almost see him, eagerly pattering along the cold corridor in his nightshirt.

ELM

Alfred, Lord Tennyson, describes the valley where Love is to be found: "Come Down, O Maid, from garden mountain high," he begs, where there are

Myriads of rivulets hurrying through the lawn,
The moan of doves in immemorial elms,
And murmuring of innumerable bees.

Elms, like lovers, prefer lush valleys to barren mountains. Stately elms were once so common that we can hardly blame Virginia Woolf when she was criticized for describing in *To the Lighthouse* rooks flying up into the high elms in Skye, where the novel is set. Later she wrote apologetically "my horticulture and natural history is . . . wrong: there are no rooks or elms in the Hebrides." Small elms *can* be found in Skye but not the large ones she had described.

Until recently, in much of Europe and North America, huge elms were widespread. Their timber, though less treasured than oak, was used for many purposes. Its crooked grain holds nails well and it is hard to split. Fibers from the inner bark were used for rope and the wood made wheel hubs, pumps, and pipes (it doesn't rot unless exposed to air). Perhaps appropriately elm wood was used for coffins: elms have a dangerous propensity to lose a huge branch, quite suddenly and without warning, even on a still summer day, killing anyone underneath. The elm "hateth man and waiteth," explained Rudyard Kipling.

Elms have always been susceptible to fatal diseases, even before the onslaught of Dutch elm disease. So many elms died in about 4000 BC that this "elm decline" is still used to date prehistoric pollen deposits. Dying elms were common enough in Shakespeare's time for Falstaffe (*Henry IV*) to be called "thou dead Elm"—a metaphor the audience would readily understand. On January 30, 1862, a wave of disease caused the *London Times* to predict elms would soon be "extinct." They recovered, only to succumb again, this time on both sides of the Atlantic, in the twentieth century.

> DYING ELMS WERE COMMON ENOUGH IN SHAKESPEARE'S TIME FOR FALSTAFFE (*HENRY IV*) TO BE CALLED "THOU DEAD ELM."

The fungus responsible for Dutch elm disease is caused by *Scolytus*, or elm beetles, the females of which burrow into dead elms to lay eggs. If the tree is diseased, the emerging larvae carry the fungus to a healthy tree (where they feed). The beetles don't usually lay eggs in healthy trees, but the more dead trees there are, the more the fungus spreads, blocking sap vessels and spreading via the roots as well. The fungus itself is sometimes controlled by a virus, which halts the disease, at least for a time. Trees themselves have no immune system and can't develop disease resistance.

Our name is derived from the Latin name *Ulmus*. "Ulmaceous" means "elmy" and can be applied to such things as John Constable's landscape paintings, rich in elm trees, or to the umbraceous ulmaceous avenues once so common in Europe and America. Few of us these days don't know of an Elm Street somewhere. Few of us, however, have seen an avenue of grown elms or even a single huge standing elm—sadly, most have been wiped out.

The ancient Romans and Greeks apparently used elm trees as props for grapevines. In *Georgics*, Virgil described the elm "clasped" by "joyful" vines. This union became a symbol of matrimonial unity, the strong elm supporting the fruitful vine. In Milton's *Paradise Lost*, Adam and Eve spend their morning on "rural work." As well as checking "Fruitless embraces," they train "the Vine to wed her Elm." The vine will wrap "Her marriagable arms" around the elm and in exchange for his support will produce ". . . Clusters [of grapes] to adorn / His barren leaves."

Elm leaves are small but thickly cover the branches, and the trees make a dense shade. The leaves are serrated like nettles (to which elms are related) and typically are uneven at the base. The smooth-leaved elm (*Ulmus carpinifolia*) has leaves that are serrated, not smooth, "resembling a horn-beam." The American white elm is *U. americana* and the English elm is *U. procera* ("tall").

Another old English name for all elms was *wych*. Now we call just one kind of small elm tree a wych elm. It's a native of the British Isles, unlike the English elm, which may not be (though scholars don't agree on this). "Wych" means "pliant" and has nothing to do with witches (*see* Hazel). Wych elms grow on mountain sides and are common in Scotland where their name is Leam (from where we get Loch Lomond, or Lake Leam). The American slippery elm (*U. rubra*) is another small elm, once used to cure many ailments. These small elms are resistant to elm disease, as are Asian elms, which are often planted nowadays to replace diseased elms. There are Chinese and Siberian elms, and the Caucasian zelkova is a beautiful kind of elm. But it's no good pretending a magnificence has not been lost, remembered now only in the names of streets, in paintings, and in poems.

EUCALYPTUS

There are many kinds of eucalyptus trees, all of them originating in Australia, and it's hard to imagine they didn't leave their native country until the very end of the eighteenth century. Wherever the climate is warm enough, eucalyptus trees grow huge so fast it seems as if they had been there since the beginning of time. They flourish in the Mediterranean, Africa, and South America. In California, they seem more part of the landscape than many native trees.

The first Westerner to describe the eucalyptus tree was William Dampier, who traveled around the world, elegantly combining piracy with botany (*see* Avocado). In 1688 his ship stopped in New Holland (as Australia was then called) and Dampier described trees that exuded a "gummy substance." Two years later Joseph Banks, a wealthy young botanist who had paid his passage to go along with Captain Cook on the *Endeavour*, also stopped in New Holland, which Banks dubbed "barren . . . like the back of a lean cow." The aborigines were suspicious of the ship's crew and, he wrote (with no apparent glimmer of appreciation) "did not copy our Mother Eve even in the fig leaf." But there were many new plants, including "gum trees" to be taken home.

A few decades later, a French ship called *La Recherche* came to Australia in search of Captain Pérouse and his two ships that had sailed out of Botany Bay, New Holland, and then completely disappeared. The search party didn't find the lost ships, but did find gum trees that seemed "as old as the world." They brought "blue gum" seeds back to plant in the empress Joséphine's garden at Malmaison.

The eucalyptus, named by a French botanist, L'Heritier, is from the Greek *eu* ("well") and *kalyptos* ("covered") because the flower buds are "well covered" by a lid called an operculum. When the bud is ready to open, the stamens (there are no petals) push off this lid and burst out, seeming more like coralline sea creatures than flowers. But they attract bees, which make eucalyptus honey. Aboriginal people sucked the nectar, as well as eating the "manna," a kind of insect scale on the leaves.

The juvenile leaves of the eucalyptus are somewhat different from the mature leaves. The former are called sessile, "without stalks," and they cling horizontally along the branchlets. These round blue discs are valued by florists because they look and smell so nice in flower arrangements. The mature leaves are long and thin, hanging loosely from the branches. When the sun is high they hang vertically or at right angles to its rays to conserve moisture and remain as cool as possible. This means that eucalyptus trees aren't very good providers of shade.

The aromatic eucalyptus oil in the leaves immediately became popular in

Europe for "cholicky complaints," which, until the trees were discovered, had been treated with oil of peppermint. Eucalyptus oil, first distilled from leaves of a tree from Sydney, was called Sydney peppermint, and the tree was named *Eucalyptus piperita*.

Eucalyptus oil was distilled not only for medicine but its smell, which, as it evaporated off the leaves, was thought to cure malaria. When the trees were planted in marshy ground it seemed that malaria, or ague, became less common, and the fragrant oil was assumed to be responsible. Probably the water that these huge quick-growing trees took up helped drain marshy land, so reducing the mosquito population; but it wasn't known until the twentieth century that mosquitoes spread malaria (*see* Cinchona).

The highly volatile eucalyptus oil means that the trees burn furiously in forest fires. But they can still survive. Under their bark are buds that sprout after the bark is burned off, and underground sections of the trunk put up new shoots. To germinate, the seeds need the heat of a fire, after which they fall into the rich ashes around the tree (but not until after the ashes have cooled). The eucalyptus tree has adapted itself perfectly to dry terrain, with roots that go far down underground in search of water.

The eucalyptus, named by a French botanist, L'Heritier, is from the Greek *eu* ("well") and *kalyptos* ("covered") because the flower buds are "well covered" by a lid called an operculum.

The trees can grow in very poor soil, and their leaves are low in nutrients. Despite this, koala bears feed almost exclusively on the eucalyptus. These marsupials (not really "bears") chew the leaves thoroughly and then take a long time to digest them, thus extracting as much nourishment as possible. Even so, koalas use a minimum amount of energy, and when they aren't eating, they spend most of the time sleeping or moving very slowly. They carefully and deliberately select the leaves they want to eat, often rejecting them. It's not known exactly why they choose particular leaves, but perhaps they can tell which are least toxic—because eucalyptus leaves contain hydrocyanic acid.

Slow to change their habits or learn new tricks, koalas have exceptionally small brains for their size. They haven't needed to be smart, as they have existed in circumstances peculiar to themselves. They don't even have to drink—all the liquid they need comes from dew and leaves ("koala" comes from the aboriginal, meaning "no drink animal"). They have very few predators and would flourish without restraint, except that the more they increase, the more eucalyptus trees they need to provide them with food. There aren't enough eucalyptus trees left to sustain a growing population of koalas. So having evolved to live under the most challenging of circumstances, koalas might now simply die of starvation.

FIG

According to Plutarch, the Greek lawmaker Solon forbade the export of figs from Athens. Those who disobeyed the law and tried to smuggle figs out might be informed against by sycophants (from the Greek *sukon* "fig," and *phainein*, "to reveal"). So it is that our word for smooth self-seekers has more to do with a fig than with, say, the apple with which they traditionally flattered their teachers.

Figs were a staple of the ancient world. The finest were eaten by the wealthy and athletes in training. Lesser-quality ones were fed to slaves. In Rome they were used fresh, cooked, and dried. Anthony's ill-fated lover, Cleopatra, who had "studied" poisons (by trying them out on condemned prisoners) decided that the bite of an asp was the easiest way to die. When she decided to kill herself she had an asp smuggled in, hidden from her guards in a basketful of fresh figs.

The Latin name *ficus* gives us the name "fig." Figs were also used medicinally, and are still put into laxatives. Pliny the Elder wrote that figs "preserve the elderly in better health, and make them look younger and with fewer wrinkles." This seems as good as any reason for eating them, though most people find figs delicious.

There are many kinds of fig, including the "strangler" fig that starts life as a vine and then puts down aerial roots, finally strangling its host tree. The sycamore fig of the Bible is an evergreen with edible fruit (*see* Sycamore). The more than six hundred kinds of figs worldwide almost all share a unique and astonishing method of fertilization, called caprification. This process was first recognized in the wild fig, *Ficus caprificus*, meaning "goat fig" (because wild figs were eaten by goats, or *capri*).

Caprification is a symbiotic relationship (essential to both) between figs and the small fig wasp, or *Blastophaga*. What we call the fig "fruit" is actually not a fruit at all but more properly a syconium (from *sukon*). This is a fleshy, pear-shaped covering within which the fig flowers and makes fruits. The tiny flowers never see the light of day but are pollinated by the wasp. Most varieties of fig have their own wasp to do the job. The female crawls into a hole at the non-stalk end of the syconium and lays eggs. There she dies and there her children mate. Then the new females brush past the male flowers as they leave the home fig to fly out and find another fig. They deposit the male pollen on the female flowers of the new fig. If a syconium contains no pollinated female flowers it drops off the tree. The ancients knew about this and hung branches of wild figs on the branches of domesticated female fig trees. During Roman times some figs evolved that could fruit

> PLINY THE ELDER WROTE THAT FIGS "PRESERVE THE ELDERLY IN BETTER HEALTH, AND MAKE THEM LOOK YOUNGER AND WITH FEWER WRINKLES."

without this process, but even today the renowned Smyrna figs have to be fertilized, either by wasps or laboriously by hand.

Figs exude acrid rubber latex, which was once used to burn off warts. Some people are highly allergic to this latex (also found in fig relatives, the mulberry and osage orange). Presumably Adam and Eve were not allergic to it because, as we well know, they sewed fig leaves together to make "aprons" or (in the 1560 Geneva "Breeches Bible") to make "breeches."

Figs do look a bit like human sexual parts, so covering themselves with fig leaves was appropriate. Ancient Greek sculptors felt no need to cover any parts of the human anatomy, and Michelangelo's Renaissance Greek-like *David* is sans fig leaf. But in the famous Los Angeles, Forest Lawn cemetery (satirized in Evelyn Waugh's novel, *The Loved One*), an "exact" copy of Michelangelo's *David*, is decorously wearing a fig leaf.

Figs, then, were often associated with sex, and not to "give a fig" is really a sexual slur. It's interesting that Buddha chose to sit under a kind of fig tree (the *F. religiosa*, or Bo tree) to achieve enlightenment. *This* fig tree became the symbol for letting go of all human desire and passions. Enlightenment aside, figs do however remain one of the most delicious fruits (or syconiums) we can ever hope to encounter.

FIR

O ur best-known fir, the Douglas fir, isn't a fir but a unique conifer first given the botanical name *Pinus taxifolia* ("yew-leaved pine"). In 1867 this tree was renamed *Pseudotsuga menziesii*, meaning "false hemlock named for the plant explorer Archibald Menzies." Menzies (*see* Monkey-puzzle) described Douglas firs in 1791 but did not bring specimens home from North America.

The Douglas fir most resembles a pine, with pendant cones (which have triple "whiskers" protruding from their scales), and it is sometimes called the Oregon pine. The wood of Douglas firs is resinous, unlike the wood of hemlocks. There is also a bigcone Douglas fir, *P. macrocarpa* ("large fruited"), the cones of which can be four to seven inches long.

David Douglas introduced the magnificent Douglas fir, as well as many other plants, to Britain. A Scottish plant collector, he is remembered as much for his adventurous spirit, quirky character, and unpleasant death as he is for his botanical introductions. Douglas explored the northwest coastal area of

America, keeping a journal of his adventures. These included having to eat his plant collections or starve and losing all his possessions more than once. In tattered clothes and worn shoes he tackled mountains that these days require expensive and elegant equipment to climb. He slept where he could and remarked in his diary that "comfort seems a superfluity . . . Here," he said, "everyone takes his blanket and, with all the complacency of mind that can be imagined, throws himself on the sand or under a bush just as if he was going to bed." That didn't save him from being nibbled by rats and fleas all night and getting so wet and cold his knees "refused to do their office" the next morning. Snow and sand damaged his vision so badly that he lost sight in one eye and had to wear frosted spectacles. He fell into a bull pit and was gored to death, aged just thirty-one.

But he collected hundreds of American plants (some of which were lost) for his British patrons. He was particularly interested in trees, telling his employer, Sir Joseph Hooker, "You will think I manufacture Pines at my pleasure." As well as the tree named for him, he sent home specimens of the Monterey pine, *Pinus radiata*, the grand fir, *Abies grandis*, and the noble fir, *A. procera*. *Procera*, meaning "tall," is apt, because this fir can reach 165 feet high.

The Fraser fir, which grows in the mountains of North Carolina and Tennessee, is named *A. fraseri*, for John Fraser who was originally a Scottish draper. In 1780, threatened with tuberculosis, he went by ship to Newfoundland for the sake of his health. He soon became interested in botany, returning to America several times in pursuit of plants, as well as going to Russia (where the Czar Paul was murdered before paying Fraser for his services). Fraser died, not from tuberculosis, but from injuries when he fell from a horse in Charleston. The fir named for him is distinguished by its cones adorned with bracts, the bristly tips of which protrude out between the scales.

The cones of true firs grow upright, like candles, coming apart before they fall to the ground. Spruce cones fall down intact. Fir trees are always almost aromatic, and their needles are flat and divided at the tip, leaving a smooth scar where they separate from the branches. Firs, unlike other conifers, need rich soil. The Latin name *Abies* comes from *abire*, "to go away." Firs go upward, rising toward the sky. Some are very tall.

The name fir comes from the Old English *furh* and German *föhre.* In Germany, fir trees were planted in front of the homes of newly wedded couples to bring them good luck. The Danish *fyr* means "fir tree," and the Anglo Saxon *fyr* means "fire." According to the sixteenth-century writer John Gerard (*see* Banana), the trees were also called firs because their resinous wood burned well, making good "firewood."

THE TREES WERE ALSO CALLED FIRS BECAUSE THEIR RESINOUS WOOD BURNED WELL, MAKING GOOD "FIREWOOD."

The legendary Greek nymph Pitys was wooed by both Pan and Boreas (the North Wind). She preferred Pan, and when blustery Boreas was rejected he blew Pitys over a cliff, where she was found by Pan lying lifeless. To keep her, even in a different form, he changed her into a fir tree, but ever after whenever the North Wind blew she moaned and shed teardrops of resin.

There are firs in North Africa, Europe, Asia, North and Central America. The common European fir is the silver fir, *A. alba* ("white"), which has pale gray bark. Native to the Alps, it is becoming rarer. Some suspect this might be due to acid rainfall. Some firs, particularly the balsam fir (*A. balsamea*) have very fragrant resin, which can also be used for glue. California missionaries called the bristlecone fir the incense tree and burned its resin for incense. Its botanical name is *A. bracteata*, because the cones have conspicuous bracts (similar to the Fraser fir). Like all firs, this tree has lovely, soft silvery foliage.

Albert Kellogg (*see* Redwood) wrote that this fir "is of the most extraordinary beauty . . . clad in light green dress of silvery sheened foliage, nearly or quite to the feet, it gives them the most exquisitely feminine expression it is possible to conceive." Although a stolid botanist, maybe he, too, glimpsed a luckless nymph in this fir's trembling silvery branches.

FRANKINCENSE

"Frankincense" means incense that is pure, or "free" (*franc*) from additives. "Incense," burned way back in history to send a fragrant smoky message to a god or gods above, comes from the Latin *incendere*, "to burn." A "censer" is the vessel used in churches for burning incense.

The ancient Egyptians used frankincense but not for embalming (for which myrrh was often used). In 1482 BC Queen Hatshepsut of Egypt brought thirty-two frankincense trees from the Land of Punt (now Somaliland) to plant around the temple at Deir el-Bahri. This is the first recorded plant-collecting expedition, depicted on the walls of the temple of Thebes (now in the Metropolitan Museum of Art, New York).

Frankincense was used by the Hebrews to burn in the temple and it is mentioned many times in the Old Testament. In the New Testament it was one of the three precious offerings brought by the Magi to the infant Jesus.

The best source of frankincense was the southern coast of Arabia, from the country of Saba (now Yemen), called Sabaea by the Romans but never conquered by them. The queen of Sheba was from Saba. Theophrastus, often referred to as "the father of botany," was a pupil of Aristotle's and wrote about the Arabian frankincense tree in his *Historia Plantarum* (300 BC). In rather an engaging account he tells us that the Sabaeans "are honest in their dealings with one another," so that no one kept watch over the frankincense trees. The Greek sailors took advantage of this and helped themselves to a valuable cargo of the precious gum, usually left "safe for the owners" until they came to get it. Perhaps, as sometimes happens, the Greeks presumed their superior civilization gave them license to behave freely?

Arab traders collected and sold frankincense. In Hebrew it was called *levonah* or *lebunah*, possibly associated with the country of Lebanon, which also produced incense from pine trees. In Arabic it was *luban*. The frankincense tree is also called the olibanum (from the Arabic, *al-luban*). The Arab traders hid the sources of their valuable commodity, making it sound extremely dangerous to collect (*see* Cinnamon). The Greek historian Herodotus (who lived in the fifth century BC) wrote about the supposed dangers of collecting frankincense. Collecting it, he said, caused the Arabs "a lot of trouble," because the trees were guarded by great numbers of "flying snakes." The traders drove these away by lighting smoky fires of storax (*see* Sweetgum). Even so, there were so many of these snakes that they would surely overrun the whole world, except that the females usually bit off the heads of the males while mating, and the young killed their mother by eating their way out of her belly, to avenge their father.

Frankincense was used in religious rites but also in perfumes. It was charred, along with other ingredients, to make *kohl*, with which Eastern women outlined their eyes in black. In John Gerard's sixteenth-century *Herball* (*see* Banana) frankincense "driveth away the dimnesse of the eye-sight" and it "also doth clense . . . the eies." It may indeed have added brilliance to the eyes of Eastern beauties.

🌿 IN JOHN GERARD'S SIXTEENTH-CENTURY *HERBALL*, FRANKINCENSE "DRIVETH AWAY THE DIMNESSE OF THE EYE-SIGHT" AND IT "ALSO DOTH CLENSE . . . THE EIES."

Frankincense trees are in the Burseraceae family, named for Joachim Burser (1583–1639). Burser's greatest contribution to botany was a collection of dried plants, which ended up in Uppsala University and was found by Carl Linnaeus, who used it to help classify plant specimens. The Arabian frankincense tree, *Boswellia sacra*, was named for John Boswell, a physician in Edinburgh who wrote *Dissertatio Inauguralis de Ambra* (1736). He was the uncle of James Boswell, author of the famous biography of Samuel Johnson. In the midnineteenth century another Edinburgh doctor, George Birdwood, named the African frankincense tree *B. carterii*, for a sea captain of the East India Company, who found it.

The frankincense tree is small and very spiny, and it grows on inhospitable terrain. Appropriate for a tree associated with the Magi, it has star-shaped flowers, white or pale green tipped with rose. Frankincense is harvested by slashing the bark so a gummy resin flows out of the wound. Although "gum" and "resin" are often used interchangeably, resin differs from gum in that it is soluble in alcohol; gum is soluble in water. At first the frankincense resin flows

out colored white, then changes to red or pale yellow. The initial white frankincense was considered the purest, and the Chinese called it milk aromatic.
Pliny the Elder, in his *Historia Naturalis* (AD 77), wrote that the soil where the
trees grew was milky white. White frankincense was more valuable than gold,
as precious as milk itself, on which we depend when we start our lives. In many
cultures our lives are also closed in fragrant mists of olibanum, so completing
a circle of milky necessity.

FRANKLIN TREE

The Franklin tree, named for the most practical of statesmen, has had an elusive history. The first botanists to see it were John Bartram and his son William when (in 1765) they were exploring the Alatamaha River in Georgia. They did not, however, collect specimens.

William, or "Billy," was twenty-six years old and his father in his midsixties when they traveled together from Philadelphia to Florida after John's appointment as "king's botanist." "I am too old to go alone," wrote John, "and I think my son William will be a fit person to accompany me as by this time I believe [he] can draw well." John still worried about William's ability to make a living and wrote to his friend Benjamin Franklin for advice. Franklin suggested William should become an engraver. John Fothergill (an English Quaker) saw William's "exquisite drawings" and offered to serve as his patron so William could write and draw.

In his *Travels* (*see* Bald Cypress) William described a Franklin tree in blossom and he drew one. "It is a flowering tree of the first order for beauty and fragrance of blossoms . . . , The flowers are very large, expand themselves perfectly, and are of a snow white colour, and ornamented with a crown or tassel of gold coloured refulgent [radiant] staminae in the centre."

The Franklin tree flowers in the autumn, and this was when William saw the tree again, on another trip to Georgia. This time he collected seeds and sent some to Fothergill. He also planted seeds in his father's garden in Philadelphia, just before John Bartram died in 1777. British soldiers were camping in what Bartram called his "darling" garden, but they did not destroy it. At about the same time Franklin wrote a last letter to his "dear friend" asking him to send plants directly to France because French botanists could no longer obtain American plants from Britain. Franklin also sent Bartram rhubarb seeds. War for plant lovers is different from war for politicians. Bartram died before replying to Franklin's last letter.

ALL THE FRANKLIN TREES NOW IN CULTIVATION ARE DESCENDANTS OF THE SPECIMENS COLLECTED BY WILLIAM BARTRAM.

The seeds in John's garden grew, and there is still a Franklin tree in that garden by the Schuylkill River. But when botanists tried to find the grove of trees on the Alatamaha River, described by Bartram, it wasn't there. All the Franklin trees now in cultivation are descendants of the specimens collected by William Bartram.

Franklin trees need a hot summer to set flowers, and the leaves turn bright red in autumn, making a stunning combination with any flowers left in bloom. The tree, *Franklinia alatamaha*, is related to the camellia and the tea plant.

Franklin himself was more of a farmer than a gardener, and his famous *Poor Richard's Almanack*, written for farmers under the pseudonym of Richard Saunders, was the first of its kind. He also invented the Franklin stove. There are, of course, many reasons why he is remembered, as well as giving his name to one of our loveliest little trees.

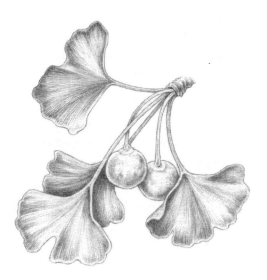

GINKGO

The ginkgo tree has leaves unlike those of any other existing tree, although fossils of such leaves are widespread. These leaves are similar to the fronds of the maidenhair fern, which is why the tree is known as the maidenhair tree.

Ginkgos are ancient, predating even conifers, to which are they similar in some ways. Ginkgos share an important characteristic with ferns and cycads (the earliest of plants). All evolved before insects, and indeed no modern insects eat them. The seeds are pollinated by "swimming" male sperm cells, which are blown from the catkins of male trees onto the female tree. There they make their way into the female ovary and pollinate the seeds.

There is only one species of ginkgo, but once there were many all over the world. It's not certain that any ginkgos survived in the wild. In China, where the tree we know originated, it was conserved in the gardens of palaces and monasteries. From there it was taken to Japan and Korea, probably by Buddhist monks. The first Western knowledge of the ginkgo was when Engelbert Kaempfer found it in Japan.

Kaempfer was on the island of Deshima, a man-made island of thirty-two acres created for traders when Japan kept all foreigners out of the country. Doctors and botanists often stayed on the island along with the officials of the Dutch East India Company. Kaempfer explained that there was a need for medicinal plants and was allowed by the Japanese to start a botanical garden on Deshima. He was able to procure Japanese plants, including the ginkgo tree, which he described in his *History of Japan*, published in 1716. By 1771 Carl Linnaeus had received a specimen of the tree and named it *Ginkgo biloba*.

The name ginkgo comes from the Japanese *ginkyo*, meaning "silver-apricot," probably deriving from the Chinese name *ngin-ghang* (meaning the same). The apricot-like fruits of the ginkgo (born only on female trees) smell quite horrible, but their nutlike kernels are edible and are still eaten roasted in China and Japan.

GINKGO LEAVES ARE REPUTED TO AID MEMORY.

Biloba means "two lobed" and refers to the unique ginkgo leaves. These have veins fanning out from the leaf base and they are not (as in other deciduous trees) interconnected. The shape of the leaf is like a lobed fan or duck's foot, and another name for the tree in China was *i-cho* ("duck's foot"). The leaf formation inspired the German poet Johann Wolfgang von Goethe to write (in 1815) a poem about a ginkgo leaf from a tree growing in front of his house at Jena. In the poem he explored whether the meaning of the twin-lobed leaf was of one divided being or two beings fused together. This, he said, applied to himself, too: he saw himself both as one and as two. After all this, it's not easy for us to forget the meaning of *biloba*. We only have to wonder if we ourselves are bilobate.

Ginkgo

Ginkgo leaves are reputed to aid memory. The Chinese have been using them medicinally for centuries, and more recently, Westerners have found they contain terpenes, which can increase blood supply to the brain. Possibly, ingesting ginkgo leaves (or medicines made from them) might help memory deficiency in the elderly—not to mention the less elderly, who are hoping to remember the names of plants.

From their first introduction these "fossil plants," as Charles Darwin himself called them, were eagerly sought by Western gardeners. An early specimen was planted in the botanical garden of Utrecht. The first American to boast a ginkgo tree was William Hamilton, who planted one in his estate, in 1784. Woodlands, on the (then) outskirts of Philadelphia, was about three hundred acres, and there Hamilton collected as many exotics as he could find, including the first Lombardy poplar (*see* Poplar). Eventually this huge exotic garden became part of a large cemetery along the banks of the Skuykill River.

The ginkgo tree was still growing in this cemetery almost two hundred years later, in 1981 (but has since been cut down). Long-lived ginkgos are not in danger of extinction now because they are a popular street tree, although usually only male trees (which don't smell bad) are used. Ginkgos seem to have a strange ability to survive. Several ginkgo trees lived on after the atomic blast at Hiroshima, even putting out new leaves the following year. One of these trees was only about a kilometer away from the epicenter of the explosion and the temple behind it was totally destroyed. Now a new temple has been built around the tree. Nearby are carved the words "No more Hiroshima."

GOLDEN RAIN

Cicely Mary Barker, who wrote *Flower Fairies of the Trees* in the 1920s, modeled her fairies on the children in her sister's kindergarten class. The Laburnum Fairy is depicted as a charming golden-haired little girl, clinging to the brilliant yellow racemes of laburnum flowers, with her bare feet perched on one of the dried, pealike seedpods. The accompanying verse explains that the showers of yellow flowers pouring off the branches clearly show why the laburnum is commonly called the rain tree.

The laburnum is not the only "golden rain tree" to be found in gardens. The koelreuteria is called by the same name, for the same reason. Panicles of golden-yellow flowers dangle down from this lovely Chinese tree, also called (confusingly) pride of India. Koelreuteria flowers, once used medicinally by the Chinese, develop into papery lanternlike fruits, inside which are three hard black seeds. These seeds are like beads, and they were often made into necklaces in China. Both laburnums and koelreuterias have heavy pendulous flower heads that almost obscure the leaves—like yellow, dripping rain, or links of golden chains.

Although the laburnum tree is a member of the pea family, it isn't, to us, a friendly one. After her verses about the Laburnum Fairy, Miss Barker warned children that the seeds "must never, never be eaten, as they are poisonous." Laburnum seeds contain a toxic alkaloid called cytisine, which causes coma, convulsions, and death. Cattle can also die from laburnum poisoning.

The ancients apparently used laburnum (in small quantities) as an emetic, and the name laburnum is the original Latin one. The Greek name was *anagyris,* and the tree's botanical name is a combination of the Latin and Greek names: *Laburnum anagyroides.* Laburnums grow in southern Europe and Asia; they were introduced to Britain in the sixteenth century. John Gerard's revised *Herball* (*see* Banana) described the tree as one that "hath little or no favour at all." Even so, its beauty made it continue to be popular in British gardens, as it still is. Other names for it were bean trefoil and golden chain tree. In France it was sometimes called *faux ébénier,* because the fine wood could be used in place of ebony. "Adam's laburnum" is a hybrid (called a chimaera) grafted with purple broom (also in the pea family). It has flowers of yellow, pink and purple, sometimes mixed. It was created in the nineteenth century in Adam's nursery, near Paris.

The koelreuteria came to Europe and Russia in the late eighteenth century. It was named *Koelreuteria paniculata* by a Finnish botanist who saw it when it first flowered in St. Petersburg in 1771. Thomas Jefferson was the first American to receive koelreuteria seeds, which he planted in his garden in October 1809.

Joseph Gottlieb Koelreuter had worked at the German University of Karlsruhe. He was an important early hybridist, who in 1760 began crossing nicotiana (tobacco) flowers and then went on to hybridize dozens of other plants. "Almost all flowers . . . carry something with them that is agreeable to insects," he wrote—a statement not as startling to us as it would have been to his contemporaries. He paved the way for studies on genetic dominance, by finding that double flowers combined with single flowers will usually result in plants with double flowers.

Laburnum SEEDS CONTAIN A TOXIC ALKALOID CALLED CYTISINE, WHICH CAUSES COMA, CONVULSIONS, AND DEATH.

In its native China the koelreuteria, or *luan* tree, was often planted around the graves of high officials. In a kind of "tomb tree" hierarchy, the graves of lesser officials and scholars were shaded with pagoda (or scholars') trees, and the graves of peasants planted with easily propagated willows. The koelreuteria isn't a legume but a kind of "soapberry" (along with litchees and akees). The pagoda tree *is* a legume, and its name *sophora* comes from the Arabic word *sufayra*, for a legume bush.

In British gardens laburnums are often trained over arches to make an alley. When the flowers bloom, the alley becomes a brilliant tunnel, dripping with dazzling yellow flowers. Walking through a laburnum tunnel is an unforgettable experience.

Probably because of its venomous reputation the laburnum tree, even though it's so beautiful in flower, is rare in American parks and gardens. Perhaps it's considered an "attractive nuisance" to children who (never having read Cicely Barker's warning) ingest the seeds—with liability responsibilities ensuing.

HANDKERCHIEF TREE

Abbé Armand David, for whom the Davidia (handkerchief tree) is named, was a Lazarist monk and the first Westerner to describe this tree with flowers "fluttering like doves." It comes from China where David had been sent to teach at a missionary school for boys. He made a museum at the school that was so impressive he was released from teaching duties to collect natural history specimens, because his "superiors found it right in view of the indirect value to religion."

Father David made three collecting trips to unexplored areas of China (*see* Apricot) and sent home numerous specimens. Among those named for him were a swan, an owl, a plum tree, a buddleia, an astilbe, and a lily. He also obtained the curious "Père David's deer" from the imperial park and sent them home to

Europe. These animals bray like donkeys and walk like mules on large splayed feet. When they died out in China they were reintroduced from an English park. Abbé David saw the handkerchief tree in 1869 and sent dried specimens and descriptions back to France. If he did collect seeds, none survived.

Like the dogwood tree, the "flowers" of the handkerchief tree are not really flowers with showy petals but large decorative bracts that surround the small flowers. The bracts of the handkerchief tree are uneven and about the size of a human hand. They stir in the slightest breeze, resembling the small, white cambric handkerchiefs used by our grandmothers when distressed. These days this tree could have been called the Kleenex tree, a name we have blessedly been spared.

As David wrote, these bracts also quiver like doves perching on the branches, and indeed another name for this tree is a dove tree. Yet another name is ghost tree, for those who are reminded of a glimmering ethereal form, with pale ghostly hands beckoning toward another world. Whatever it's called, anyone who has encountered a *Davidia involucrata* in full bloom never forgets the sight. The Latin *involucrum* means a "wrapper" or "sheath" and refers to the bracts that enclose the flowers before they open. An involucre is a circle of bracts found in several kinds of flowers (including daisies).

Augustine Henry was also unsuccessful in introducing the tree to Europe. Henry was an Irish doctor who went to China in 1881 as an employee of the Imperial Chinese Maritime Customs Service. Henry spent much of his time during his twenty years in China collecting plants. He found a Davidia tree near Ichang and sent dried specimens and seeds back to Kew, but the seeds never germinated.

It wasn't until 1899 that an expedition, sponsored by the British Veitch nursery, sent Ernest Wilson to China specifically to find and collect the legendary handkerchief tree. Wilson traveled for fifteen hundred miles aided by a sketch

Henry had made of an area as large as New York State. Remarkably, after a journey lasting over six months, Wilson actually found Henry's tree—just too late. It had been cut down. The trunk and branches formed the beams of a newly built house. Wilson recorded in his diary on April 25, 1900, that he had slept very badly that night. But he didn't give up. The next month, in a different location, he came upon more trees and sent home seeds. This time they germinated and the Veitch nursery raised thirteen thousand seedlings. Meanwhile, a French missionary had also sent home seeds, one of which grew into a tree. This tree, to Wilson's chagrin, flowered five years before the Veitch seedlings.

Anyone who has encountered a Davidia involucrata in full bloom never forgets the sight.

It takes about a decade for a handkerchief tree to bloom, and apart from the flowers, it's not particularly spectacular. There aren't many found in gardens, East or West. It seems that quick-growing trees suit our lifestyles best. Like the Chinese home owners described by Wilson, we sometimes cut fine trees not only to build our houses but also to clear spaces where we think we want our yards. We then plant quick-growing trees around our new houses, just where *we* think they should be. Rarely do we let a tree dictate where the house should be.

All this creates uniformity in our environment, and we don't know what will be the result of this kind of dominance. Abbé David himself wrote *over a hundred years ago* that "it is really a pity the education of the human species did not develop in time to save the irremediable destruction of so many species which the Creator placed on our earth to live beside man, not merely for beauty but to fulfill a useful role necessary for the economy of the whole." Sadly, a hundred more years has not yet been enough to "educate" us.

HAWTHORN

The hawthorn, or May tree, used to bloom on May 1. In 1752 the calendar was changed and the month of May arrived two weeks earlier, but the May trees still observed the old calendar, blossoming often *after* the May Day celebrations were over. However, they continued to be called May trees.

May Day was a very important country festival, and for a village maiden to be chosen as Queen of the May was tantamount to stardom. In Tennyson's poem "The May Queen," the honor utterly turns a young woman's head, and she is horribly unkind to her faithful lover: "They call me cruel-hearted, but I care not what they say, / For I'm to be Queen o' the May, mother, I'm to be Queen o' the May." She gathers "garlands gay" and probably washes her face with "May Dew" to keep her beauty. However, with the kind of justice so appreciated by the poet's nineteenth-century readers, Tennyson's heroine is soon dead, although she does have time to repent of her unpleasant behavior *and* bequeath her gardening tools to her little sister!

The scent of May blossom is almost fetid (some say it's "sexy"), and in some cultures it's considered "unlucky" to bring the flowers indoors. They are beautiful, though, smothering the branches in white. The fruits, or "haws," are botanically *pomes*, meaning they have a construction similar to an apple. They are quite edible, some varieties being more palatable than others. There are hundreds of species of hawthorn (which are related to roses) partly because they hybridize so readily.

In Britain hawthorns were used way back for hedges. Indeed the name "hawthorn" comes from the Old English *hagathorn*, meaning "hedge thorn." Thomas Hyll, who wrote *The Gardener's Labyrinth*, in 1577 (*see* Ash), described how to make a hedge of prickly plants including "Whitethorne" (hawthorn). He instructs the gardener to make a mixture of seeds in water until it is the "thickness of Honey." This mix should then be spread "diligently" onto an old rope—if the rope is "stark rotten," so much the better. Then the rope is laid along a trench and in due course a "most commendable" enclosure surrounds the garden. The long thorns and the hawthorn's tough zigzag twigs made an almost impenetrable barrier.

Settlers to America found New World hawthorns, and three varieties were sent back for Carl Linnaeus to name in his 1753 *Species Plantarum*. They were the *Crataegus coccinea*, or "scarlet" hawthorn, the *C. viridis*, or "greenthorn," and the *C. crus galli*, or "cockspur." The scarlet hawthorn's berries were eaten by both settlers and Native Americans. Jon Josselyn in *Two Voyages to New-England* (1663) wrote they were "not as astringent as the Haws in England." They make good jelly. The cockspur thorn sent back to England by John

Bartram (*see* Franklin Tree) was popular for hedges because of its very long sharp thorns. *Crataegus* comes from the Greek *kratos*, "strength," for the hawthorn's very hard wood.

Hawthorns were one of the trees associated with Christ's crown of thorns. This was thought to give them spiritual powers and the branches were sometimes carried on board ships to protect the sailors. One famous and lucky ship was even named the *Mayflower*. The sacred Glastonbury thorn was a hawthorn bush said to have sprouted when Joseph of Arimathaea (who had buried Jesus in his own intended tomb) came to Britain bearing a cup of Christ's blood, planning to found a Christian church. Wearily he stuck his staff into the ground while he rested, and it burst into flower, even though it was midwinter. So he built Glastonbury Abbey on the site.

The name "HAWTHORN" comes from the Anglo-Saxon Old English *HAGATHORN*, meaning "hedge thorn."

Hawthorns are best propagated by taking cuttings or layering. Layering is half cutting the branches and then pinning them onto the ground with the cut section, where new roots will develop, buried. It was a common way of making hedges. To sprout from seed, hawthorns need an acidic environment, which they get when the fruit is partly rotten. They remain on the tree after the leaves have fallen until they are quite soft—which is how birds prefer to eat them.

HAZEL

When Shakespeare described Kate in *The Taming of the Shrew* as "straight and slender and as brown in hue / as Hazel-nuts," every person in his audience would have been able to make the comparison. In Europe and parts of Asia, hazelnuts were an important food from prehistory until quite recently.

In England, Nutcrack Night was on Halloween, when the harvested nuts were cracked, accompanied with fortune telling and general jollity. The nuts, as well as the trees, were associated with magic. A worm in a nut prognosticated ill fortune. Forked hazel twigs were almost always used by rhabdomancers (diviners) in search of precious metals or (often more successfully) underground sources of water.

Hazelnuts, popular in cakes and candy, are more usually known in America as filberts. The name filbert has several postulated origins, the most obvious being that in England the nuts were harvested on St. Philibert's Day, August 22, when they ripened. They would then be dried until Nutcracker Night. Another suggestion is that they were named for the nymph Phyllis, reputedly turned into a tree (*see* Almond). "After Phyllis philliberde / This tre was cleped," wrote the fourteenth-century poet John Gower.

"Filbert" might also come from the German *Vollbart*, meaning "full beard." Each filbert nut is enclosed in a frilled husk which sometimes extends beyond the end of the nut, rather like a hairy beard. The nuts can be rounded or elongated. The rounder ones look a lot like human heads with a short husk like a little cap or bonnet (a *haesel* in Anglo-Saxon). When there were few toys children used plants for dolls, doubtless including little bonneted hazel heads.

Sometimes hazels are classed as shrubs because of their multiple trunks, but they can grow to about thirty feet high. They were one of the first trees to recolonize in Britain after the Ice Age, and as far as we know, the earliest humans ate the nuts. The hazel trunks were used for multiple purposes in the past. Unlike most wood, hazel branches split lengthwise very easily and can then be shaped and bent or woven to make fences or walls daubed with clay. The inside wood is pure white and the bark dark and mottled. They still make decorative walking sticks with the bark carved in places to expose the inner wood.

FORKED HAZEL TWIGS WERE ALMOST ALWAYS USED BY RHABDOMANCERS (DIVINERS) IN SEARCH OF PRECIOUS METALS.

In the King James translation of the Bible, Jacob used hazel rods to outwit Laban, his father-in-law. Laban had agreed to let Jacob have any "speckled and spotted" offspring born to his flocks. So Jacob peeled the bark of hazel rods (as well as chestnut and poplar) to make "pilled white strakes," which he then soaked in the animals' drinking water. This made most of the cattle, goats, and sheep give birth to "ringstraked" young, which Jacob could keep. Soon his flocks were greater than Laban's, and God's promise to "favour Jacob" was fulfilled—with a little help, so it was believed, from hazel magic.

William Butler Yeats found magic, too, when he "cut and peeled a hazel rod," catching with it a silver trout, which then became

> ". . . a glimmering girl
> With apple blossom in her hair
> Who called me by my name and ran
> And faded through the brightening air.

There was not, however, quite enough hazel magic for "Wandering Aengus" who could never find his girl again—"Though I am old with wandering."

The best hazelnuts originated in Asia Minor. Pliny mentioned hazelnuts from Abellina, and the common hazel is *Corylus avellana*. The Greek *korys* means a "helmet" or "hood." There are two hazels native to North America, but their nuts are small and they have hard shells. Native Americans ate them, but settlers soon imported European or Turkish (*C. maxima*) trees. Hazelnuts hybridize readily, and amateurs can't easily identify the different species. In spring the male trees bear long tasseled flowers we call catkins or lamb's tails. The female flowers are small and red and bloom close to the branches. They are wind pollinated and each catkin can produce four million pollen grains! The pollinated female flower grows a long stem, at the end of which will be the nut.

The contorted hazel, *C. avellana contorta*, has no nuts but does have catkins on its twisted branches. All these hazels are male, and all derive from a single twisted branch found in a hedgerow in Gloucestershire, England. It is a garden favorite, known as Harry Lauder's walking stick, after the singer who entertained soldiers during both world wars. As the famous comical character Roderick McSwankay he carried a twisted cane while he sang.

Another garden favorite is the witch hazel, which is a hazel only in name. It is sold as a "shrub," but it grows quite as large as many small trees. It's worth a bit of space in either a garden or a book. Witch hazels are native to North America and Asia. The North American witch hazel (*Hamamelis virginiana*) was sent to Britain in the eighteenth century, and the Asian witch hazel (*H. mollis*) was introduced to Western gardens a century later. They are often hybridized. The name witch most probably comes from *wych* or *wican*, meaning "flexible," for their springy branches, similar to those of hazels. Some say that the botanical name *Hamamelis* comes from *hama*, "together," and *melis*, "apple," because certain witch hazels fruit and flower together; others that it is the Greek name for a fruit tree.

In the very earliest spring the American witch hazel *H. vernalis* and the Asian varieties flower even earlier than snowdrops. The other witch hazels flower at the beginning of winter, when they and all other deciduous trees have lost their leaves. The flowers, resembling thin yellow ribbons, miraculously emerge from the bare branches when no other flowers are around. If it gets too cold, the petals coil up for a few days until a warm spell makes them unfurl again. They are sweet scented and can go on doing this for weeks. Extract of witch hazel bark was used by American Indians who taught settlers that it was a cure for many ailments. Scientists now claim that there are no real therapeutic properties in witch hazel extract. But gardeners, who understand magic, know better.

HEMLOCK

The common name for the hemlock tree seems to come from the plant that the Greeks imported from Asia Minor or Crete, and used to execute criminals. That is, poison hemlock, *Conium maculatum* (the Greek plant *koneion*, with a "spotted" stem) called *hymlic* in Old English. Socrates drank a cup of the poison when he was condemned to death by the citizens of Athens. The poison paralyzes the body from the feet up, leaving the victim's mind quite clear. This would be indescribable torture to anyone who was afraid of death, but Socrates, we are told, calmly took a bath and then drank the poison, asking the gods to bless his journey to the next world. He walked around as long as he could, asking his friends to be quiet and have patience, until the poison traveled from his feet to his heart.

The poison hemlock and the hemlock tree aren't related—the first is a parsleylike plant, the second a coniferous tree. It is surmised that early settlers in America thought the drooping branches of the hemlock tree looked a bit like the feathery leaves of the hemlock plant. Another suggestion sometimes made is that the crushed leaves of the plant and the tree smell similar, but this seems impossible, since the leaves of the hemlock plant smell unpleasant, and the leaves of the eastern hemlock smell pleasantly "piney." Anyway the settlers called this new tree Hemlock fir or Hemlock spruce. This would have been the common or eastern hemlock *Tsuga canadensis*, which covered the eastern coastal areas with thick dark woods. The hemlock is one of the rare trees whose seedlings can germinate in deep shade, and hemlock woods are dense, dark, and gloomy. Maybe the gloomy association of the herbaceous hemlock contributed to the name.

The hemlock was mentioned by Peter Collinson in 1736. He said he had "2 fine plants in my Garden," which were hemlocks but, when they were sent to him, were "call'd spruce." Peter Collinson, an English Quaker, corresponded and exchanged plants with the Quaker botanist of Philadelphia, John Bartram. They never met, but after years of writing to each other John Bartram could call Collinson "one of my dearest friends" (*see* Horse Chestnut).

The needles of hemlocks, like those of spruces, grow from a small protrusion, leaving a rough surface on the twig if they are removed. They are flat and blunt, with silver resin canals underneath. The bark is rich in tannins and, in the past, was widely used for curing leather. More recently hemlocks were the chief source of rayon. Like spruces, hemlocks can grow in damp soil. But their cones are small, much like those of larches. They are native to Asia and North America, but not Europe. Western American hemlocks and Japanese hemlocks didn't reach eastern American or European gardens until the mid-nineteenth century. They immediately became popular, and now there are many varieties, including weeping, dwarf, and prostrate hemlocks.

David Douglas (*see* Fir) had described the western hemlock *T. heterophylla*, "with different leaves," but he didn't send home specimens. In 1852 John

HEMLOCK WOODS ARE DENSE, DARK, AND GLOOMY.

Jeffries, another Scottish explorer-botanist sent the western and the mountain hemlock (*T. mertensiana*) to the East Coast. The latter was named for Karl Heinrich Mertens, the son of Franz Karl (for whom the Virginia bluebell was named). Jeffries was employed by the Oregon Association, and in 1854 he completely disappeared, never to be heard of again. There was plenty of speculation about his (probably unpleasant) fate. Soon after, the western hemlock arrived in England, where Queen Victoria unsuccessfully asked that it be named *albertiana* for her husband Prince Albert.

The hemlocks were separated from other conifers and given the name *Tsuga* by Elie-Abel Carrière, a French botanist, author of *Traité Général des Conifères* (1855). He isn't remembered for much else, but he worked hard to plant trees in France, claiming that floods were caused by cutting down forests and that trees were essential to the good of humans. The book he wrote on this subject was called *Les Arbres et la Civilization*. Books on the same subject are still being published. And land is still being cleared of trees. The name *Tsuga* is the common Japanese name for the hemlock tree. Parts of Japan were still covered in thick hemlocks forests in the nineteenth century. Carrière re-sorted the hemlocks and the pseudohemlocks (like the Douglas fir) and gave them the Japanese name.

In 1860 a party of Englishmen climbed the sacred volcano Mount Fuji in Japan. When they reached the summit they raised the Union Jack, sang the national anthem, fired their pistols twenty-one times, and drank champagne in honor of Queen Victoria's health. Among this party was John Gould Veitch whose grandfather had founded a famous nursery garden in Exeter. He brought home seeds of the Japanese hemlock *T. diversifolia* ("diversely leaved"), and of a pine named for himself. He also brought home Boston ivy, a Japanese vine that later smothered and gave its name to the buildings of the Ivy League colleges of the eastern United States.

HOLLY

Holly has always had magical or spiritual connections. Most hollies are broad-leaved evergreens (some are deciduous). Their vividly shining leaves stand out magically in somber winter woods, and it's not surprising that the Romans used them as decoration for their winter solstice celebrations, or Saturnalia. The early Christian church first forbade its members to bring evergreens indoors at Christmastime as the pagans did. When this didn't work, the church adopted the custom instead.

The Middle English name for the tree was *holyn*. In Old German it was *hulis*, names probably connected with the word "holy." The holly was particularly suitable as a Christian symbol because it was thorny (like Christ's crown of thorns), was covered in red berries like drops of crucifixion blood, and was bitter to taste, so symbolizing the Passion. In Germany it was called *Christdorn* and in Norway *Kristtorn*. It became a part of Christmas celebrations long before Christmas trees, retaining some magical "pagan" associations. It was extremely bad luck to bring holly indoors before Christmas or leave it there after Epiphany. Each *leaf* left inside would bring its own episode of misfortune. We who hang whole wreaths of holly had better be careful.

The botanical name *Ilex* was that of the holm (or holly) oak known to the Romans. Carl Linnaeus thought the holly's leaves were similar to those of this oak and so named it *Ilex*. The descriptive name of the English holly, *aquifolium*, means that the leaves are pointed. There are, however, many hollies that have smooth-edged leaves. The English hollies have prickly leaves low down and smooth ones high up the tree, beyond the reach of browsing animals. In his poem "The Holly Tree," Robert Southey, one of the so-called Lake Poets, wrote that the sharply pointed leaves of "youth" diminished, "Till the smooth temper of my age should be / Like the high leaves upon the holly tree."

Even though the spiny lower leaves of the holly were supposedly divinely protected, their sharpness doesn't seem to deter all animals, at least not in North America, where deer browse on the prickly bitter leaves with gusto.

Hollies are widespread in all continents but Australia, and there are many kinds. The leaves and bark contain not only tannin but caffeine, and in both North and South America were used to make tea. Early European settlers described Native Americans drinking infusions of "black drink," which formed part of a cleansing ritual. Mark Catesby, who went to Virginia in 1712, where he collected plants and made exquisite drawings of birds (*see* Catalpa), wrote that during these spring rituals the participants "drink and disgorge with ease." The commonly named yaupon holly, is *Ilex vomitoria*. The common American holly is *I. opaca* ("not glossy"). Its prickly leaves and red berries have made it popular for Christmas decoration since settlers first arrived, even though its leaves aren't as shiny as those of English holly.

In South America the leaves of the smooth-leaved holly, *I. paraguariensis*, are brewed to make tea, or *yerba maté* ("herbs in a gourd cup"). The Jesuits dominated maté production in the seventeenth century, making groves of easily harvested pruned trees, which if left alone can reach sixty-five feet. Maté is still an important South American crop.

Hollies flower on separate trees, male and female, and are pollinated by insects, usually bees. One male tree can pollinate many females, and in Old England the jolly red-berried females were thought to be male: "Holy and hys mery men they dawsyn and they syng / Ivy and hur maydens they wepyn and they wryng," explained a fifteenth-century carol. The ivy has dull black berries.

> IT WAS EXTREMELY BAD LUCK TO BRING HOLLY INDOORS BEFORE CHRISTMAS OR LEAVE IT THERE AFTER EPIPHANY.

The toyon tree that grows in California has bright red berries used for decoration at Christmas. It isn't a holly, but it might have been the origin of the name for Hollywood, California. Hollywood was founded in 1887 by Horace Wilcox, a prohibitionist who envisioned a community based on sober religious practices. The town was supposedly named by Wilcox's wife, Daeida, either because she just liked the name or perhaps for the abundant "Christmas berries" of the region. It subsequently compensated for its sober beginning, celebrating not only Christmas but just about anything.

The diverse uses for holly included sweeping chimneys with prickly bunches of its leaves, and using its light wood in all sorts of carpentry. The Chinese holly, *I. cornuta*, was called in Chinese *gougan*, or "dog's bone," for the bone-white wood. This holly was introduced to Britain in the mid-nineteenth century by Robert Fortune (who also brought back forsythia).

Perhaps the most widespread use of holly, now and in the past, is for hedges. It grows slowly, is evergreen, and makes a prickly barrier, so it's perfect for the purpose. In his garden at Say's Court the diarist John Evelyn had a holly hedge that was four hundred feet long, nine feet high, and five feet wide. It did not, however, prove substantial enough to survive Peter the Great, who in 1698 rented Evelyn's house while in Britain to study "the building of ships." According to Evelyn's servant, the czar and his retinue were "right nasty," and they amused themselves by riding through and battering down the huge hedge. Evelyn wrote sadly of his hedge once "glittering with its armed and varnished leaves." One wonders what the Russians found so entertaining. Perhaps they masochistically compared each other's scratches in their battle with the "Holy and hys mery men"? Whatever the motive, the result was, as Evelyn wrote, that the hedge was quite ruined, "thanks to the 'Czar of Muscovy'" and his men.

HORNBEAM

. . . the recreants came behind
In a place where the hornbeams grow,
A path right hard to find,
For the hornbeam boughs swing so.

The textile designs of William Morris are, perhaps not surprisingly, more appreciated these days than his poetry, laced with romantic Death. "Shameful Death" (written in 1858) is no exception. Hornbeams may have been more familiar to Morris's readers than they would be to most of us, who wouldn't know one if we saw it, although they are native to Britain, Europe, Asia, and North America. Small trees with twisted boughs, they often have several pale, fluted trunks. Their leaves are not unlike beech leaves, and they bear male and female flowers on the same tree.

Because they are dense and small, hornbeams make good hedges. If we know them at all, we may have seen hornbeam hedges in gardens such as the famous Hidcote Manor garden in Gloucestershire, England (made by the American major Lawrence Johnson and now owned by the National Trust). John Evelyn (*see* Ash) wrote that a hornbeam hedge "grows tall, and so sturdy, as not to be usurped by the *Winds* . . . and flourishes into glossie and polish'd *verdure* which is exceedingly delightful." He added, touchingly, that clumps of hornbeams supported up by frames were good for "the *People* to sit and solace in."

The hornbeam, or hardbeam as it was sometimes called, has very hard wood, often used to make yokes for oxen. The trunks don't grow big enough to make planks, but the wood was prized for spindles, cogs, or anything that needed to wear well. It was also called ironwood and reputedly blunted any tools that were used to shape it. The botanical names for the hornbeam are *Carpinus betulus* ("beechlike") for the European hornbeam, and *C. caroliniana* for the American hornbeam. *Carpinus* is the tree's Latin name, used by the Romans.

Confusion arises with the hop hornbeam, in America sometimes called the eastern hornbeam, which isn't the same tree as the *carpinus*. Hop hornbeams don't have particularly hard wood, and they can grow to sixty feet. The hop hornbeam and the hornbeam have similar foliage and bark, but the hop hornbeam has fruits that look like the flowers of hops—hence its name. These fruits are pendulous, with tightly closed scales, and the hop hornbeam's botanical name *Ostrya* comes from the Greek word for "oyster," also tightly closed (until we steam it). The American hop hornbeam is *Ostrya virginiana*, the Old World (European and West Asian) hop hornbeam is *O. carpinifolia* ("with leaves like a hornbeam").

Although the fruit of the former look like the flowers of the latter, the hop hornbeam has no connection with the hop vine, the flowers of which are used to flavor beer. (This vine is actually related to cannabis). The female hop flowers give beer a pleasantly bitter taste and make it keep better. The smell of hops is said to induce sleep, and George III, who suffered from insomnia, was helped by a hop pillow. Using hops in beer wasn't common until the end of the sixteenth century. Everyone drank ale, beer, or cider because the water wasn't safe. Indeed when William Wood recounted the benefits of the New World (in *New England's Prospects*, 1634), he wrote that the water was so pure "dare I not prefer it before good Beere, as some have done, but any man will choose it before bad Beere." William Wood also described the "Horne" tree, with wood so hard "as is almost incredible."

Another American tree, growing in the southern desert, is the ironwood, which has even harder wood than the hornbeam, so dense it won't float. Even though hornbeams are sometimes called ironwoods, they are different trees. The botanical name, *Olneya tesota*, comes from a Rhode Island botanist, Stephen Olney, and the Spanish word *tieso* for its "stiff" evergreen foliage. The wood can endure for over a thousand years.

> WILLIAM WOOD ALSO DESCRIBED THE "HORNE" TREE, WITH WOOD SO HARD "AS IS ALMOST INCREDIBLE."

Hornbeams are not common in the wild anymore. Desert ironwoods are also quite rare, threatened by irrigation that takes their water elsewhere. How nice it would be if this were not so and if our water was as safe to drink from streams as it was in the seventeenth century. We feel safer if we drink bottled water these days, but judging from the cans and bottles littering our highways, we still drink lots of beer as well.

HORSE CHESTNUT

Poor little Stephen Dedalus "shivered as if he had cold slimy water next his skin. That was mean of Wells to shoulder him into the square ditch because he would not swop his little snuffbox for Wells's seasoned hacking chestnut, the conqueror of forty." This chestnut, in James Joyce's *Portrait of the Artist as a Young Man*, was a "conker," the nearly inedible seed of the horse chestnut. It is not a relation of the edible sweet chestnut.

The seeds of the horse chestnut *ought* to be edible, so smooth and brown and delicious do they seem. It is possible, though not recommended, to eat them if they are roasted and then placed under running water for several days. After this treatment the very hungry, and some animals, do eat them. Pigs (supposedly more intelligent than most farm animals) won't touch them, but they have been fed to cattle and horses. Indeed John Gerard's *Herball* (*see* Banana) claimed that "the people of the East countries do with the fruit thereof cure their horses of the cough, shortness of breath and such like diseases." That's where this tree got its common name. The botanical name, given by Linnaeus, is *Aesculus hippocastanum. Esca* means "food" and *hippo* means "horse." Originally *Aesculus* was the Latin name for a kind of oak bearing edible acorns. In America, horseshoe-shaped scars left on the branches, where the fallen leaves were attached, is sometimes given as the derivation of the common name.

Horse chestnuts are native to Asia Minor and first came to Britain at the beginning of the seventeenth century, along with other ornamentals like lilacs and tulips. The tree grows very fast and soon became popular in British gardens. It can reach a hundred feet high. With its spreading branches it makes a good shade tree, but its chief glory is in spring when the sticky buds open and the tree is covered in upright spikes of white flowers, decorating the branches like candles. The individual flowers resemble miniature orchids.

Peter Collinson sent seeds of the horse chestnut from London to his American friend John Bartram in Philadelphia (*see* Hemlock). He wrote in 1763, "To see a Long avenue of Trees 50 feet High being Perfect Pyramids of Flowers from top to bottome . . . is one of the grandest and most Charming Sights in the World." The next year John Bartram's own horse chestnut bloomed, and Collinson wrote, "I am greatly pleased the long expected Horse Chestnut has gratified thee with its beautiful flowers."

The spectacular flower clusters are replaced by prickly fruits that open to drop the seeds. These were once called Constantinople nuts, or *oblionkers*. The game of "conkers" may have got its name from this or, because it was originally played with shells (French *conques*), possibly "conkers" came from this. A conker was threaded on a string and each player struck his weapon against his rival's, until one of them cracked. The conqueror (another possible derivation of the name) could last (as we have seen) for over forty battles. A "conk" could also mean a "head." In this era of PlayStations, it seems rather a simple game to arouse much passion but, if James Joyce is to be believed, was once loaded with meaning.

The horse chestnut has an American native relative that is similar but much less spectacular. Buckeyes (so called because the round brown fruits with a white marking resemble the eye of a buck, or deer) only grow to about forty feet. Even so the Ohio buckeye, *A. glabra* ("without hairs"), became the state tree there and Ohioans are sometimes known as Buckeyes. The smell of this tree's bark gives it the common name stinking buckeye. The leaves of both buckeyes and horse chestnuts are fanlike with several leaflets, but the leaflets of most horse chestnuts have no stalks. The flowers of buckeyes can be white, pink, or red. The red buckeye is *A. pavia*, for Peter Paiv, a Dutch botanist at Leyden University, and buckeyes were first named pavias by Linnaeus, until they were included with horse chestnuts. Horse chestnut seeds contain aesculin, a poisonous substance. Sometimes a paste was made of them for binding books, since the toxin deters insects. The timber doesn't splinter and was once used for artificial limbs, particularly for wooden legs.

HORSE CHESTNUT SEEDS CONTAIN AESCULIN, A POISONOUS SUBSTANCE.

Henry Wadsworth Longfellow was familiar with the trees around him, often including them in his poetry (*see* Birch and Larch). But he did not specify, and scholars can't agree, on whether the chestnut tree in his famous poem "The Village Blacksmith" was a horse chestnut or a sweet chestnut. Both trees can grow very large and "spreading," and when the poem was written in 1839, horse chestnuts were well established in North America, and sweet chestnuts had not yet been decimated by blight (*see* Chestnut). Those who believe the immortal tree was a horse chestnut say that after the tree was cut down (to "improve" the corner of Brattle Street, Cambridge) a chair was made from its wood and given to Longfellow. When the wood of Longfellow's chair was later analyzed, it was horse chestnut. Others still aren't convinced. Whatever kind of chestnut it really was, huge spreading trees on the corners of city streets seem to be as rare today as blacksmiths working "from morn till night."

JAPANESE CEDAR

The Japanese people live rather formally, and often close together, and their gardens as well as their lives tend to be regulated. One of the ways they seek relaxation and rejuvenation is through *shinrinyoku*, or "forest bathing." This is not bathing in water but in deep, quiet forests, often made up of cryptomerias, or "Japanese cedars," as we call them.

Cryptomerias aren't cedars but unique members of the swamp cypress family (*see* China Fir). They are evergreen conifers and can reach huge proportions, attaining 150 feet in height. They are also extremely long lived. Their flower parts are concealed within the scalelike needles, and that's where the name *Cryptomeria* comes from. The Greek *krypt-* means "hide," and *meris* means "a part." There is only one species, *Cryptomeria japonica*, although there are garden cultivars.

Other names for this tree are Japanese redwood (more botanically correct than Japanese cedar), peacock pine (for the feathery branches), and goddess of mercy fir.

This tree has spiritual associations. The leaves were burned as incense and the straight trunks made pillars for temples. Its Japanese name, *sugi*, also means "upright," perhaps because it embodied a human striving for uprightness of character. Japanese cedars were often planted around shrines and tombs, and indeed the genus name *Cryptomeria* comes from the same root as a crypt, or tomb, where we bury our own dead. An incredible avenue of sugi trees was planted in the seventeenth century to join a Shogun burial site to Tokyo (then Edo). The avenue is twenty-two miles long and consists of thirteen hundred trees.

THEIR FLOWER PARTS ARE CONCEALED WITHIN THE SCALELIKE NEEDLES, AND THAT'S WHERE THE NAME *CRYPTOMERIA* COMES FROM.

Robert Fortune sent sugi seeds to the London Horticultural Society and it became a popular ornamental tree in Britain. In 1858 the United States patent office received seeds and planted them in the government experimental garden in Washington, D.C. But in the West we only see specimen trees, never thick forests as in Japan.

The Japanese sugis were also important timber trees, with rich red-brown heartwood and pale-yellow sapwood. Fortune described the timber as "remarkable for the number of beautiful rings and veins which show to great advantage when the wood is polished." When buried, sugi wood turns dark green, and it was used by the Japanese like precious stones, called *jindai-sugi*.

The idea of "forest bathing" is immensely appealing in this noisy world in which most of us have to live. No car, no bicycle, no gun, no radio — not even a dog (harder for some of us). Just silent trees, reaching to the sky. This would be rejuvenation indeed.

JOSHUA TREE

Joshua, Moses's successor, is best known for capturing the city of Jericho. He and his army danced outside the city playing trumpets, until the walls collapsed. Some say the excessive vibrations caused the walls to crumble, others that the hand of God shoved them over. Anyway, Joshua went on to conquer the Promised Land and (we are told) "utterly destroyed all that breathed, as the Lord God of Israel commanded."

This kind of leadership may seem a bit drastic to us but was obviously inspiring to some. In 1857 Brigham Young summoned a group of Mormons in California to join him in Utah. These "Latter-day Saints" journeyed from San Bernardino toward the Mohave Desert. Along the way they saw these strange trees that looked as if they were beckoning them onward toward *their* promised land. So they called them Joshua trees.

The Joshua tree (also called the praying tree) isn't a true tree but a giant yucca, and its botanical name is *Yucca brevifolia* ("short leaved"). It has no woody core or bark, but a fibrous stem. Unlike palm trees (which don't have a woody trunk either), this stem can increase in size as the tree grows (*see* Date). Joshua trees can reach forty feet tall with a trunk of three feet in diameter. They have no taproot, but their fibrous roots spread in a mass around them. The wood is light and strong.

Joshua trees grow in the region of the Mohave Desert, but mostly in only a few areas. They need a cold winter and are generally found three thousand feet above sea level. Their evergreen leaves are spiky and leathery, with sharp points and a waxy surface that conserves water. The bark is hoary and deeply furrowed. The way they grow is strange. After it flowers, the terminal bud at the end of a branch dies and is replaced by shoots below it. This gives the tree an angular structure, with branches that look jointed and seem to be eerily gesticulating.

The name yucca came from a plant sent to John Gerard in the sixteenth century. In his *Herball*, Gerard named it, "supposing it to be the true *yucca* . . . wherewith the Indians make bread, called *Cassava*." The plants aren't the same, but Gerard's name was retained. Yuccas have an astonishing relationship with the small pronuba yucca moth, on which they rely for pollination. The female moth lays her eggs in the ovary of a yucca flower and her young eat some, but not all, of the fertilized seeds before they emerge. The seeds have been fertilized by the moth who packed pollen into the female stigma of the flower, as if conscious that this step is essential to the survival of the yucca (and of her own kind). It's a better miracle than many.

The large green-white flowers of the Joshua tree are edible, and native American tribes made a kind of cake out of the seeds. The roots are red at the tips and were once used for dye. Apart from humans, desert creatures use the tree for sustenance and shelter. Woodpeckers make nesting holes in the soft trunks.

The first English-speaking botanist to describe the Joshua tree seems to have been John C. Fremont, who called it "the most repulsive tree in the vegetable kingdom." Fremont was in the Corps for Topographical Engineers and went to Utah and Nevada in the 1840s. Apparently it was a tough journey. The expedition ran out of food and had to eat their dog. Another time a mule slipped over a cliff, and they lost all the maps and specimens it was carrying.

JOHN C. FREMONT CALLED IT "THE MOST REPULSIVE TREE IN THE VEGETABLE KINGDOM."

Now, of course, these lands are no longer deserted and dangerous. Joshua trees survive in parks, mainly the Joshua Tree National Monument, established in 1936. Even in a park setting, they are odd trees. Mary Austin described them in *Land of Little Rain* (1903): "After death, which is slow," she wrote, "the ghostly hollow network of its woody skeleton, with hardly power to rot, makes the moonlight fearful."

It's believed that giant sloths originally dispersed the Joshua tree's seeds, but now the large fruits mostly depend on rolling down mountain slopes to spread. Even if we spread the trees artificially they are very sensitive to climate change, and global warming could threaten or eliminate present populations. Maybe we should consider the eerily beckoning branches as a plea for help.

JUNIPER

In the King James translation of the Old Testament the prophet
Elijah, fleeing the wrath of Jezebel, went into the wilderness
and collapsed exhausted "under a juniper tree." He prayed, "It
is enough now. O Lord, take away my life." Instead, when he woke up he
found an angel had left food and water beside the tree—and this lasted him
for forty days.

More recent translations of the Bible call Elijah's tree a broom, but there
were plenty of junipers in the Middle East, as well as white broom. Both juniper and broom favor arid places, and junipers will send down deep roots where
almost nothing else can survive, even growing above the normal tree line.
Rocky mountain juniper is called *Juniperus scopulorum* ("of rocks") because it
grows on cliffs.

The Middle Eastern juniper of the Bible could have been *J. sabina vulgaris*,
named for the area in Italy where it was abundant. The Sabine hills were evi-

dently well populated with women as well as junipers. These women, so the tale goes, were victims of a ruse by Romulus, who thought to increase the new city of Rome's population by arranging a mass rape of them (after inviting them to a party). The name *sabina*, or savin, for this juniper has now been replaced by the name *J. oxycedrus* (from the Greek *oxys*, "sharp"), perhaps because it looks like a pointed cedar or perhaps for its prickly foliage. Another juniper that grows in this area is *J. phoenicea* ("from Phoenicia"). This has brown, rather than bluish, "berries."

Junipers are conifers (cone bearers), and they are the largest group in the cypress family. Their cones, however, are unique in that the scales on them have fused and are soft—so they really resemble berries, which is what we call them. *Juniperus* is the ancient Latin name. The common juniper, *J. communis*, is widespread in the cooler parts of Europe, and juniper berries were used medicinally from ancient times. The juniper tree seems to have been universally respected for magical powers. In Germany it was customary to take off one's hat when passing a juniper tree (or an elder) and the German for juniper is *Wacholder*, or "awake tree." It was supposed to be dangerous to fall asleep under a juniper tree (a tradition started by Pliny), but doing so brought Elijah a good fortune. At any rate, the King James translators thought so.

John Evelyn, in his *Sylva, or A Discourse of Forest-Trees* (1664), thought that Pliny was wrong about sleeping under a juniper. He wrote that juniper berries were "one of the most universal remedies in the world." At about the same time, a physician at the University of Leyden, Sylvius Francisius (also known as François du Bois) accidentally discovered gin. He was particularly interested in chemical substances in the body and tried distilling juniper berries in spirits, in order to obtain a diuretic remedy with the properties of juniper berry oil. This cheap beverage turned out to be more than a diuretic. It was sampled and brought home to England by soldiers returning from the Low Countries, eventually becoming a social problem. Dutch gin is made from beer distilled twice, with juniper berries included in the second distillation. It is different from American and British gin, distilled from malt wine with flavorings added. The word "gin" comes from the French *genévrier*, or "juniper."

Junipers are slow growing. A favorite landscaping tree, there are many hybrids available. They can be columnar or prostrate, the latter being popular as a ground cover.

Thujas, or arborvitae ("tree of life"), aren't true junipers, but their name comes from the Greek name for "juniper," which was from the Greek *thyô*, or *thuo* ("I sacrifice"). *Thuos* means "incense." The fragrant wood was burned in sacrificial services. Our word "perfume" originally referred to fragrances rising "through smoke."

Thujas include specimens from China, Japan, and North America. The Japanese arborvitae was one of the five sacred trees of the Kiso forest. In feudal times a commoner who cut down a sacred tree could be executed. North American arborvitae trees came to Europe during the reign of Francis I, and supposedly got their common name because some starving French sailors were saved from dying by eating them.

The American western white cedar and western red cedar are both thujas. The red cedar, or *Thuja plicata* ("plaited," for its juvenile growth), was particularly used in the past for totem poles. It is an awesome tree and can reach 135 feet high. It is also a favorite food of deer, which can decimate stands of seedlings. Destroying these members of the cypress family hardly seems fair of the deer, because Kyparissos, as we remember (*see* Cypress), asked to be turned into a cypress because he had accidentally killed a deer. Poor thanks for his remorse.

The German for juniper is Wacholder, or "awake tree."

LARCH

Give me of your roots, O Tamarack!
Of your fibrous roots, O Larch-tree!
My canoe to bind together
That the river may not wet me!
*   And the Larch, with all its fibres,*
Shivered in the air of morning,
Touched his forehead with its tassels,
Said, with one long sigh of sorrow,
"Take them all, O Hiawatha!"

Although the outcome might not have been much different, at least Hiawatha *asked* the Larch-tree if he could destroy it. Henry Wadsworth Longfellow knew that American Indians used the roots of the American larch to sew together their birch bark canoes (*see* Birch) and he also knew that in their culture they were expected to ask permission to use whatever was needed from the wild.

Today we plant larches in gridlike rows, and we are not likely to ask their permission before "harvesting" them, in millions, for telephone poles, fencing, and paper pulp. Excellent trees for our purposes, they grow in conditions where other conifers wouldn't thrive. In the northern regions of America, Asia, and Europe they survive on high mountain slopes, reaching the edge of the tree line. Indeed, some of the most northern trees to be found are larches. In milder climates they grow tall very fast.

Larches, like all conifers, are botanically nonflowering plants, or gymnosperms (meaning "naked seed"). They are wind pollinated and their seeds are not enclosed within a fruit or seed pod like those of flowering plants (angiosperms) that later evolved. The female cones of conifers open to catch the pollen from male cones. Larches bear male and female cones on the same tree. Unlike all but a few conifers (*see* Bald Cypress), larches are deciduous. Their needles turn a lovely golden brown before they fall in autumn. In spring the trees are clothed with soft bright green new needles.

The American larch (*Larix laricina*) is also called a tamarack tree, a name that comes from the French Canadian *tamarac*, probably of Algonquin origin. The Roman name for the larch was *larix*, and *laricinus* means "larchlike." An early English botanist, William Turner, whose *Herball* was published in 1551 (*see* Birch), wrote that the "Larix or larex groweth in the highest toppes of the Alpes higher than the firres do . . . It may be called in englishe a Larch tree." At that time larches had not yet been imported to Britain.

The European larch (*L. decidua*) was probably introduced to Britain by the elder John Tradescant. In 1618 King James sent an ambassadorial party to Muscovy (Russia), and Tradescant, a gardener and botanist, went along in search of new plants. It wasn't a very easy trip. At one time the cabin leaked and "it rayned doune thourow all my clothes and beds to the spoyll of them all." Tradescant lost some of his newly collected plants by mistakenly watering them with salt water, but "4 sorts of fir trees" did make it home, one of which is thought to be the European larch.

The larch was eagerly received by British gardeners. The second Duke of Atholl planted millions of larch trees around his estate in Perthshire, Scotland. Dunkeld, where they grew, became famous for its larch-covered hills. In 1887 when newly introduced Japanese larches were also planted there, they hybridized with the duke's trees and made a new larch, *L. × eurolepis* (a "European" larch mixed with a slender, or *lept-*, Japanese one). This tree was more resistant to insects and the fungus diseases to which larches are susceptible. The new hybrid was called the Dunkeld larch and widely planted for timber. It's hard for anyone except an expert to identify the many kinds of larch, which include dwarf, pendulous, and weeping, and they all hybridize readily.

American Indians used the roots of the American larch to sew together their birch bark canoes.

The golden larch of China isn't a true larch. Its botanical name *Pseudolarix amabilis* means "lovable false larch," and it surely is, with the most wonderful golden foliage in fall. It's deciduous, like true larches. Unlike common larches its cones aren't retained on the tree after the seeds drop. The cones themselves are flared, rather like artichokes, and the tree is valued as an ornamental rather than as a timber tree. Robert Fortune unexpectedly came across golden larches growing next to a monastery high in the mountains of China and sent specimens home to Britain, in 1853. Their Chinese name was *jin song*, or "golden pine." Chinese gardeners, way back, grew dwarfed larches in pots, but they can reach 130 feet high and 8 feet in girth. They grow much more slowly than true larches.

Larch resin was used for caulking boats. In northern Europe and Asia larch bark was sometimes grated, mixed with broth, and eaten. A fungus called agaricus that grows on Russian larches (*L. siberica*) was once used medicinally. Most important, though, was larch "turpentine" often made from boiling the cones. John Josseyln, writing to describe the New World to prospective settlers (*see* Hawthorn), wrote that this "comes nearest of any to the right Turpentine." He explained that American turpentine "is singularly good to heal wounds and to draw out the malice . . . of any Ach, rubbing the place therewith." This would have been a comfort to people preparing to leave their familiar medicines and arrive in a foreign world of unknown flowers and trees. To us it would be the equivalent of going to a drugstore with strange labels we could not comprehend.

LEMON AND LIME

C itrus fruits, which are related to the herb rue, are a recommended part of almost everyone's diet. They include oranges and grapefruit as well as citrons, lemons, and limes. The name citrus comes from citrons, which are like thick-skinned lemons and were the earliest of the family to reach the Western world. Their Greek name was *kitron* and the Latin name *citrus*. Citrons were used way back (and still are used) in the Jewish ceremony of the Feast of Tabernacles, during which a citron, or *etrog*, is circulated for participants in the ritual to smell and thank God for the fragrances of life. Some etymologists say the citron took the place of cones from the cedar of Lebanon and its name is connected with *kedros* (Greek for "cedar").

The classical world certainly knew the citron (*Citrus medica*), but we are not sure if it knew lemons as well, and the two fruits may have been confused by later writers. In *Georgics*, Virgil wrote that these fruits (sometimes translated as "lemons" but much more likely "citrons") were a good antidote to the "deadly drugs of stepmothers." Citrons came from Media and may have been brought home by Alexander the Great in 330 BC. Pliny referred to "median apples," which were probably citrons.

Partly because of their name it's hard to trace the origin of lemons. In Chinese they were *limung* or *ningmeng*, and in Arabic *laymun* (from the Persian *limun*). Some scholars say Arabic traders took lemons to China from India (and that the Chinese name came from the Arabic); some say the Arabs took lemons (already named) from China to the Middle East. There are still wild lemons in the Himalayas, but no one knows where the tree really originated or if (which is probable) it is a hybrid citron. Crusaders to the Holy Land brought lemons home with them, but during the Middle Ages they were rare and expensive. More sensitive to cold than oranges, they don't grow well in most parts of Europe.

By the time of Louis XIV, lemons were grown in hothouses, and the court ladies of Versailles reputedly rubbed lemons on their mouths to make their lips seductively red. They were used in French cooking from about that period. By 1636 the Dutch painter Jan Davidsz de Heem had gone to live in Amsterdam, because lemons (and other fruits) were readily available there, to draw from life. Curls of lemon rind, like loops of gold, often appear in Dutch paintings.

Botanically, a citrus fruit is a hesperidium. This refers to the supposed connection of citrus fruits (probably oranges) with the "golden apples" that grew in the mythical garden of the Hesperides, or "the daughters of evening." Hercules managed to slay the snake/dragon guarding the tree and procure "apples" from it. A hesperidium is a kind of berry, containing juice sacs covered with *albedo* ("white"), and an outer skin, or *flavedo* ("yellow"). The flavorful "zest," or cut peel of lemons, may have come from the Latin *scindere* ("to cut"), but its origin is uncertain. It has given us the term "zest for life."

Limes were often confused with lemons and are very like them but more acidic. They are picked green but if left would ripen to yellow. Their name *C. aurantiifolia* ("golden leaved") refers to their lighter tinted leaves. All citrus trees are small, thorny evergreens. Limes, unlike lemons, don't mind a humid climate and grow very well in the West Indies and Mexico.

THE COURT LADIES OF VERSAILLES REPUTEDLY RUBBED LEMONS ON THEIR MOUTHS TO MAKE THEIR LIPS SEDUCTIVELY RED.

Limes are particularly associated with "limeys," or British sailors who were given a ration of lime juice to prevent scurvy. In 1753 James Lind, a Scottish naval surgeon, in his *Treatise on the Scurvy*, made a connection between scurvy and the ascorbic (meaning "anti-scurvy") properties of citrus fruits. Lind actually recommended lemon, not lime, juice. He was, unknowingly, right since limes contain much less ascorbic acid (vitamin C) than lemons, and the British navy only used limes because they grew in the British West Indies. Scurvy still occurred on land and sea until the twentieth century when vitamin C was isolated and its effectiveness proved.

The Italian name for citrus fruits is *agrumi*, which means "bitter." That's why a defective car is called a lemon — buying one leaves a sour, or bitter, taste in your mouth. A "lemon law" endeavors to rectify this.

LINDEN

On January 10, 1777, Carl Linnaeus, having reached three score years and ten, died at eight o'clock in the morning. His tomb is in Uppsala Cathedral, carved with his name: Carolo Linné, *Botanicorum Princeps* ("Carl Linnaeus, Prince of Botanists").

His name, although still familiar three hundred years later (even to non-botanists), was only a generation old, and it commemorated the linden tree. Until Linnaeus's father, Nils Ingemarsson, wanted to enter the church, his patronymic name was good enough for a farmer living in southern Sweden, but to enroll at a university a surname was required. Near the family estate of Linnegard grew a huge linden tree, called in Swedish *lind*, so Nils called himself Linnaeus, or "Linden-tree man," after the tree. Some other family members took the name Tiliander, from *tilia*, the linden's botanical name.

In America lindens are usually called basswoods. The name basswood comes from *bast*, which is the inner bark of the tree. This bark was soaked until the fibers separated and could be used for weaving coarse cloth or rope. American Indians used bass fibers from American lindens to make cloth and baskets. In Europe, too, bass was a main source of rope until hemp (cannabis) was introduced from China, in the fifth century AD. There are three main New World lindens, indigenous to the central and eastern states. The *Tilia americana* is a magnificent tree with huge leaves, and it can grow to 130 feet.

Lindens are widespread over Europe. The two most common species are *T. cordata* (for "heart-shaped" leaves), also called the small-leaved linden, and *T. platyphyllos*, which is "wide leaved" or large leaved. The large-leaved lindens were once supposed to be the female trees and the little-leaved lindens male trees. The "common" linden, *T. vulgaris*, is a hybrid of the small and large-leafed lindens. The old English name for the tree was *linde*, from the Old Nordic name.

UNDER ITS DENSE SPREADING BRANCHES PEOPLE MET TO METE OUT JUSTICE, SOMETIMES USING THEM AS A GALLOWS.

Until the sixteenth century the linden was sometimes called a Pryp tree. The origin of this name is obscure, though it may be connected with the Greek name for the linden, *philyra*. Philyra was a nymph whom Kronus desired and seduced. When interrupted in flagrante delicto he protected his identity by quickly turning himself into a stallion. In due course poor Philyra gave birth to a centaur, half man, half horse. She was so appalled when she saw her child she begged the gods to help her — so they changed her into a linden tree. Her child, Chiron, grew up to be wise and good, particularly learned in medicine. In Germany linden tisanes were thought to be so efficacious that the word *lindern* means "to soothe."

In Shakespeare's time the linden was called a line-tree. In *The Tempest*, Ariel hangs "glistering apparel" on "this line" (which isn't a clothesline). Stephano drunkenly grabs a jerkin, addressing the tree as "Mistress Line." In the seventeenth century "line" changed to "lime," which of course has nothing to do with the citrus tree of that name. Today in Britain lindens are usually called lime trees.

Linden leaves made fodder for cattle. Their flowers, which are intensely fragrant, attract bees, and sometimes the lindens are called bee trees, or humming trees. In the famous remembrances of Marcel Proust he recalls "the taste of the crumb of madeleine, soaked in her [his aunt's] decoction of lime-flowers." He sometimes helped make the tea, shaking the amount required into the water, and noticing how "the drying of the stems had twisted them into a fantastic trellis, in whose intervals the pale flowers opened . . . the leaves assumed . . . the most incongruous things imaginable."

In spring, especially in Germany, it was customary for couples to dance around a linden tree, in a festival called the *Lindenbluten fest*. Women hung votives on the branches and ate linden leaves as an aid to pregnancy. There was another, grimmer, side to the tree. Under its dense spreading branches people met to mete out justice, sometimes using them as a gallows. Some thought that dragons lived inside lindens, like the German *Lindwurm*, or "linden-tree serpent."

Linden trees can live a long time and grow very large. They were a favorite "coppicing" tree (*see* Alder). After a tree had been felled it put up new shoots that would be cut every twenty-five years to provide a sustainable source of wood. In the town of Dedham, Essex, a sixteenth-century law allowed people to "croppe lindens without forfeit . . . *so that they kille not.*"

Lindens hybridize very readily, and these days European, Asian, and American hybrids are found in gardens, parks, and woods worldwide. They would be more popular as street trees were it not for the "honeydew" excreted by aphids feeding on the leaves. This sticky substance drops liberally from linden trees, making everything underneath gooey.

Linden wood is soft and elastic with an even texture. It can be cut crosswise and carved into paper-thin surfaces and intricate folds. A group of German Renaissance artists working in an area of southern Germany, where large-leaved lindens grew, is known as the lime wood sculptors. One of these was Tilman Riemenschneider who left many of his works unpainted, so their astonishing carved details are not covered. It seems fitting that some of the loveliest carvings the world has ever seen should be these German lime wood carvings of the Virgin Mary. Linden trees, sacred to the Norse mother goddesses Freya and Frigga, were always revered by women and thought to protect mothers and children. Asking for intercession from a Virgin Mary fashioned from a lime wood tree might, one hopes, have given extra power to a woman's prayers.

LOCUST

Europeans coming to Virginia in the seventeenth century knew their Bible well and had read of the locust tree with its long, dark beanlike pods. William Strachey, author of *Historie of Travaile with Virginia Britannia* described a tree with feathery leaves "which beares a cod like to the peas . . . we take yt to be locust."

The locust of the Bible is *Ceratonia siliqua*, also known as the carob tree. Its name comes from the Greek *keras* ("horn"), for its horn-shaped pods, and *siliqua* (Latin for "pod"). The seedpods were sometimes called St. John's Bread and were probably the "locusts" that John the Baptist ate in the wilderness. Confusion apparently arose when a transcriber of the Bible changed the Hebrew word for "carob pod" to "locust" by substituting the Hebrew "g" for the "r" in *cherev*.

Carob pods were (and still are) used in the Middle East to feed cattle, and their covering, a mucilaginous pulp, is sweet and syrupy. It is used to make carob, a chocolate-like substance. The seeds themselves are almost uniform in size and shape and were once used as a standard weight measurement or "carat" and still describe the size of a diamond. A Talmudic legend tells of a rabbi who planted carob seeds to make trees for his grandsons but then fell asleep and reawakened generations later to find the trees grown up in a strange new world. This was the origin of the famous American tale of Rip Van Winkle.

The American locust tree is similar in appearance to the carob, and its leaflets also droop in wet weather and at night (*see* Acacia). It's also a legume, a member of the Fabaceae family, but a different species. Settlers called it a black locust, but when it reached Europe it was first called *Acacia americana* and then given the botanical name *Robinia pseudoacacia*. That means it's like an acacia but false.

THE SEEDPODS WERE SOMETIMES CALLED ST. JOHN'S BREAD AND WERE PROBABLY THE "LOCUSTS" THAT JOHN THE BAPTIST ATE IN THE WILDERNESS.

The name *Robinia* was for two French botanists, father and son. The father Jean was the king's doctor and director of the Royal Gardens under Henry IV. Henry's consort Marie de Medici was passionate about flowers and embroidery. Jean Robin collected as many unusual flowers in the garden as he could find and then had them drawn by the court artist Pierre Vallet for the queen and her court ladies to copy and stitch. The young Robin, Vespasian, was a gardener but also traveled and collected plants. He specialized in acclimatizing foreign plants in the Jardin du Roi in Paris, where he planted a robinia in the early 1600s. The tree, which grows easily almost anywhere, acclimatized with no trouble and spread widely. It is a common tree in China, called *yanghuai*, or "foreign scholar's tree." It is used as a street tree, but its wood, which resists insects, is also grown for building.

Because of the very fragrant white flowers that hang in drooping clusters, black locusts are sometimes called honey locusts. Real honey locusts, with their sharp thorns, pinnate leaves, and beanlike pods, are similar to acacias and locusts, but the honey locust is the *Gleditsia triacanthos* ("three spined"). The genus is named for Johann Gleditsch (1714–1786), who was the director of Berlin's Botanic Garden. The garden had started as a physic garden in 1679 but was completely neglected. Dr. Gleditsch tried to restore it but couldn't get the Academy of Sciences to fund his efforts, and the gardeners wouldn't do as he ordered, so he didn't achieve much and wild pigs continued to break through the fences. The next director, Carl Ludwig Willdenow, professor of botany at Berlin University, finally restored the garden. The genus *Willdenowia* called after him is a little-known greenhouse plant from Africa. So, although more successful, botanically speaking he was much less well rewarded than Dr. Gleditsch, whose tree grows worldwide and has hundred of cultivars (hybridized forms).

In China, the pods of the *G. sinensis* ("Chinese") were dissolved in water and used as a substitute for soap. In America, Civil War soldiers were said to have pinned their cloaks with the very long thorns of the *G. triacanthus*. Nowadays gleditsias are used mostly as ornamentals, and spineless varieties have been bred for gardens. Both robinias and honey locusts have many hybrids, some with yellow leaves, or green leaves tipped with bright yellow. The latter make the tree look as if it has another flowering season.

MAHOGANY

The first of four fifty-euro gold coins honoring Austrian physicians was issued in 2007. On one side of the coin is a profile portrait of Gerard van Swieten (1700–1772), clasping a book and gazing toward the medical staff of Aesclepius (a rod entwined with a serpent). On the reverse side is the image of the *Swietenia mahogoni*, the mahogany tree.

The tree was named for the empress Maria Theresa's physician. The empress persuaded Dr. Swieten to move from the Netherlands, look after her health, and reform the School of Medicine in Vienna. The doctor founded a chemical laboratory, made a botanical garden, and established a system of training and examining medical students, thereby replacing a health system that had often relied on religious doctrines and practices. The Vienna Medical School became prestigious throughout Europe.

Although the bark of mahogany has astringent properties, the actual tree *isn't* important medicinally. But Nikolaus von Jacquin became director of the botanical garden at Vienna and named the mahogany in honor of Swieten. Jacquin had seen mahogany trees when he went to the West Indies to collect plant specimens in 1757. The ship he was on was captured by the British who imprisoned Jacquin, but when he was released he visited Jamaica and Cuba, where he saw these trees. The name mahogany most likely came from African slaves on Jamaica. The mahogany tree looks like (and is related to) an African tree the slaves called *M'Oganwo*, or *M'Ogani*, in the Yoruba language (of a Nigerian tribe of whom many were enslaved).

There is another African tree, the *Khaya*, that has fine wood, comparable to mahogany and is sometimes called African mahogany. Other trees with dark wood are also sold as mahogany but the true mahoganies are of the *Swietenia* genus, specifically *S. mahogoni*. Two other mahoganies, *S. humilis* ("low") and *S. macrophylla* ("large leaved"), hybridize readily. Gerard Swieten's name was also given to the "Ceylon" satinwood, from southern India, *Chloroxylon swietenia* (*chloros* "green," *xylon* "wood"), another tree, not a mahogany, prized for paneling and veneer.

THE NAME MAHOGANY MOST LIKELY CAME FROM AFRICAN SLAVES ON JAMAICA.

Mahogany was known to Europeans long before it was named by slaves. The trees grow in the West Indies, Florida, and South America. Spanish conquerors sent home the wood from the New World for paneling, fine furniture, musical instruments, and shipbuilding. As well as having beautiful color variations, mahogany doesn't split. It was said that mahogany-planked ships in the Spanish Armada resisted shattering when hit by cannonballs. The French name for mahogany is from *acajou*, a Brazilian name. The French also call the cashew nut (a tropical tree, too, but unrelated) *acajou*. The Spanish called (and still call) mahogany *caoba*, another South American name.

In *Les Misérables*, Victor Hugo describes the old Vaugirard cemetery (where

Jean Valjean plans to be buried alive) as "a poor place" with a drunken grave digger. The bourgeoisie, or well-to-do, preferred the Père-Lachaise cemetery. To be buried there was *comme avoir des meubles en acajou* ("like having mahogany furniture"). Victor Hugo's nineteenth-century readers would have completely understood the comparison. The Père-Lachaise cemetery is still prestigious and includes the tombs of Gertrude Stein, Isadora Duncan, Chopin, and Jim Morrison. Victor Hugo himself is buried at the Panthéon.

MANGO

All things chickeney and mutt'ny
Taste far better when served with chutney,
This is the mystery eternal:
Why didn't Major Grey make colonel?

Major Grey was an officer in the Bengal Lancers and either he or his Bengali cook created this mango-based chutney, the recipe for which was sold to the Crosse and Blackwell Company. The Anglo-Indian condiment and the limerick written about it (by John F. Mackay) is a good illustration of what the mango means to people in different parts of our world. In the West, at least until recently, mangoes at best were a condiment; at worst travelers described them (wrote American botanist and explorer David Fairchild in *The World Goes Round My Door*) as a "ball of tow soaked in turpentine which you have to eat in the bath." Not so in Asia. Apart from the fact that store-bought chutney would be disparaged there, the mango tree is sacred to both Hindus and Buddhists and it is India's national tree.

From about 4000 BC mangoes were collected where they grew wild, in the foothills of the Himalayas, and eaten. They were unknown in the classical world, making their way slowly west via Africa and Persia. Marco Polo did not mention them. But in the first century AD a Chinese traveler to India, Hwen T'sang, discovered mangoes there and called them *an-mo-lo* from the Sanskrit *amia*. The Chinese began importing and enjoying mangoes.

By the tenth century mangoes had reached Persia, with the name *man-gay*, from the Tamil name *man-kay*. Meanwhile in India they were domesticated and cultivated. By the sixteenth century the Mogul ruler Akbar made a large mango orchard at Darbanga, which he called Lakh Bagh (*lakh* meaning "one hundred thousand" and denoting the number of trees in it). Akbar, it was said, had the trees watered with milk and treacle to make the fruit sweeter. Although the fruit can be sweet and delicious it can sometimes have a turpentine flavor.

Mangoes are related to cashews, pistachios, and poison ivy (*see* Sumac) and give some people a rash when they handle or eat them.

THE MANGO TREE IS SACRED TO BOTH HINDUS AND BUDDHISTS AND IT IS INDIA'S NATIONAL TREE.

There are many Hindu and Buddhist legends connected with the trees that are often associated with fertility. The green and new red leaves are considered lucky in India and are used in wedding ceremonies. Sometimes mango leaves are hung above a doorway to celebrate the birth of a baby boy. The evergreen trees make a deep shade, and Buddha himself was said to have rested in a mango grove. The trees can grow to sixty feet and can produce fruit for forty years.

Mangifera indica means "mango-bearing (tree) from India." These are tropical trees, which don't grow in Europe, but they do well in South America, probably first brought to Brazil by Portuguese traders. A sixteenth-century Portuguese explorer, Afonso de Albuquerque, gave the name Alphonso to what is still considered one of the best mangoes (there are hundreds of varieties). As well as exploring and trading, Afonso endeavored to convert Hindus and Muslims to Christianity. He made a plan (unsuccessful) to steal the body of the prophet Muhammad and hold it until all Muslims left the Holy Land. He also suggested diverting the course of the Nile River as a way of subduing the Egyptian people.

Mangoes didn't reach North America until the nineteenth century. David Fairchild imported mangoes, as well as other tropical plants, to Florida. The hybrid mangoes he grew were very different from the "balls of tow" he had once described. In another book, *World in My Garden*, he gave a lyrical description of his Haden mango, an offspring of the India Mulgoba mango. He wrote that the Haden mango (named for the husband of a widowed friend) was "One of the most gorgeous of all the fruits in the world . . . A delicate mottling of scarlet which spread like a wash over a background of gold and deepened to a spot of purple, but where a branch of the tree had shaded it the fruit was bright green. The color has to be seen to be understood."

Anyone can see, and taste, a mango these days for they are sold in most supermarkets. David Fairchild was indeed successful in making them accessible to all Americans. Sadly though, the Florida of the early twentieth century, described by him with equal tenderness, is fast becoming lawns, golf courses, and condominiums.

MANGROVE

The buccaneer/writer William Dampier (*see* Avocado) described mangrove trees in his *Voyage to New Holland*, published in 1699. He wrote that they "grow so mixt one amongst another, that I have, when forced to go thro' them, gone half a Mile, and never set my Foot on the Ground, stepping from Root to Root."

Mangrove trees can grow right on the ocean's edge, sometimes completely submerged by tides. The classical writer Theophrastus described Alexander the Great's sailors mooring their boats to the exposed branches of submerged mangroves until the tide ebbed and then having to move the cables to the roots. The trees not only prevent soil erosion, they also can actually build up new land by catching debris between their tightly knit roots. If they are cut down to make open waterfront, these new beaches erode, eventually destroying a natural protective barrier against hurricanes and huge tidal waves. Tourist beaches made from cleared mangrove swamps retain no barrier to stop a tsunami rolling inshore unhindered. We have seen this occur.

"Mangrove" probably comes from a Senegalese word for "tree," adopted by the Portuguese as *mangue* and combined with the English "grove." The name covers trees with shared characteristics, developed in order to survive. Mangroves grow worldwide but only in tropical waters, and they have adapted to conditions not tolerated by other trees. They can even grow in pure sand and be totally submerged under salt water. In Florida there are three species normally referred to as mangroves: the red mangrove, *Rhizophora mangle*, the black mangrove, *Avicennia germinans*, and the white mangrove, *Languncularia racemosa*. Red mangroves, named for a red layer under their thin gray bark, have stiltlike roots that hold the trees firmly in the water. Kneelike joints absorb oxygen, which travels through spongy tissue to the roots in the mud below. Mangroves are sometimes called walking trees.

The botanical name *Rhizophora* comes from *rhizo* and *phoros*, meaning "root bearing." This refers to the way the fruits hang down from the branches and grow a sharp shoot *before* they drop from the parent tree (unlike other trees whose fruits germinate after they have dropped away). When these fruits drop, their spiked shoot pierces into the mud below, and rootlets quickly grow from it into a new tree.

If they don't land in the mud, the fruits float away from the parent tree. The shoot continues to elongate until its weight pulls it down vertically, and it can anchor itself and put out roots. The germinated fruits can float horizontally for a very long time. This ability of the seeds to germinate on the parent plant is called viviparity. Mammals that give birth to living young are viviparous. Most plants, other than mangroves, aren't viviparous, although some qualify by reproducing from bulbils.

The *Avicennia* mangroves were named for the Arabic physician Ibn Sina (980–1037), whose name was Westernized to Avicenna. As a reward for curing the Sultan of Bukhara, he was given free use of the court library and he soon became knowledgeable in science, mathematics, and philosophy. He wrote a medical text that was used until the sixteenth century and was reputed to be the first doctor both to describe parasitic worms in humans and cover pills with gilt or silver to make them seem more effective.

Black mangroves grow in shallower waters farther inland than red mangroves. The bark of a mature black mangrove is black. To get air to their mud-bound roots, black mangroves put up pencil-like roots called pneumatophores which surround the trees like snorkels, allowing them to "breathe" air. When water covers these aerial roots the air is pushed out of holes in the pneumatophores and then replaced with fresh air when the water recedes. Since salt water can enter these holes, the tree gets rid of it by exuding salt through its leaves, rather as some seabirds lose excess salt through their bills. The black mangrove has very fragrant white flowers that make wonderful honey, and beekeepers sometimes move their hives to the coast during the honey season.

THEY CAN EVEN GROW IN PURE SAND AND BE TOTALLY SUBMERGED UNDER SALT WATER.

The flowers of the white mangrove, *Laguricularia racemosa*, have a fluffy calyx (like a "hare's tail," *lagurus*). The bark is light colored. These mangroves generally don't need aerial roots because they live above the high-water mark. Like all mangroves, their wood is rich in tannic acid, which protects them from termites. All mangroves regenerate much more slowly than other trees if they are cut or damaged. The white mangroves are at the final edge of the mangrove barrier between land and sea. Behind them grow land plants; to seaward of them the other kinds of mangrove support an intricate chain of creatures. The rotting swampy vegetation feeds worms, which in turn feed small shrimps, which feed fish.

Mangrove forests stink. Mosquitoes breed copiously in the wetlands around them. Alligators lurk among them. To most humans they hold none of the romance that make other woody groves so compelling. Impenetrable, they don't fit our dreamy tourist vision of tropical beaches. On these beaches we can protect ourselves (we hope) from the sun's rays with barrier creams. But making too much room to bask in the sun can destroy the natural barriers of the beach itself.

MAPLE

In Murasaki Shikibu's eleventh-century Japanese novel *The Tale of Genji*, Prince Genji makes a seasonal garden for each of the four ladies he loves; the autumn garden is for the Lady Aki-nonomu, his daughter. In it "all of the autumn colors were gathered together," and when they saw it the ladies of the court "who had been seduced by the [Lady Murasaki's] spring garden (so it is with this world) were now seduced by the autumn."

Most of this seductive color would have been from the bright leaves of the Japanese maple. Many Japanese maples are red year-round, and almost all turn dazzling shades of scarlet in autumn. The Japanese celebrate their brilliant color with festivals, similar to those for spring blossoms (*see* Cherry). They love to tell a story about Sen-no-Rikyu, a famous sixteenth-century Japanese tea master, who had just finished sweeping the garden in preparation for a tea ceremony. It looked clean and soulless, so he flung two or three of the red maple leaves he had swept up onto the clear mossy ground.

Not all maples turn red in autumn, but many do. The color comes from anthocyanins, produced as cholorphyll is withdrawn from the leaves and the tree shuts down for the winter. The sharp points of these blood-red leaves are probably the origin of the maple's ancient Latin name, and our botanical name, *acer*, meaning "sharp." The Indo-European root *ac* also gives us the adjective "acute." Maple wood was used to make spears and lances, and in ancient Greece the tree was dedicated to Phobos, or "Terror," the son and companion of Ares, the god of war. The leaves were sometimes used to treat a "sharp" pain. When Linnaeus classified the maple he did not change its Latin name.

Carl Peter Thunberg, a Dutch botanist stationed on the island of Deshima when the rest of Japan was closed to foreigners (*see* Paulownia), brought the first Japanese maple west. This maple, *Acer palmatum* ("like the palm of a hand"), has green leaves that turn scarlet in fall. In spite of imperial edicts, Thunberg was able to collect Japanese plants, partly by sifting through hay brought to feed the livestock on Deshima (and collecting the seeds in it) and partly by trading information with young Japanese botanists. In exchange for plants he taught them rudimentary Western medicine, and the Linnaean system of classification. He wrote *Flora Japonica* in 1784.

In North America, too, busloads of tourists travel north to admire the autumn foliage — most of it from the fiery leaves of maple trees. Maples grow across northern continents, including northern Africa and Asia. Most maples are deciduous, with hand-shaped, or palmate, leaves. All have seeds called samaras (from the Latin name). These winged seeds have been used by countless children worldwide to spin like tiny propellers. The blade looks (said Gerard's *Herball*) like the "innermost wings of grasshoppers." The English name maple goes back a long way to an Icelandic root *möpurr*. In Old English we have *malpulder*, exemplified in *Mapulder-shed*, or Maplestead, still a town in Essex, England.

Maple wood, which is pale and without resin, is particularly good for bowls and utensils since it imparts no flavor of its own to food or drink. An ancient cup made from maple wood was called a mazer. The most desirable mazers were made from a knotty protuberance on the tree. This woody bump, or boss, is thought to be caused by a disease of the tree and was sometimes called a "mazle" or "meazle," giving us the word for "measles," a human disease characterized by a bumpy skin.

The European maple, the only maple native to Britain, is *Acer campestre*, or "field maple." Early on, another maple, the *A. pseudoplatanus*, or "false plane," was imported to Britain, where it was called a sycamore (*see* Sycamore) and spread widely. The famous Tolpuddle martyrs, the earliest gathering of trade unionists, met under a sycamore maple. When their leader George Loveless was convicted and deported to Australia he took a leaf of the tree with him, pressed between the leaves of his Bible.

Settlers in America immediately encountered and admired American maples and sent them home. The red maple, *A. rubrum*, is, as its name implies, one of the most brilliant fall maples. In the mid-eighteenth century John Bartram, the Quaker botanist, sent scores of trees, including maples, to Peter Collinson in London. Bartram also sent animals, including a "Great Mud Turtle," which, Collinson said, "near bit my finger." He added, understandably, "Pray send no more Mud Turtles one is enough."

In spite of the beautiful native maples in North America, Alexander Hamilton introduced the Norway maple, *A. platanoides* ("like a plane tree"), to his estate Woodlands, near Philadelphia (*see* Ginkgo). This maple spread rapidly, taking over woods in some places. Its autumn leaves are pale yellow or orange, not brilliant scarlet like the fall leaves of red and sugar maples. There are hundreds of maple cultivars, which gardeners, rightly, love and their characteristics and different names fill whole books. Some maples won't hybridize with each other, notably the red and sugar maples, which grow in woods together but remain distinct.

Maple syrup, the sap of the sugar maple *A. saccharum*, fascinated early Europeans, seeming like a manifestation of the golden age described by Virgil: "who would not marvel to see realized . . . in the frozen forest of Canada, those enchanted pictures that the ancient poets have left us of the golden age, when they painted for us the trees distilling honey through their bark?" asked Henri Louis Duhamel du Monceau in *Traité des Arbres et Arbustes* (1755). The sap was mostly gathered by Indian women and children during a joyous annual festival when the children would be allowed to spill hot syrup on the snow to harden into candy. Before metal kettles, the sap was reduced by dropping hot stones into containers of it, or leaving it to freeze, removing the ice and collecting the syrup left beneath.

Sugar cane was expensive to grow and needed slaves to work the fields. One of Thomas Jefferson's projects was growing sugar maple trees to provide maple sugar as the main sweetener used. "What a blessing to substitute a sugar which requires only the labour of children," he wrote optimistically in 1790. He planted sugar maple seedlings at Monticello, but they mostly died. Maple sap needs frosty nights and warm days to flow properly, so he could not have succeeded even if his trees had flourished.

In the United States we think of maples covering hillsides, enflaming them in autumn and providing millions of American breakfasters with syrup. Several states and the country of Canada, too, honor the maple tree as their symbol. Everyone knows and loves a maple tree. They are emblematic of the enormous generosity of a great land.

MONKEY-PUZZLE

In 1834 Sir William Molesworth purchased a rare, recently introduced tree for his estate of Pencarrow, in Cornwall. He paid the handsome price of twenty-five pounds sterling for the sapling, and it was planted in a ceremony to which he invited some friends. As the story goes, one of the guests, a lawyer called Charles Austin, handled the prickly leaves of the little tree and then remarked (with feeling), "It would be a puzzle for a monkey." And the tree got its common name.

More likely the sharp prickles developed to confuse dinosaurs. The monkey-puzzle, or *Araucaria*, is a very ancient tree, found in the Arauco province of Chile. It is thought to have once been widespread, before our continents divided. It is related to the Norfolk Island pine and the Australian wollemi pine, both of which also grew in prehistoric times.

The first seeds of the monkey-puzzle to reach Europe were collected by Archibald Menzies in 1795 (*see* Strawberry Tree). Menzies was the doctor/ botanist of the ship HMS *Discover*, under the command of Captain Vancouver (for whom the island is named). They traveled down the Pacific coast and stopped in Chile, where the British Viceroy invited the officers to dinner. Menzies spotted some curious nuts among the nuts and fruits handed around for dessert, and he slipped some into his pocket. When they returned to the ship Menzies planted the nuts in "a glazed frame erected on the quarter-deck," wrote Vancouver. The ship's captain and botanist had their problems, Vancouver confining Menzies to his cabin for three months because of an argument over whether the sailors were spending too much time, or not enough time, caring for the plants. But five of the strange nuts germinated and reached Kew gardens safely.

At first the gardeners at Kew called the tree an Araucarian pine. The people of Arauco, who live where these trees grow in Chile, are the Pehuenche Indians. Their name in English means "people of the monkey-puzzle tree." The nutritious nuts, or piñons, are an important part of their diet. Many of these people still revere the tree, calling it their mother. The botanical name is *Araucaria araucana* from the family Araucariaceae (*see* Wollemi Pine).

The new trees excited English gardeners, who soon wanted to purchase more than were available. In 1844 William Lobb (*see* Redwood) was sent to collect more seeds. It wasn't long before no fashionable Victorian garden was complete without a monkey-puzzle tree. Lobb's employer, the Veitch nursery, published a *Manual of Coniferae* and described "a magnificent vista of these strange wonderful trees with their dark plexus of branches and rigid bristly foliage." Many outgrew the modest front gardens of suburban villas where they were planted. They can still be seen occasionally, incongruously dwarfing the "gentlemen's residences" of the time.

In 1884 Marianne North, a Victorian painter who traveled all over the world to paint the native flora, went to Chile to find and paint a monkey-puzzle in its native land. She wrote in her journal that this tree was "known in England as the puzzle-monkey tree, rather unreasonably, as there are no monkeys in Chili [*sic*] to puzzle . . . Probably they [left] in disgust at the general prickliness of all the plants there." She painted the monkey-puzzle (along with some llamas), particularly admiring its bark "which is a perfect child's puzzle of slabs of different sizes, with 5 or 6 distinct sides to each, all fitted together with the neatness of a honey comb." This bark can be seven inches thick and helps protect the tree from extremes of temperature.

🌿 NO FASHIONABLE VICTORIAN GARDEN WAS COMPLETE WITHOUT A MONKEY-PUZZLE TREE.

Marianne North donated the monkey-puzzle painting and all her others to Kew gardens and also paid for a building to house them. The pavilion, named for her, is still in the gardens. It is crammed with paintings, each surrounded by a frame fashioned of wood from the different countries they represent. It is well worth a visit.

In their native country, far from Victorian gardens, monkey-puzzles are truly magnificent. The few remaining forests of them can take the observer back to a time when there were no humans on earth yet, and no monkeys either.

MULBERRY

The story of Pyramus and Thisbe in *A Midsummer Night's Dream*, acted by Bottom, Quince, and Shakespeare's other comical workmen, was originally a Persian legend, retold by Ovid. In it the lovers select a meeting place under a mulberry tree, but Thisbe arrives first and is scared away by a lion. She drops her veil that "Lion vile with bloody mouth did stain." Pyramus finds the veil, presumes his love is dead, and "bravely broach'd his boiling bloody breast . . . / His dagger drew, and died." Thisbe finds the body and kills herself. In some versions of the legend, the pale fruits of the mulberry become stained with the lovers' blood and turn dark crimson forever after.

The Persian *Morus nigra*, or black mulberry, does come from Persia and also drops black fruits, which stain everything they touch with bloodlike juice. This tree was probably brought to Britain by the Romans, and Shakespeare was familiar with it. A black mulberry tree in his garden at Stratford-on-Avon is said to have been planted by Shakespeare himself.

If the Pyramus and Thisbe legend is based on real trees, the Persians might have heard about a white-berried mulberry. *M. nigra* is a different species from the *M. alba*, or white mulberry, that originated in China where it was cultivated to feed silkworms. The silkworm, *Bombyx mori*, only eats mulberry leaves. It will eat the leaves of the black mulberry but thrives best on white mulberry leaves. According to a Chinese legend, silk was discovered by the empress Xi Ling-Shi in about 2640 BC. She was seated under a mulberry tree enjoying a cup of tea when a silkworm cocoon fell into her cup. The empress extracted the cocoon and a long silken thread started to unwind from it. Not long afterward another empress, Si Ling-chi, was said to have invented the loom for weaving this fabulous thread.

> THE SILKWORM, *BOMBYX MORI*, ONLY EATS MULBERRY LEAVES.

The Chinese made and exported silk (along the famous Silk Road) but jealously guarded from the West the secret of how it was made. In about 552 AD the Byzantium emperor Justinian "saw with concern . . . that the wealth of his subjects was continually drained by a nation of enemies and idolators," wrote Edward Gibbon, in *The History of the Decline and Fall of the Roman Empire* (1776–1788). Justinian was delighted when two Persian monks came to him "having deceived a jealous people by concealing the eggs of the silkworm in a hollow cane and returned in triumph with the spoils of the East . . . the worms were fed with mulberry-leaves . . . and trees were planted to supply the nourishment of the rising generations."

The culture of silk, along with the white mulberry tree, slowly spread across Europe. Muslim conquerors took both the trees and the silkworms to Spain and Sicily. The Greeks and Romans had already spread the black mulberry tree because they ate its fruit and made wine from its juice. Although silkworms prefer white mulberry leaves, most people find the white fruit insipid. The white mulberry fruits have stalks; black mulberries are unstalked.

The silk industry was well established in Europe, particularly in France, by Tudor times. The first Stuart king of Britain, James I, hoping to start a silk industry, had hundreds of mulberry trees planted during his reign. In 1609 he issued a letter to the lords-lieutenants of every county with "Instructions for the increasing of Mulberie Trees." The king himself planted a Mulberry Garden near his palace. It seems, however, that most of the trees he planted were black mulberries. Whatever the reason, the silk industry never flourished in England as it did in France.

In the New World settlers were pleased to find the American mulberry, *M. rubra* ("red mulberry"). Native Americans ate the fruit (usually dried) and made cloth from the fibrous bark. But silkworms didn't like the leaves of red mulberries, so white (as well as black) ones were imported to start an American silk industry. Eliza Pinckney Lucas, a stalwart lady who first raised American indigo on the southern plantation she inherited from her father, also planted mulberry trees. She managed to obtain just enough silk to make three silk dresses, which she wore when she visited England in 1741.

In the nineteenth century a new kind of mulberry, the *M. multicaulis* ("many stemmed") was imported to North America from the Philippines, again with the hope of establishing a profitable silk industry. An 1828 pamphlet on the subject suggested that "each of us commence operations by the erection of a cocoonery of a suitable size proportionate to the number of trees we possess . . . The expense is so trivial compared with . . . the certainty of Profitable returns that everyone should complete his arrangements without delay." No silk industry ensued (*see* Tree of Heaven), but a lot of these new mulberry trees were sold by nurserymen and planted. Most of them didn't withstand the climate and died.

The name *morus* (*mûrier* in French) most likely is simply the ancient Latin name, but some say it might come from the Greek *mora*, "delay." Others say it has the same root as "moron." The latter seems unlikely because, as Pliny the Elder said, the mulberry is the "wisest of trees," prudently delaying until the weather is dependably warm to open its spring leaves. When the new mulberry leaves had emerged, wrote John Evelyn, gardeners could bring their potted plants "boldly out of the Greene-house." The Italian *moro* means both "mulberry" and "dark or black."

Americans mostly don't eat even the fruits of the black mulberry, although birds love them. In cities where mulberries are common street trees, we sometimes see the fruits squashed on sidewalks, leaving bloodlike stains. When Shakespeare's play is over, "Moonshine and Lion are left to bury the dead," and the mulberry, the scene of the tragedy, lives on. Some mulberries live for hundreds of years, while generations of humans come and go, playing their plays of life, and death.

MYRRH

Myrrha was the daughter of Cinyras, king of Cyprus. In spite of asking the gods to help her resist, she fell in love with her father and, with her nurse's help, tricked him into sleeping with her. After several nights Cinyras discovered that he had been making love to his own daughter and tried to kill her. She ran away and wandered for nine months in the deserts of Arabia, finally reaching the land of "Sabaea" just as she was about to give birth. Again Myrrha prayed for help, and this time the gods answered by transforming her into a tree. Through its bark the beautiful (but hapless) Adonis was born. "She still weeps, and warm drops flow from the tree . . . the myrrh that drips from her trunk retains her name. Men will speak of it for eternity," declares Ovid's *Metamorphoses*.

Most probably Myrrha was named for the tree, not the other way round.

For myrrh was a very valuable commodity known to Arab traders long before classical times. Its name comes from the Arabic *murr*, or "bitter," meaning the same in the Hebrew *mor*. Myrrh trees were said to have been brought by the queen of Sheba as a gift to King Solomon. The "beloved" of the Song of Solomon holds her lover between her breasts like myrrh. In the book of Esther, when the Persian king wanted to replace his recalcitrant wife he had a bevy of virgins "purified" for six months with oil of myrrh. When Esther was duly chosen, she managed to charm her husband sufficiently for him to accept her Jewish father and abstain from killing all the Jews in Persia. The "toilet of Esther" getting ready to charm the king was a popular theme of Renaissance artists.

ITS NAME COMES FROM THE ARABIC *MURR*, OR "BITTER," MEANING THE SAME IN THE HEBREW *MOR*.

Myrrh was one of the three valuable gifts brought to Jesus in Bethlehem. Marco Polo wrote in his *Travels* that the kings came from Persia, and it was said there that if the gift of myrrh was acceptable it would prove to them that the baby was a healer. The gold would show he was a king, and the frankincense a god (*see* Frankincense). The baby did accept the myrrh, as well as the other offerings. The Old French word *mire* meant an apothecary. Myrrh was also used to embalm bodies. When Jesus died, women brought myrrh as well as other aromatics to the tomb. According to the Oxford English Dictionary, a *myrrophore* is "a woman carrying spices to the sepulcher of Christ, as represented in art."

Myrrh trees grow on the southern coast of Arabia, in what is now Oman and Yemen. They are spiny, small and gnarled, and grow where practically nothing else thrives. The tree has red flowers, pointed fruit, and a fissured bark. If the bark is wounded it exudes a protective gummy substance that is antibacterial and traps insects. This resin dries to a golden-yellow substance, highly aromatic. It was brought by the Arabs on camels across the desert.

The botanical name of the myrh is *Commiphora abyssynica* ("camphor from Abyssinia"). It is not related to the aromatic camphor tree. In the book of Genesis, "Ishmeelites came from Gilead with their camels, bearing spicery and balm and myrrh," when they came across Joseph and his unbrotherly siblings. Joseph was sold to the traders for twenty pieces of silver and, along with the spices, taken to Egypt. But that is another story.

NEEM

The neem tree, *nim balnimb* in Hindi, has been venerated in India for thousands of years and is mentioned in ancient Sanskrit writings. It was used to cure and alleviate so many ailments that it was sometimes known as the village pharmacy. The twigs could be used for cleaning teeth, the bark made dye, the seeds fed livestock, and the tree itself provided welcome shade.

Neem trees grow to about fifty feet high and their ashlike leaves are evergreen or semi-evergreen. Native to India, they were taken to Africa by British colonists. They also grow well in Saudi Arabia, South America, and the southern United States.

The flowers are sweet scented and the small fruits, with a single seed, are green turning to yellow. The fruits and seeds yield bitter oil with healing properties and gave the tree another name, margosa, from the Portuguese *amargosa*, meaning "bitter." The oil was used to eliminate head lice, to heal skin ailments, as a contraceptive spermicide, and when mixed with water, to protect crops from insect pests.

Indian farmers traditionally used neem seeds soaked in water on their crops, even if they couldn't name azadirachtin, the chemical compound responsible for its efficacy. The botanical name of the neem tree is *Azadirachta indica*, from the Persian-derived *azad-dirakt*, meaning "free" or "noble" tree. *Indica* means "of India." It was known that locusts didn't attack neem trees (although they devoured every other plant around them). Neem leaflets made wonderful book marks because the books they were placed in seemed to be protected from insect damage.

When Western scientists "discovered" and isolated azadirachtin, it seemed that it might be used in insecticidal products with few side effects on the environment. This, it was thought, could revolutionize farming and certainly help in our endless struggle to feed ourselves as populations grew. By the end of the twentieth century, neem oil was being used by gardeners and became a potential a source of big profits. Attempts to patent this miraculous substance followed. Those who strove to do so argued that they were only trying to patent the isolation of the tree's chemical components, not the tree itself. Their opponents protested that the chemicals had been effectively used in India for centuries, did not have to be invented, and that trees cannot be patented. If only the name of the noble *Azadirachta* could elicit the noblest of human motives—but this isn't always easy when large fortunes are at stake.

IT WAS USED TO CURE AND ALLEVIATE SO MANY AILMENTS THAT IT WAS SOMETIMES KNOWN AS THE VILLAGE PHARMACY.

NUTMEG

Nutmeg is a popular color described by fashion designers for fall wear. But of course it's also a spice, often ground into comforting beverages like eggnog or toddy, particularly associated with warmth during the winter holiday season.

Nutmeg originated in the Banda Islands. Antonio Pigafetta kept a record of his 1520s voyage on the *Victoria* under Ferdinand Magellan. He described the ship crossing the Atlantic, rounding South America and sailing the unknown Pacific seas for three months. Only one out of five ships returned home to Spain and most of the sailors (including Magellan himself) died. But the Western world had finally discovered the Moluccas, or Spice Islands. Pigafetta wrote of seeing a tree with fruit similar to a "quince apple." This was the nutmeg tree.

Nutmegs weren't unknown in Europe before this, but they were rare and valuable, brought to Europe by Arab traders. The Arab physician Avicenna (*see* Mangrove) described the "nut of Banda," and nutmegs were used in the

Byzantine Court. Like many exotics, they were thought to be aphrodisiac. "Nutmeg" probably came from the Arabic *misk* ("musk"). In Old Latin it was *nux moschata* ("musk-scented nut"). In French the name became *muscade nois* (meaning "perfumed nut"). *Muscade* shares its word origin with *muguet*, the intensely fragrant lily-of-the-valley. By Chaucer's time in England it was called "Notemygge to put in ale . . . Or for to lye in cofre" (or used to scent chests).

The Portuguese acquired the Spice Islands and monopolized the spice trade until the seventeenth century when the Dutch East India Company took over (*see* Clove). Dutch growers decimated the native population and used their own slaves to grow and harvest nutmegs, which soon became obtainable throughout Europe.

Nutmeg trees have smooth shiny leaves, and their fruit is pear shaped. Nutmegs aren't nuts but seeds of the nutmeg fruit. The trees can grow to about thirty feet and live nearly a century but don't fruit for their first decade. The seedlings need shade. There are male and female trees and in modern groves about one male to every twenty females is enough to pollinate the flowers, which are small and greenish. Some people called nutmegs harem trees.

Nutmeg fruit is edible and sometimes made into preserves. It's a favorite food of fruit-eating pigeons, whose beaks can stretch to ingest it whole. These pigeons have very rough stomach linings and, unlike many birds, don't have to eat grit to separate the nutmeg fruit from the kernel. By excreting the seed whole they spread the trees.

The Dutch attempted to keep their monopoly by confining nutmegs trees to the island of Pulo Run. Dutch and British fought fiercely for ownership of this tiny island and the right to raise nutmegs there. In the 1667 Treaty of Breda the Dutch retained the island of Pulo Run and ceded to the British New

Amsterdam (the island of Manhattan) — a piece of real estate that turned out to be worth a lot of nutmegs.

Between the fleshy fruit and the kernel is an aril, or covering, which is another spice we call mace (also meaning "perfumed"). In Gerard's *Herball*, this aril is described as "of a perfect crimson colour, and [it] maketh a most goodly show." He goes on to say that the mace "forsaketh the Nut . . . and loseth that brave crimson dye, which it had at first." Usually this was (and is) done by human hands — the mace is cut off and, dried, has a yellowish hue and a slightly different flavor from the kernel.

In French the name became *muscade nois* (meaning "perfumed nut").

Nutmegs have to be grated just before use to get the best flavor. In the eighteenth century, when nutmegs were at their most popular, personal nutmeg graters, sometimes made of silver, were carried by the well-to-do. Perhaps their aphrodisiac reputation made them good to have at hand. Whether or not this property was merely suggestive, nutmegs can cause pleasing hallucinogenic sensations and can, if ingested in quantity, even cause death. In the old days nurses used to grind nutmeg into warm milk to soothe babies. In modern America, prison inmates sometime manage to obtain this spice in lieu of other more obvious narcotics.

The Dutch used to dip nutmegs in lime to prevent them from germinating elsewhere, and they are often still dusted with lime, giving them a characteristic ashy exterior. A "wooden nutmeg" is a fraudulent object, once supposedly substituted for the real thing by dishonest traders who presumably discouraged prospective customers from scratching the surface to see if it had a fragrant smell.

Nutmeg

The botanical name for nutmeg is *Myristica fragrans*, meaning "myrrh-like fragrance." Unlike myrrh, nutmegs were not known in biblical times and were not part of the offerings brought to the Nativity stable by the three kings (*see* Myrrh). The little Lord Jesus, as the Christmas carol tells us, did not cry—so there would have been no need to offer this baby grated nutmeg in milk.

OAK

I might with rev'rence kneel and worship thee,
It seems idolatry with some excuse
When our forefather Druids in their oaks
Imagin'd sanctity . . .

So extolled William Cowper in "Yardley Oak" (1786).
In many of the places where humans have lived, and prayed, there have been oak trees. A large oak has often been a center for meetings and worship.

Oaks were sacred to many gods: the Norse Thor, the Roman Jupiter, the Slavic Perun, the Celtic Dagda, and the Hebrew El. The Druids crowned their sacrificial victims with oak-leaf garlands, and some people think the name "druid" comes from the Gaelic *darach*, "oak tree." The Icelandic for "oak" was *eik*, and the Middle English was *oke*.

Oak

The Latin name for "oak" is *Quercus*, and the common English oak is *Quercus robur*, for "robust." In the past oaks were often used as permanent boundary markers. They are among the largest trees on earth (although not the very largest) and can live a very long time (although not as long as some other trees). Oaks are, however, more adaptable than most trees and are widespread. Different oaks can grow in totally different climates and terrains, from stinking swamps to stony hillsides. They can be evergreen or deciduous.

As well as worshipping oaks, people sometimes avoided them, especially during thunderstorms, because they were believed to attract lightning. This is true to a certain extent, because of their great height and the relative dryness of their fissured bark. When an oak is hit by lightning the electric current seeks moisture behind the thick bark, and the tree tends to explode apart. Jove, as we know, hurled lightning bolts when displeased, and oaks were *his* tree. Thor, also associated with oaks, gave his name to thunder (as well as Thursday). "Beware of an Oak, it draws the stroke, / Creep under the Thorn, it will save you from harm," warned an ancient saying. It's still true that sheltering under bushes is safer than cowering by oak trees (or any trees) during a storm — though prickly thorns might not immediately suggest the sacred and protective crown of thorns, as once they did.

The eighth-century Benedictine monk Boniface was sent by Pope Gregory II as a missionary to Germany, where he found an obstinate group of pagans worshipping an oak tree. Boniface ordered that the tree be cut down. While the worshippers were helplessly watching, a supernatural blast of wind arose, ripping off the top of the oak, which crashed down, splitting into four equal parts when it struck the ground. The pagans, satisfactorily for Boniface, interpreted these four parts as a sign of the crucifix, manifesting the power of Christianity. After the pagans were converted, the oak wood was used to build an oratory dedicated to St. Peter. Boniface himself was murdered, in 754 AD, by another group of potential converts. He was later sanctified.

Oaks have served humans so very well, in so many ways. Their wood has made houses, floors, and most important, ships. The transoms of ships were built around crotched oak branches, V-shaped joints stronger than any that could be made by men. The British navy depended on large oaks and had pretty much used them all up by the American War of Independence. The British thought poorly of American oaks until the USS *Constitution* (affectionately called Old Ironsides by American sailors) proved otherwise. Constructing that impregnable ship required fifteen hundred American oaks, but at that time there were still plenty left to supply the new nation's navy.

Before aniline dyes were invented certain colors were obtained from oak trees. The kermes oak, *Q. coccifera*, was used in ancient Greece where a rare scarlet dye was obtained from its oak galls, which are spherical growths on oak trees, made by insects. The female kermes wasp forms a gall as a place to lay her eggs. These galls were soaked in vinegar to extract the red dye from them. At first the Spartans used no dyes for their clothes, but later they took to dyeing their battledress red, so the bloodstains wouldn't show up. Oak galls mixed with iron were used to make ink. Sadly, though, after a few centuries the iron oxidizes, and the writing disappears, threatening many old manuscripts that had survived until recently.

The American black oak, *Q. tinctoria*, was also used, as its botanical name

suggests, for dye, this time yellow, from the yellow inner bark. The American white oak, *Q. alba* ("white"), is so called because of its pale wood. White oaks are different from red oaks, the latter being indigenous only to North America. The main difference is that red oaks have leaf veins extending beyond the leaf margins to form bristles around the edge of the leaves.

Another difference is that red oak acorns take two years to mature. *Q. rubra* has brilliant scarlet leaves in fall. Another common red oak in the United States is the pin oak, *Q. palustris*, meaning "of swamps," although it can grow elsewhere. It is a popular street tree. The leaves have pinlike edges, typical of red oaks, but most probably the name pin comes from its tough, thin lower branches, often used to pin together carpenter's joints. Another explanation came from André Michaux, who, in 1785, was sent by the French government to study American trees. He wrote that these thin branches gave the tree the "appearance of being full of pins."

> IN MEDIEVAL FORESTS THE RIGHT OF "PANNAGE" WAS A RIGHT TO GRAZE PIGS UNDER THE TREES.

Evergreen oaks include the holm, or holly oak ("holm" being an old name for holly). The tree of southern plantations was *Q. virginiana*, which is often romantically draped with Spanish moss, or *Tillandsia*. This was charmingly named by Linnaeus after Elias Tilliander who was so "harassed by Neptune" when crossing the gulf of Bothnia that he returned to his home in Sweden overland, avoiding crossing the sea but traveling two thousand miles, instead of two hundred, to do so. Draped over high branches, Spanish moss, Linnaeus decided, doesn't need water.

The city of Albuquerque in New Mexico was named (in 1706) for its Spanish viceroy, the Duke of Alburqurque, whose name meant "white oak" (later one "r" was dropped). Another oak named for a person is the Oregon white oak, *Q. garryana*. Nicholas Garry was the deputy governor of the Hudson Bay Company and the explorer botanist David Douglas (*see* Fir) was "much indebted" to him for help, which included using the company's guides on his travels. Poor Garry died insane, but at least he has a tree, as well as a popular shrub, named for him.

The acorns of the Oregon white oak were eaten in great quantities by local tribes. "As might be expected, they are far from being of a palatable flavor," wrote Douglas, somewhat uncharitably. An acorn-eating culture is called a balanoculture, from the Greek *balanos* ("acorn"). Acorns, once their tannin has been leached out by soaking them in water, are extremely nutritious. Humans often enjoy, and can benefit from, small amounts of tannin. Tea and red wine both contain tannic acid and are said to be healthful as well as being delicious.

Most wild oak trees are planted by jays or squirrels, which relish the acorns but bury a lot for future use and then forget to retrieve some of them. Pigs like acorns, too, and get nice and fat on them. In medieval forests the right of "pannage" was a right to graze pigs under the trees. June and July, however, were "forbidden" months, since deer would then have fawns lying in the underbrush. As well as acorns, pigs eat helpless young animals with relish — a comforting rationalization, perhaps, for humans addicted to bacon.

OLIVE

T he olive is a tree the least known in America," wrote President Jefferson from Paris on July 30, 1787. "And yet the most worthy of being known. Of all the gifts of heaven to man, it is next to the most precious, if it be not the most precious. Perhaps it may claim a preference even to bread, because there is such an infinitude of vegetables, which it renders a proper and comfortable nourishment."

Jefferson planted both olive seeds and suckers many times in his gardens at Monticello, Virginia. He thought that in the warm southern climate it would be easy to cultivate olive trees and produce oil, but these trees only set fruit under very specific conditions. They can flourish with very little rain, because they have deep roots and narrow waxy leaves that conserve moisture. They won't survive in damp climates however warm, and they must have a cool winter period of dormancy before they can flower and fruit. By 1813 Thomas Jefferson had to admit that olive oil could not be produced in the southern states, and that if any of the trees he had planted "still exist it is merely as a curiosity in . . . gardens." He unjustly blamed this failure on "the nonchalance of our Southern citizens."

Jefferson was, however, unaware that on the California's coast, where the climate suited them, olive trees were growing and producing oil. These trees had been planted in Spanish missions along the coast. The first mission was that of San Diego de Alcala, founded by the Franciscan father Junipero Serra in 1769. It took a while to establish this mission, and the others north along the coast to Sonoma, because, perhaps understandably, it wasn't easy to convince the local Indian communities that living in a mission and raising crops was necessarily a life preferable to the one that they had led before (even if they were assured of eternal salvation). However, by the time Father Serra died in 1784, the converted Catholics working under the fathers raised enough food for the communities and a surplus to trade with passing European ships. They produced animal hides as well as olive oil to exchange with these ships for glass, iron, and other goods. They had no contact with Jefferson's world, so it's not surprising he thought olives were unknown in America.

THE ROMANS RUBBED THE (PERFUMED) OIL ONTO THEIR SKIN AND THEN SCRAPED IT OFF, IN LIEU OF SOAP.

Spanish conquerors brought olives to Mexico from Spain. The Arabs had brought olives to Spain from the Middle East. In the Koran (24: 35), it is written, "Allah is the Light of the Heavens and the Earth. The similitude of His light is as a niche wherein is a lamp . . . kindled from a blessed tree, an olive." The Greeks and Romans both grew olive trees and used their oil, but more often for burning in lamps and oiling their bodies than in food. The Romans rubbed the (perfumed) oil onto their skin and then scraped it off, in lieu of soap. Pliny said that the two "liquids" agreeable to the human body were "wine within and oil without."

The Israelites had used olive oil, too, to burn in the temple and to anoint their kings. In the book of Hosea the beauty of God is "as the olive tree." After the Flood a dove brought Noah an olive leaf to show that the water had receded and the trees were emerging from beneath it. Ever since then the dove and the olive branch have been symbols of God's forgiveness and of peace. The flag of our United Nations displays an olive branch, in the hopes it can maintain peace between the nations. The Hebrew for olive is *zaylt*. The Arabic for "olive oil" is *zayt*. The garden where Jesus spent his last night praying was the Garden of Gethsemane, which means "the garden with the olive press."

In spite of the botanical name *Olea europaea*, olive trees don't originate in Europe but more probably in Mesopotamia or in the Middle East. Greek legend said that the goddess Athena first offered the olive tree to the Greeks and that the city of Athens was named for her to thank her. The god Poseidon had offered the horse, which was turned down.

Next to the city of Athens was an ancient olive grove given to Academus, who had rescued Helen when she was kidnapped by Theseus. (She was later abducted by Paris and the Trojan wars followed.) In the fourth century BC, Plato lived next to this olive grove and he and his followers walked there discussing philosophy. John Milton, in *Paradise Regained*, vividly described the beauty of

> The olive grove of Academe
> Plato's retirement, where the Attic bird
> Trills her thick-warbl'd notes the summer long.

A place of learning where academics live is still called an academy. They are often places of great beauty.

The narrow, silvery leaves of the olive are similar to those of the Russian olive, or oleaster. It too thrives in dry places, sometimes even growing in sand or gravel, but this small tree (or large shrub) from Asia, is no relation to the true olive. True olives (like lilacs, which *are* in the same family) can live very long. They regenerate from suckers at the base if the main tree dies or is cut down. A few olive trees are thought to be over a thousand years old.

As food products, olives and olive oil are probably more popular now than in the past. Olives are extremely bitter, and it's laborious to make them fit to eat. In fact one wonders how it was ever discovered that they *could* be palatable. They have to be soaked for a long time in brine and lye before they can be used. Green olives are unripe black olives. The oil must be extracted with huge presses. Jefferson had suggested producing oil for "bettering the condition of . . . slaves" rather than as a luxury food. He said that vegetables that "would otherwise be useless" would be "rendered edible by the aid of a little oil." As it turned out, the slaves themselves introduced sesame oil from Africa and by 1811 Jefferson wrote that "we now use it [sesame oil] and make from it our own salad oil preferable to such olive oil as is usually to be bought."

We ourselves are not apt to think of olive oil as something to make the inedible edible. It's an essential part of Mediterranean cooking, revered more than ever because it is low in cholesterol. The precise virginity of olive oil perplexes many a gourmet who only wants the very best, and it's not unusual to find seals of purity (or alleged virginity) on expensive little bottles of the stuff. The Athenians seem to have got it right—we still value olive oil but have more or less given up horses.

ORANGE

On June 25, 1666, Samuel Pepys visited the garden of Lord Brooke in Hackney. "I first saw oranges grow," he recorded in his *Diary*," some green, some half, some quarter, some full ripe, on the same tree . . . I pulled off a little one by stealth (the man being mightily curious of them) and eat it, and it was just as other little green oranges are."

Ripe oranges, in spite of their name, which they gave to the color itself, aren't necessarily orange colored when ripe and can even be green. The already ripened fruit gets its bright color when temperatures fall. Unlike many fruits, though, oranges don't continue to ripen after they are picked, so being "tree-ripened" is not an option! Also, as in Lord Brooke's tree, the oranges ripen at different times. On the tree's northern side the oranges are said to be less sweet than those that mature on the south side.

Oranges aren't mentioned in the Bible (in spite of the suggestion by some scholars that they might have been the "fruit of knowledge"), and the classical world only knew the citron (*see* Lemon and Lime). The oranges Pepys "first saw" would have been the sweet oranges, *Citrus sinensis* ("from China"), which had long been cultivated in China but weren't brought west until the beginning of the seventeenth century.

Bitter oranges, or *C. aurantium* ("golden"), the ones we now call Seville oranges, had come to Europe a long time before this, probably brought by Arab traders. They weren't eaten but used medicinally and for their perfume. They were introduced to Spain by the Moors and spread to Portugal where they grew so well that they acquired the name *bortugal*, still used in the Arab world. Orange trees blossom and form fruits at the same time, and the tree doesn't lose its leaves. So it was often planted in Muslim gardens as a symbol of longevity and rebirth (*see* Cypress). The name orange comes from the old Arabic *naranj*, which came from the Persian *narang*. Some say (but don't explain why) that this name came from a Sanskrit word, *nagarunga*, meaning "fruit favored by elephants."

Oranges spread to Italy and France and are often seen in Renaissance paintings. Our tradition of decking brides with orange blossom originated as a symbol of their (supposed) purity, their commitment, and their hopes of fertility.

In China, oranges of many kinds have been grown and eaten for centuries. A collection of Chinese stories from the sixth century BC, *Yanzi Chunqin*, described the proper way to peel an orange. In 304 AD another Chinese manual even described controlling citrus pests by moving the nests of certain ants into citrus groves. The Chinese name for orange was *jyn*, but the name didn't migrate to Persia with the fruit.

Orange blossom is incredibly fragrant. The Japanese prince Genji made a garden for one of his "Ladies," planted with orange trees "whose scent re-awakens forgotten love." The prince "forgets" and "remembers" different loves throughout this very long eleventh-century novel. Fragrant oils can also be extracted from orange peel and leaves. John Parkinson, in *Theatrum Botanicum* (published in 1640), wrote that orange leaves were "very acceptable" in salads.

Bitter oranges make the best fragrant oil. Bergamot oranges were (and are) an important ingredient of Earl Grey tea. Neroli or orange blossom oil is use for many perfumes. It was named for a seventeenth-century French princess who married the Duke of Nerola and held a salon in Rome. She later went to Spain as a royal lady-in-waiting and, presumably not because of her perfume, greatly influenced government policy there.

Oranges (the bitter kind) were brought to the New World by Christopher Columbus. Sweet oranges are less hardy and were first planted in greenhouses or "orangeries" both in Europe and North America. But in the nineteenth century successful orange orchards were established in Florida and California, becoming, and remaining, very big business. Some oranges (like Sunkist) are trade names. Others commemorate people, like William Chase Temple, who was general manager of a Florida citrus grove. The popular Washington navel orange got its name when seedlings of a tree found in Bahia, Brazil, were sent to the U.S. Department of Agriculture in Washington, D.C. A Mrs. Luther Tibbett acquired two of these plants and launched this fabulous orange.

ON THE TREE'S NORTHERN SIDE THE ORANGES ARE SAID TO BE LESS SWEET THAN THOSE THAT MATURE ON THE SOUTH SIDE.

An early orange orchard, in Mandarin, Florida, was owned by Harriet Beecher Stowe. She taught Sunday school and gave reading lessons to the children of the plantation. Her reputation apparently helped sell the oranges, which were packed in boxes stenciled with her name. Businesses these days also sometimes use social programs as a part of their marketing strategy. Mandarin oranges are ancient oranges from China where, it is said, they were consumed by mandarins, a privileged group who wore orange-yellow robes. Tangerines are a kind of mandarin that originated in Tangiers. Clementines, another kind of mandarin orange, were first raised (in about 1902) by a priest, Father Clementine, in his Algerian garden. All these small oranges have to be cut rather than picked from the tree, or their loose skin will rupture. The botanical name of tangerines and mandarins is *C. reticulata* ("net veined").

The Protestant House of Orange, a German principality, was not at first connected with the color orange. The name came, not from the color or the fruit, but from the Roman town of Arausio, later Orenge and then Orange, in Provence. A prince of Orange was rewarded for his services to the Holy Roman Emperor, Charles V, with territory in the Netherlands. In 1689 Prince William and his wife, Mary, came over from Holland to establish the succession of the House of Orange to the British throne. They were hated by the Catholic Irish, who included the color orange as a symbol of the Protestants with their "orange" beliefs.

This lovely color has more recent unpleasant associations. During the Vietnam War, Agent Orange, the herbicide containing dioxin, was used to defoliate areas of the jungle so the trees could not be used for cover. The poisonous spray was kept in drums painted with an identifying stripe colored bright orange—a far cry from the life-giving connections of this beautiful little tree.

OSAGE ORANGE

The fruits of the Osage orange are bright greenish-yellow balls, about the size and shape of oranges, but with a curious brainlike formation. Actually each ball is not a single fruit but a cluster of fruits called a syncarp (similar to the pineapple "fruit"). In the early seventeenth century the doctrine of signatures, shaped by spiritual philosophy, postulated that the form of plants could indicate which parts of the body they could cure. Under this system of thought, Osage oranges would probably have been used to cure afflictions of the brain (*see* Walnut). But in medieval Europe Osage oranges, which are native to the American Midwest, had not yet been discovered by European botanists.

Meriwether Lewis first sent seedlings of "Osages Plum and Apples" to Jefferson in March 1804. Lewis described the fruits (which he did not see) as highly aromatic. The cedar-scented balls are still used as a cockroach repellent and their sticky white juice is said by some to burn off warts. Both a male and a female tree are needed to produce the Osage "apples" or "oranges," which, in spite of their name, are not edible.

Lewis obtained his specimens from the Osage Indians, near St. Louis, Missouri. The hard, pliable wood was used by them to make hunting bows, and consequently French settlers sometimes called the tree *bois d'arc*, or "bow wood." This became "Bowdark," or "Bodark," orange (or apple), a name still used in some areas of North America.

Botanically, Osage oranges are usually called *Maclura pomifera*. *Pomifera* means "apple bearing" and *Maclura* is for William Maclure who lived from 1763 to 1840. The naturalist Thomas Nuttall named the tree for Maclure, probably because Maclure had called Nuttall "a frank affable man," a compliment that needed acknowledgment. Nuttall himself found the western dogwood, which was named, for him, *Cornus nuttallii*. *Cornus* means "horn," and refers to the dogwood's very hard wood.

The alternative name for the Osage orange was *Toxylon pomifera*, from *toxicum*, the Latin for "poisonous" (*see* Yew). This name was given in 1817 by Constantine Rafinesque, who claimed to have first classified the tree. Rafinesque was a showy character who boasted that although he had no college degree, he knew more languages "than all the American colleges united." His contemporary John Torrey (*see* Yew) wrote in a letter on March 12, 1818, that Rafinesque's work was "the most curious medley I ever saw . . . But Raf. will probably not stop here—I expect he will soon issue proposals for publishing the botany of the *moon*!" Rafinesque, upset when his "official" botanical name was usually dropped in favor of Nuttall's, was perhaps somewhat compensated when the big-eared bat was called *rafinesquii* and Thomas Nuttall called the desert chicory *Rafinesquia*.

In his diary Maclure wrote that he had seen the Osage orange and thought "it would make an excellent hedge." He was right. Osage oranges are very thick and thorny and in the pre-barbed-wire era made an excellent barricade. An old rule for farmers was that a fence should be "horse high, bull strong, and pig tight." An Osage orange fence was all of these, and it was much easier and cheaper to plant a hedge than construct stone walls or wooden palings. The trees grew rapidly, "nearly ten feet in one year," wrote Maclure. Soon farmers were surrounding their fields with these hedges, and providing Osage orange seedlings became good business, too. You can often see the remains of these hedgerows along old roads, where in autumn the pools of their curious green fruit are soon to be squashed into a brown rotting mess by passing cars.

Even where farms were surrounded by his namesake, Maclure did not become a household name. It's a pity he is not better remembered, because in many ways he seems to have been ahead of his time—ours, too, for that matter. He traveled widely, and his diary is full of pithy comments about the world, ranging from hygiene ("so necessary to health") to prejudice ("The astonishing contradictory variety of tastes and manner [in the world] can only be equaled by the astonishing obstinacy with which each society insists that they have reason, and all the others are wrong"). A rich and a self-made Scottish immigrant, he used his money to improve the world. He endowed the Philadelphia Academy of Science with twenty thousand dollars as well as his huge library. He was an early patron of the Pestalozzi system for teaching young children. He warned against "impostors who live by the stupidity and ignorance of the people" and was probably hoping to help by leaving five hundred dollars to any "laborers' club" that would establish a library of more than a hundred volumes. If his executors found any takers we do not know. We do know that impostors can still successfully exploit ignorance, over a century and a half later.

PAPAW

The name papaw, or pawpaw, is applied to two different fruits, not related. One is native to tropical South America, the other native to central and eastern North America.

The name papaw probably comes from the Spanish *papaya*, which in turn came from the Caribbean *abábai*. Papayas, the tropical fruit, are thought to have originated in South America and spread to the West Indies. They were first described to the West by Hernando de Soto, who was captain of a Spanish ship sent to reenforce the Spanish conquest of Peru. Later, De Soto explored Mississippi and, in 1541, wrote about his travels there. He would have been exposed to both kinds of papaw, and was responsible for giving the North American *Asimina triloba* the same common name as the West Indian *Carica papaya*.

Tropical papayas, once discovered by Western explorers, spread rapidly wherever colonists went, and they now grow in most tropical countries. They are strange, ancient trees with huge pulpy fruits that might once have fed dinosaurs. They don't have branches but a sprouting leafy crown at the top, with the fruits dangling down beneath it. They are sometimes called tree melons because papayas are about the size and shape of small melons. In Cuba they are called bomb fruits, and they are also (impolite) slang for female breasts.

Sexually papayas are odd. The female flowers contain no nectar but fool pollinators that search for it and so transfer pollen from the nectar-bearing male flowers. The trees themselves can be inconsistently male, female, or hermaphrodite.

The sweet fruit doesn't travel well and is often made into papaya juice. The seeds are edible but peppery. Perhaps most significant is the enzyme papain produced by papayas. Papain aids digestion and also tenderizes animal flesh. It is the ingredient of commercial meat tenderizers. Local people used to cook meat or fish wrapped in papaya leaves. Papain is also thought to heal wounds. The origin of the botanical name *carica* is obscure, though some etymologists say it came from the erroneous belief that the tree originated in the ancient land of Caria (in Asia Minor).

PAPAIN AIDS DIGESTION AND ALSO TENDERIZES ANIMAL FLESH.

The origin of the North American papaw's genus name, *Asimina*, is equally obscure. It may be a French version of the American Indian name, *assimin. Triloba* means "three lobed" and applies to the strange meaty brown flowers of this papaw.

Even after De Soto described the papaw in Mississippi, it remained unknown to most Westerners until Mark Catesby included it in his 1747 *Natural History of Carolina Georgia, Florida and the Bahama Islands.* Catesby made notes of the plants (and birds) that he saw but didn't finish the drawings and engravings for his book until he had settled again in England. Sometimes this caused problems. Peter Collinson, who knew Catesby, wrote to his friend

John Bartram asking him to send specimens of the papaw because Catesby "neglected when in Virginia to Draw the Papaw & as this is a Curious plant, in Flower & Fruit & not Figur'd by any Body . . . he begs a short Discription of its Colour."

Bartram responded and described the tree to Collinson, saying, "Ye papas will bear ye shade as well as most . . . [It is] of swift growth . . . but by degrees these other trees of slower but more permanent growth advances above and overcomes them like many human monarchs." This is as near to politics as the letters between the "king's botanist" and the Quaker gardener get (*see* Hemlock).

The color of this papaw's flower is brownish, and its smell is unpleasant to humans but attractive to the insects that pollinate it. The fruits, often called custard apples, are like small bananas, hanging in pairs, and more akin (if you will) to the human male than female anatomy. The seeds, unlike those of the South American papaya, are poisonous and were used, crushed, to control head lice.

Not many people eat local custard apples these days, preferring fruits or juices (including papaya juice) shipped from afar, and the papaw tree is no longer valued for its fruit. That's a pity, not so much because of well-nourished Americans, but because papaw leaves are the staple food of zebra swallow-tail caterpillars. Trees, even unusual ones, come and go, but these days it seems butterflies mostly go and don't come back.

PAULOWNIA

The paulownia, or princess tree, is named for Anna Pavlovna, the youngest daughter of the ill-fated Russian czar Paul I, who was assassinated in 1801, when Anna was only six years old. Anna was close to her brother, the new czar Alexander, and the family continued to live on the beautiful estate of Pavlovsk, famous for its gardens. Napoléon wanted to marry Anna but her mother refused to let her, and she married William II of the Netherlands instead.

William, like Anna's own family, was a keen gardener and collector of new plants. William patronized the German doctor and plant collector Philipp Franz von Siebold, who was employed by the Dutch East India Company.

At the time Japan was closed to all foreigners (*see* Maple), but the East India Company was allowed a trading base on Deshima, a tiny man-made island. Siebold was an eye doctor and could perform cataract surgery. His grateful patients gave him access to new plants, but eventually he was caught collecting maps of Japan and was imprisoned, then expelled. He settled for a time in Holland where King William commissioned him to form the Royal Society for the Encouragement of Horticulture. Siebold established a garden to "acclimatize" foreign plants. Between 1830 and 1842 he wrote a two-volume tome, *Flora Japonica*, illustrated with copies of Japanese drawings. It was he who named the newly imported *Paulownia* for the queen who loved plants.

There are several paulownias native to China, where it had been cultivated in gardens and used in medicine for thousands of years. Its Chinese name was *tong*. Some species have white or pale pink flowers, but the paulownia most familiar to Americans has purple foxglovelike flowers that appear before the leaves. This is the *Paulownia tomentosa*, which was either native to Japan or cultivated for a long time there. The Japanese name was *kiri*, or empress tree, and we sometimes call it the empress tree, too. In Japan the light, tough wood was used to make sandals or clogs and was so valuable that when a baby girl was born an empress tree was planted beside the family house. By the time she was old enough to marry there would be enough wood to make her marriage chest, with some left over to sell for her dowry.

IN JAPAN THE LIGHT, TOUGH WOOD WAS USED TO MAKE SANDALS OR CLOGS.

The paulownia, which had come to Europe in the mid-1800s, arrived in America soon after. There is a story that seedlings were spread inadvertently because the seed pods were used to pack around shipments of fragile imported porcelain and then thrown out. Whether or not this is true, the paulownia is one of the fastest-growing trees around, and it spread rapidly across the United States. It is now regarded as "invasive," especially in warm regions, and it is a frequent inhabitant of vacant city lots. Sometimes the trees poke between ravaged buildings. The fragrant lavender flowers drop down onto the cracked sidewalks below and lie for a while, making a breathlessly beautiful carpet, surrounded by desolation.

PEACH

I n Renaissance paintings the allegorical figure of Truth was
sometimes depicted as a naked figure being unveiled by Father
Time (illustrating that "Truth is the daughter of Time," or
Veritas filia temporis). In her hand Truth often holds a peach with one leaf attached, demonstating that the heart-shaped fruit and tongue-shaped leaf speak
the truth when united.

Peaches were called Persian plums or Persian apples by the ancients, and
their botanical name is *Prunus persica*, from the mistaken belief that they
originated in Persia. More likely they came to Persia from China, where they

had been cultivated and revered for thousands of years. The peach was the Chinese symbol of longevity and was believed to have grown in the land of Queen Xiwangmu where those who ate it became immortal. But since these mythical peaches only blossomed every three thousand years and bore fruit after another three thousand years, the truth of their immortal powers remained mainly symbolic. The Chinese name for peach is *tao*.

Peaches could be grafted onto almond trees, to which they are closely related, and they probably had a common ancestor somewhere in central Asia from whence peaches moved east to China and almonds moved southwest (*see* Almond). From the ancient classical world peaches made their way across Europe wherever the climate suited them. By the thirteenth century, their name had evolved from the tenth century *persicarius* to *peske* and then *peshe*. The French name is still *pêche*. A thirteenth-century account of the English king John's death in 1216 attributed it to eating too many peaches (others said it was too many lamprey eels!). If peaches were the cause, they must have been imported, because peach trees are thought to have been first brought to England by Catherine of Aragon when she came from Spain to marry Henry VIII in 1509.

The fruits were used for eating and making brandy and had medicinal virtues. Nicholas Culpeper in his *Complete Herbal* (1652) asserted that "Venus owns this tree . . . the fruit provokes lust." Peaches are still somewhat associated with love, and a "peach of a girl" might well provoke lust.

Since peaches grow readily from seed they could be spread quickly and early on were carried by settlers to the New World. The American climate suited peaches admirably. Native Americans took to peaches, and by 1663 William Penn wrote that there was "not an Indian plantation without them." It was appropriate that they grew their own peaches by then because in 1655 a massacre had been caused by the different conception of "ownership" perceived by settlers and Native Americans. In New Amsterdam an Indian woman was caught eating a peach in the orchard of Hendryck van Dyck who promptly shot her dead. The next day a thousand members of her tribe raided the town and killed or carried off two hundred inhabitants.

Peaches grew, and still grow, particularly well in California. The early American peaches were yellow and "freestone" (the stone easily separating from the flesh of the fruit). In 1850 Charles Downing introduced a white peach from Shanghai that was named Chinese cling because the fruit adhered to the stone. The flesh was pale, not yellow. In 1870, so the story goes, Chinese cling peaches hybridized with yellow freestone peaches in the Georgia orchard of Samuel Rumph. He called this new peach 'Elberta' after his wife, Clara Elberta Rumph.

A nectarine is a peach with a smooth skin not, as is sometimes thought, a cross between a plum and a peach. Peach trees occasionally bear nectarines and vice versa. Nectarines were known in Europe in the seventeenth century but weren't grown commercially until the nineteenth century, in California. Their name means they are "like nectar," drunk by the gods. Nectarines with their thin skins travel less well than peaches. That might be why Roald Dahl selected a giant peach rather than a nectarine to carry James Henry Trotter and his friends on their bumpy adventures.

NICHOLAS CULPEPER IN HIS *COMPLETE HERBAL* (1652) ASSERTED THAT "VENUS OWNS THIS TREE . . . THE FRUIT PROVOKES LUST."

PEAR

According to Suetonius in *Lives of The Twelve Caesars* the emperor Claudius's eldest son, Drusus, died "just before coming of age" when he was "choked by a pear which he had playfully thrown into the air and caught in his open mouth." This bizarre accident seems rather unlikely if we think of the large, luscious pears known to us today. In classical times, though, pears, which were only eaten cooked, *were* small and hard enough to lodge in the throat.

Pears appear in Assyrian carvings, but it seems that the Romans cultivated and spread them. By the first century AD the naturalist Pliny the Elder mentioned about forty different varieties of pear. Pears were probably introduced to Britain by the Romans and certainly taken to Gaul by them. The trees need a cool winter but prefer hot summers, and they do particularly well in Italy and France. The Latin name for the fruit, *pirum*, is the root of our "pear," the French "*poire*," and the Italian "*pera*," suggesting further that they were spread by the Romans.

The best-known pear in medieval England was the Warden pear, which was brought from Burgundy to the Cistercian Warden Abbey. Another French import was the Caillou pear, shaped like a pebble (*caillou*) and probably rather hard as well. In medieval England pears were often used to make pear cider, or "perry." Juicy dessert pears were developed in Italy and France and very soon associated with love. In Chaucer's *Canterbury Tales* the Carpenter's wife is described as "ful more blissful as to see / Than the newe pear-jonette tree." Chaucer's adulterous Merchant's wife even declares (as she climbs a pear tree to meet her love) that "I must have of the pears that I see, / Or I must die, so sore longeth me . . ."

✿ APPLES CAN BE ELONGATED AND PEARS CAN BE ROUND, DEPENDING ON THE PATTERN OF GROWTH.

Perhaps their "pyriform," or pear shape, such as that of wide-hipped women, contributed to the seductive image of the pear. Shakespeare compared "old virginity" to a "French withered Pear." The Christmas "Partridge in a Pear Tree" is clearly sending a stronger message to "my True Love" than mere Christmas greetings.

The most famous French pear was (and still may be) the Williams, or *bon chrétien*, pear. One story is that it was brought to France in 1482 by an Italian hermit, St. Francis of Paola, who had been summoned to the court of Louis XI to cure the king of eczema. The hermit gave the king a little pear tree to tend, with instructions to eat its fruits as soon as they were ripe. The king died before the pears had ripened, but the "good Christian" pear survived. Later it was renamed the Williams pear (we don't know for whom) and then was imported to America in the eighteenth century by Enoch Bartlett of Massachusetts and given his name. Bartletts are still one of America's most popular pears.

There are no pears native to America. Settlers brought over seed and stock and pears did well here. In 1774 Paul Dudley, describing the New World, said he saw pear trees forty feet high and six feet in girth. Occasionally a distinctive seedling would appear, like the Seckel pear, which was discovered on Jacob Weiss's farm outside Philadelphia in the 1760s. The farm was purchased by a Mr. Seckle who marketed this pear, still popular today.

Asian pears are much more "sandy" than European pears. These "grit" cells are present in all pears, but absent in apples, and they break down, becoming softer, as the pear ripens. Pears are picked before they are fully ripe and then ripened off the tree. There is only a very short period when a pear is ripe enough to eat but not overripe (some say it's about ten minutes). Asian pears can be hybridized with Western pears to resist some diseases. Pears grown in America were very susceptible to the fire-blight fungus, which was partly controlled after Asian pears came west in the nineteenth century. Peter Keiffer, a nurseryman in Pennsylvania, managed to develop a pear that was quite resistant to fire blight.

The Chinese like their pears crisp, and don't mind them gritty, but often cultivate them just for the blossom. An unforgettable image (in the Chinese *Story of the Stone*) described winter frost "like pear blossoms, scattering on the ground," while a girl "with green sleeves" recites verses about the cold. The Chinese also used pears medicinally and grew dwarf pears in tubs around their houses.

Some Asian pears, notably the Bradford pear, were cultivated in the West not for their fruit but as ornamentals. The Bradford pear was so popular it once threatened to dominate American streets, with its pyramid form, lovely fall foliage, and beautiful blossoms. It was planted everywhere, but the upright branches break easily, especially with snow on them, so it isn't used as much now as it once was. It got the name Bradford from the U.S. Department of Agriculture's director.

Pears are closely related to apples as well as to quinces and rowans. They can be grafted onto all these trees with varying success. Their difference with apples is not (in spite of "pear-shaped" ladies) in their shape, for apples can be elongated and pears can be round, depending on the pattern of growth and whether the fruit grows faster along its long axis than its radial axis.

Pears, however, can play one very good party trick. They can be "captured" in a bottle. This is fun for any gardener who has a pear tree. When the pear is embryonic it is slipped into a bottle, preferably round bottomed. The bottle is tied firmly onto the tree, making sure rainwater can't get inside. Within the bottle the pear continues to grow, protected from insects and diseases. If all goes well, it reaches full size and can then be harvested like a "ship in a bottle." Pear liqueur or brandy is poured around it, making an impressive drink to serve to guests. The French (who seem to have invented the trick) call it *poire captive*. Most people wonder how it got into the bottle. Try it, it's easy to do.

PERSIMMON

At the beginning of the seventeenth century Captain John Smith sailed from Maine down the East Coast of America. He claimed the land he saw for England, naming harbors and landmarks as he passed (including three islands off Cape Anne, called by him after three Turks whose heads he had severed, in another adventure). Smith described many of the fruits and vegetables of the New World, including the persimmon. He wrote, perhaps with feeling based on experience, "If it be not ripe it will draw a man's mouth awrie with much torment."

The botanical name of the persimmon is *Diospyrus*, meaning "divine grain." Persimmon trees are a kind of ebony and also have hard dark wood (*see* Ebony), but they are best known by their fruits. The American persimmon is *Diospyrus virginiana*, and the Asian persimmon is *D. kaki*. As Captain Smith warned, both these trees bear fruit that is palatable when ripe, but impossible to eat until then. The tartness of the unripe fruit is from tannic acid. As the fruit ripens, the acid is transformed by enzymes.

🌿 THE BOTANICAL NAME OF THE PERSIMMON IS *DIOSPYRUS*, MEANING "DIVINE GRAIN."

Those who knew this didn't always resist a playful deception. Peter Kalm, sent to explore North America by his teacher, Carl Linnaeus (*see* Alder), described how his "poor credulous" servant was offered an unripe persimmon (which can look tempting). He tasted it and it "contracted his mouth so that he could hardly speak." The servant wouldn't even *try* ripe persimmons, and one can hardly blame him.

Persimmon wood was often used for spindles, because it didn't shatter. Later, golf clubs were made from it. But the trees don't grow taller than about fifty feet, so the timber isn't useful for construction. The Algonquin name for the fruit is *putchamin*, from which comes the English name.

Kaki is the Japanese name for the Asian persimmon. Its fruit is larger and less acidic than the American fruit. Kakis are sometimes grafted onto American persimmon stock, which is hardier. Kakis are about the size of a large tomato. Some are self-pollinating and have no seeds and some are pollinated by insects. They were brought to Europe and America in the mid-nineteenth century, perhaps by Commodore Matthew Perry who, forcefully, persuaded the Japanese to be more welcoming to foreign traders. Most likely kakis originated in China, even though they are called Japanese. Some varieties have a horizontal ridge dividing the top from the bottom half of the fruit, rather like a global equator. In 1736 a Jesuit priest called persimmons he saw in China "fruit of two stories." The Chinese name for persimmons is *shi*.

American persimmons aren't eaten as much now by humans as they were in the past. They are, however, a favorite food of some wild animals, particularly possums and raccoons. Sometimes the trees are called possum trees.

Persimmons shouldn't be eaten until they drop off or can be shaken off the tree. In the southern folksong "Bile Them Cabbage Down," a possum and a raccoon have a "relationship," which includes a proposal of marriage and a chase across the countryside. It must have been after the first frost for it describes,

> Possum up the 'simmon tree
> Raccoon on the ground.
> Raccoon say to the possum
> Won't you shake them 'simmons down?

These animals anyway seem to know when a persimmon won't produce the "torment" described by Captain Smith.

PINE

Pine trees played an important part in the American Revolution, and before the Stars and Stripes were adopted as its symbol, the first revolutionary flag depicted a white pine tree. When colonists came to America they left behind European forests with few large trees. Tall trees that could be used as masts for ships were especially rare, and the masts of British ships sometimes had to be made from the trunks of several Scots pines joined in sections. Even these pines became sparse in Britain and were often imported from Russia or Sweden. The discovery of a supply of "British" timber in the colonies was invaluable.

When, in 1605, George Weymouth, a British naval captain, brought home a trunk of "Weymouth pine," it was received with joy. Soon the first saw mill was set up in New England to log these vast trees. We call them white pines, or *Pinus strobus*. *Pinus* is an ancient Latin name, probably connected with the Greek *pitus*, "pine." *Strobus*, "a spinning top," refers to the crown's shape. Even before roads and heavy machinery the American logging industry boomed. In winter teams of horses or oxen pulled the huge trunks across the snow to the nearest river. Pine wood is light and buoyant as well as being very strong, and the logs could be floated to harbors, from where they were shipped. To the indignation of the colonists, the Crown claimed the largest trees "for Masting our Royal Navy." Any settler caught using them might have all his land confiscated. The biggest trees were marked with a royal blaze, and spies watched to prevent cheating. One of the first triumphant acts of the new American government was to stop the export of mast wood to Britain.

The new nation now had exclusive rights to exploit its own forests. It exercised these rights so successfully that by the end of the nineteenth century the vast forests that had covered the Northeast had been almost used up. Pine trees made ships, houses, furniture, and even matches. The resin made pitch, tar, rosin, and turpentine. Sailors, who used pine pitch to caulk their vessels and to keep their pigails together, were called tars. Dancers and musician increased friction on their shoes and bows with rosin. In 1860 an Englishman, Frederick Walton, invented linoleum, a floor covering made of linseed oil, resin, and cork dust that increased the demand for pine sap. We still treasure amber jewelry from fossilized pine sap, some even containing the carcass of an insect that fed on its sweetness eons ago. No wonder that ancient pine forests disappeared. We can grow new pine trees rapidly, but the giant pines the colonists found are few and far between.

The pine family, or *Pinaceae*, includes, as well as other conifers, pines, firs, and spruces, which are easily confused. Pines themselves are widespread, can grow in poor soil, and adapt to very different climates. They are often distinguishable from firs by their cones, which hang down, rather than pointing up. The only pine native to Britain, the Scots, or Scotch, pine, is often called a Scotch fir.

Pinecones are the mature female reproductive organs of the tree (*see* Larch). The flowerlike male conelets produce an abundance of pollen, which can cover the ground and every other surface, with yellow dust. Superstitious early sailors complained when the decks of their ships were powdered with "raining brimstone," thought to bring misfortune. The female cones capture this windblown pollen and then enclose the germinated seeds tightly, sometimes for years, until they ripen. For the Romans a closed pinecone was a symbol of fertility. A wand tipped with a pinecone was called a thyrsus. The exuberant Greek god Dionysus sometimes held a thyrsus in one hand and a wine cup in the other.

In Shakespeare's time pinecones were called pineapples, a name that was later transferred to the tropical pineapple, shaped like a pinecone. The pineapple has no botanical connection with pines and is not a tree but a perennial plant. Its botanical name *ananas* means in the Guarini language "excellent fruit."

Pine needles are distinctively joined in bundles of two to five by a papery sheath at their base. These needles were eaten in spring by American Indians, and in the 1540s the men of the explorer Jacques Cartier's expedition were saved from dying of scurvy by friendly Canadian Indians who gave them infusions of pine needles. *Adirondack* is an Indian word meaning "bark eater," and pine bark can be used to make a kind of tea, as well as providing tannin.

American pines include the lodgepole pine, so named by Lewis and Clark because the trunks were used for Indian tepees and lodges. Like many conifers (*see* Redwood) this pine has serotinous cones, ones that have to be opened by the heat of forest fires. On the same expedition, the ponderosa ("heavy") pine was found, and the explorers described hungry Indians eating the seeds, leaves, and inner bark of this tree. They also ate the fruits of the pinyon pine, *P. edulis* ("edible"), so popular these days for pesto sauce.

The tree that most excited David Douglas (*see* Fir), and nearly cost him dearly, was the sugar pine, *P. lambertiana*. He named this for Aylmer Bourke Lambert, who was vice-president of the Linnaean Society and wrote, in 1803, *A Description of the Genus Pinus*. Douglas had little use for armchair botanists, or society in general, and quarreled bitterly with his patrons at the Royal Horticultural Society, but he had met Lambert, a rich independent botanist and must have respected him. The tree's huge cones, wrote Douglas, were shaped like "sugar cones," which was the way sugar was sold at that time. When trying to collect some of these cones, which are about a foot long, Douglas was surrounded by a group of suspicious Native Americans. He saw one of these men sharpening a flint knife and this "gave me ample testimony of their inclination." Brandishing his gun saved him. Douglas was an excellent shot and once proved his ability before another hostile group by tossing a hat in the air and shooting its brim clear off. But he made friends, too, and the Indian name for him was the Grass Man, because of his insatiable pursuit of wild plants.

THE BRISTLECONE PINE IS, AT THIS TIME, THOUGHT TO BE THE OLDEST LIVING PLANT ON EARTH.

The bristlecone pine is, at this time, thought to be the oldest living plant on earth. One bristlecone pine, growing in the White Mountains of California, is known as the Methusela tree and thought to be about forty-seven hundred years old. These pines live on very poor soil, their sparse waxy needles conserving moisture and staying on the tree for up to twenty years. Much of the tree's wood is dead wood, and there is very little foliage. Their botanical name is, appropriately, *P. longaeva* ("long lived").

Ancient pines exist in Japan and China, too, where they have always been revered. In Japan, pines were, along with cranes and turtles, a symbol of longevity, even immortality. Pines were carefully planted in Japanese gardens to complement water or the rising moon or to cast a strange shadow on a bare wall. They could be pruned to enhance the sense of the garden. Sometimes they were kept dwarfed, as bonsai.

In China, too, pines were an integral part of the garden. T'ao Ch'ien, a fifth-century Chinese hermit poet, described returning to his garden after leaving "the world's dust." He was happy to be alone, walking "around my lonely pine tree, stroking it." Li Li-weng, a seventeenth-century artist and gardener, wrote, "When one sits in a garden with peach trees, flowers and willows, without a single pine in sight, it is like sitting among children and women without any venerable men in the vicinity to whom one may look up."

POMEGRANATE

On June 29, 1678, John Evelyn noted in his *Diary*, "There were brought into service a new sort of soldiers called Grenadiers who were dexterous in flinging hand grenades . . . they had furred caps with coped crowns . . . which made them look very fierce." These elite soldiers were the tallest and strongest to be found, and the weapon they hurled was a grenade, or round ball, full of tiny fragments, capable of doing extensive damage when it exploded. Ironically it got its name from the lovely, life-giving fruit of the pomegranate tree. The name pomegranate comes from the Latin *pomum*, "apple," and *granatum*, "with many seeds." The botanical name *Punica* ("Carthaginian") comes from the Romans who probably first obtained the pomegranate from Carthage.

Pomegranates, probably originating from the area around present-day Iran, were brought to Turkey, Greece, Egypt, and North Africa well before recorded history. An intact dried pomegranate was found in the 1470 BC Egyptian tomb of Djehuty, Queen Hatshepsut's butler. In the Old Testament pomegranates (*rimmon* in Hebrew) are mentioned many times, notably when the Jews in the wilderness complained to Moses of having to wander in an "evil place" where there were no delicious pomegranates as in Egypt. Moses, however, assured his followers there would be pomegranates (as well as milk and honey) in the Promised Land. And indeed pomegranates grow wild in Israel, even though they are not native there.

The renowned traveler Sir Richard Burton, who visited Mecca and Medina, and scandalized his nineteenth-century contemporaries with his translation of the *Arabian Nights*, said he had tasted pomegranates that were virtually seedless and "as large as an infant's head" (age of infant not specified).

The seeds are, however, the most characteristic feature of pomegranates, and they were responsible for the association of the fruit with fertility and rebirth. In Persia, a bride would squash a pomegranate on the threshold of her new home and count the seeds that fell out, hoping for as many children as seeds. In Greek mythology pomegranates were sacred to Hera, goddess of childbirth and marriage. The legendary Greek nymph Persephone was kept in the underworld by Hades until her mother Demeter, goddess of growing things, managed to free her. Unfortunately, just before leaving Hades, Persephone ate a pomegranate and inadvertently swallowed six seeds, thereby binding herself to Hades for six months of every year and creating the season of winter when she was obliged to go underground again.

But Persephone, or spring, returns each year,

and the pomegranate is also a Christian symbol of resurrection. The Unicorn Tapestries, at the Cloisters Museum in New York, show the beautiful unicorn, mortally wounded, with a bloodlike stream of pomegranate seeds pouring from the gash in his white flank, and we know he will live again.

Pomegranates need a hot climate for their fruit to ripen, but can survive in cooler climates. They thrive in Mediterranean countries, and Shakespeare knew they grew in Italy, where Romeo and Juliet lived out their tragic story. At dawn, Romeo says the lovers must part, because he hears the lark. Juliet, clinging to him, argues with false hope, that the bird he hears is not a lark but a nightingale "on yon Pomegranate tree."

THE NAME OF THE RED STONE GARNET COMES FROM THE OLD FRENCH NAME OF THE FRUIT, *GRANATE*.

Pomegranates flourished in Spain. The Moors brought the art of tanning "morocco" leather with pomegranate bark to Spain, and Spanish leather became a luxury. Moorish kings, and later Queen Catherine of Aragon, used the pomegranate as a heraldic symbol. The fruit is topped by a spiky calyx that looks a bit like a crown. The seeds are packed into compartments like jewels, and indeed the name of the red stone garnet comes from the Old French name of the fruit, *granate*.

Its hard skin makes the fruit easy to transport, and Spanish sailors took pomegranates to South America where they spread. In 1777 William Bartram wrote in his *Travels* that in the deserted town of Frederica, Georgia, "pomegranates and other shrubs grow out of the ruinous walls of former spacious and expensive buildings." In U.S. southern states and California pomegranates grow well.

They are a tricky fruit to eat since the edible pulp has to be separated from the numerous seeds (unless you like to chew them). In India and Europe the juice was pressed out. A drink called *grenadine* was particularly popular in France. In Iran pomegranate juice, *robb-e anar*, is used in cooking and coloring rice, but not until recently in North America has it been particularly popular. Now with the enthusiasm of the newly converted, Americans have taken to pomegranate juice as the antioxidant cure for many of our ills.

Perhaps we aren't drinking enough pomegranate juice, though. We still hurl grenades at one another, these days often using machines, not men, to do the heavy lifting. Grenades travel faster and farther the modern way but still explode into piercing, dangerous fragments, small like pomegranate seeds.

POPLAR

The last of the twelve labors of Hercules was to bring Cerberus, the guard dog of the underworld, to earth and then return him. While he was successfully doing so, Hercules wore a wreath of poplar leaves. When he could relax and remove the wreath, the upper side of the leaves had darkened (from, it was said, the scorching fires of hell) and the underside of the leaves were white (blanched by the perspiration from his brow).

Botanically speaking, this legend fits rather well. The upper surfaces of white poplar leaves are dark and leathery, adapted to absorbing scorching sunlight and repelling moisture. The way the tree exudes moisture is via the pale woolly underside of the leaves, which metaphorically "perspire." White poplars, native to Africa, Turkey, and Siberia, have leaves that are pale beneath and dark on top. They are lobed, unlike the typical heart-shaped leaf we associate with populars. The gray poplar (*Populus* × *canescens*), native to Europe but growing widely in the United States, has similar leaves but less deeply lobed. It is thought to be a hybrid between white poplars and aspens. Aspens, a kind of poplar, are native to America and Britain (*see* Aspen).

The white poplar (*P. alba*) sometimes looks as if its branches are covered in snow. The trunk becomes paler as the tree ages, but the bark, which looks like birch bark, does not peel. The Dutch name for the white poplar was *abeel* (from the Latin *alba*, "white"). The famous Flemish botanist Matthias de L'Obel (for whom the lobelia is named) got his name from the similar-sounding name of the white poplar, "abele." His family motto was "Candore et Spe," from the white underside of the poplar leaves signifying "candor," and the green upper side "hope."

Poplars include the white poplar, black poplar (*P. nigra*), and the balsam poplar (*P. balsamifera*), with aromatic leaf buds. The balsam poplar is sometimes called the balm of Gilead. Its resin can be used medicinally, but it has no botanical connection with the Old Testament balm of Gilead, which caused Jeremiah, despairing of the spiritual health of his people, to cry, "Is there no balm in Gilead?"

The American cottonwood is also a poplar (*see* Cottonwood). The seeds of the Chinese "necklace poplar," *P. lasiocarpa* ("hairy fruited") look like strings of beads until they burst open in midsummer releasing copious amounts of white fluff. Poplars hybridize easily and there are many kinds.

Poplars, closely related to willows, often grow near water. They do not grow in woods. The black poplars include the well-known Lombardy poplar (*P. nigra* 'Italica') coming, as its name suggests, from northern Italy. It is a fastigiate (tall and pointed) mutant of the European black poplar, and most Lombardy poplars are male, propagated from suckers.

In classical mythology poplars descended from the Heliades, who were

Phaëton's sisters. Phaëton had managed to get hold of and drive the chariot of Helios, the Sun, for one day. But he was quite unable to control the fiery horses, which galloped too near the earth, almost destroying it with fire. Before this could happen Zeus struck down Phaëton. His sorrowful sisters stayed by the river where he fell, weeping night and day until they turned into poplar trees. Their tears became amber droplets.

Black poplars originated in Central Europe and Asia but came to Britain before records were kept. In John Gerard's *Herball*, both white and black poplars were described as rare, with only "here and there a tree." The Lombardy poplar came to Britain in 1758 and was brought to America in 1784 by William Hamilton for his estate near Philadelphia called Woodlands (*see* Ginkgo). Hamilton, who visited London soon after the Revolutionary War, said of his new country that he would "endeavour to make it smile in the same beautiful and useful manner" as Britain. Lombardy poplars, easily propagated and quick to grow tall, became popular, and President Jefferson lined Pennsylvania Avenue in Washington with them.

MATCHES ARE MADE FROM POPLAR WOOD, WHICH BURNS SLOWLY.

Andrew Jackson Downing, author of *Landscape Gardening and Rural Architecture* (published soon after his death in 1852), wrote that the name poplar came from the Latin *Arbor populi*, or "people's tree," because it was "peculiarly appropriated to those public places most frequented by the people." (Actually the Latin words for "poplar" and for "people" are of different genders). In Old French it was *poplier*. In Middle English it was a "popul tree" or a "popple." However, Downing thought that this tree "has been planted so indiscriminately . . . in close monotonous lines . . . that it has become tiresome and disgusting."

Poplars are susceptible to canker and fungus diseases. They also take up large quantities of water and can be a problem if grown too near drainage systems, which they themselves can completely drain. Particularly Lombardy poplars are often planted to make windbreaks. Europeans discovered that it is best to space these trees, rather than planting them close together, because although gaps between the trees reduce gusty winds, a solid wall of trees can create turbulence. Not all American landscapers know this.

Poplars have soft wood and are often used for paper pulp. They also make good floorboards because the wood doesn't shrink much. Matches are made from poplar wood, which burns slowly. Maybe poplars seek water because they fear the fire which so nearly consumed the whole earth when Phaëton madly drove the sun chariot. But his weeping sisters did not escape being consumed by the fire of millions of matches, struck and burned, one by one.

QUINCE

W hen the Owl and the Pussycat went to sea and were married

By the Turkey who lives on the hill.
They dined on mince and slices of quince,
Which they ate with a runcible spoon.

For a very long time quinces have been a part of nuptial celebrations or at least of love. They were tossed into bridal chariots in ancient Athens. They may have grown in the Middle East in Old Testament times, for some scholars believe that the "apples" that "comfort" the lover in the Song of Solomon were quinces, perhaps brought by traders from the Caucasian mountains where they are thought to have originated. Juliet's nurse refers to "dates and quinces in the pastry" in Shakespeare's *Romeo and Juliet*.

The classical name for quince was *mela Kydonia*, or "apple from Kydonia," in Crete, where the finest quinces grew. The French name was *cooin* (now *coing*) and in Old English became *quine*. By Tudor and Stuart times a confection of quinces called a *quidony* was popular.

Quinces are closely related to apples and pears and indeed were once classified as pears and given the name *Pyrus cydonia*. The fruits are pear shaped and yellow, and they have a "sandy" texture like that of unripe pears. They are the most common rootstock used for grafting pears. In spite of these affinities they won't hybridize with pears but are a separate tree, now called *Cydonia oblonga*.

Quinces have to be cooked to be palatable. In the *De Materia Medica* of Dioscorides (written in the first century AD), a concoction of quinces and honey is called *melomeli*, "apple in honey." The quinces were packed into jars with honey and left until the mixture softened. Sometimes spices were added. The mix was used medicinally or to aid digestion at the end of a meal. Arab cooks sometimes added rose water. The Arabs probably brought quinces to Spain and Portugal, where the quince mixture was known as *membrillo*, or *marmelo*.

MARY QUEEN OF SCOTS WAS SAID TO HAVE BEEN GIVEN QUINCE MARMALADE WHEN SHE BECAME SEASICK CROSSING FROM FRANCE TO SCOTLAND IN 1561.

This preparation, imported to Britain, became "marmalade," which was made of quinces long before oranges were used. Mary Queen of Scots was said to have been given quince marmalade when she became seasick crossing from France to Scotland in 1561. She is said to have taken her medicine and murmured wittily, "Marmalade pour Marie malade." (She must have been feeling a bit better by then).

By the time of Samuel Pepys quince marmalade was evidently made by housewives at home. On November 4, 1663, Pepys wrote in his *Diary* that he came "home to dinner, and very pleasant with my wife who is this day . . . making Marmalett of Quince . . . I left her at it." Most people are glad to escape when someone else is making marmalade.

Quinces contain so much pectin that the marmalade or jelly can be stiff enough to cut or shape into forms. Indeed the "slices of quince" eaten by the enamored owl and pussycat were very likely slices of quince jelly. When cooked, quinces turn a lovely pale pink, and they were often baked in pies, with or without apples. Settlers took quinces to North America and made "quince cheese." They also made glue from the seeds, which become mucilaginous when boiled.

The seventeenth-century herbalist Nicholas Culpeper thought highly of quinces. He wrote (in his *Complete Herbal* of 1652) that they give out a substance "almost like the white of an egg." This he recommended for "sore mouths." He advised that smelling quinces, which a have a strong applelike fragrance, was an antidote to poisoning. What is more, he believed that the downy skin of quinces could be crushed and "laid as a plaister, made up with wax, [and] it brings hair to them that are bald, and keeping it from falling, if it be ready to shed."

In John Gerard's *Herball* (*see* Banana), a woman "which eateth many Quinces during the time of her breeding, shall bring forth wise children and of good understanding." Neither herbalist mentions a "runcible" spoon or whether eating quinces improves fur or feathers. Or indeed what a union between a quince-eating owl and pussycat would "bring forth." Edward Lear just leaves the happy pair dancing on the beach, by the light of the moon.

REDBUD

According to the New Testament book of Matthew, Judas Iscariot bitterly repented for betraying Jesus and tried to give back the silver he had been paid. The priests refused to accept the money, which Judas "cast down" on the floor of the temple. He then went and "hanged himself." The priests used the money to buy a field in which to bury "strangers."

No actual tree for Judas's suicide is mentioned in the Bible, but legend assumed he had hanged himself on a tree, and the fig, poplar, and elder were all thought to be possibilities, some much less likely than others. The redbud, or *Cercis siliquastrum*, ended up with the name Judas tree, and it does fit best, being both sturdy and native to Palestine. Some scholars, rejecting the tradition, say the name came from Judaea (where it grew) rather than Judas. There is also an account in the biblical book of Acts that Judas did not hang himself but died in the potter's field that had been bought with the tainted silver pieces. Even so, we know the redbud as a Judas tree.

Siliqua is the Latin for "pod." These trees have beanlike seedpods and are in the pea family. Unlike many trees in this group they don't have nitrogen-fixing nodules on their roots (*see* Acacia). Unlike some other members of this family the seeds are edible and the flower buds are considered tasty. In the Middle East they were pickled and used like capers. Peter Kalm, sent to North America by Linnaeus (*see* Alder), called the American redbud the "sallad tree."

The American redbud, *Cercis canadensis* (more common in northeastern America than Canada in spite of the name), is related to and very like the Mediterranean tree. There is also a Chinese redbud (*zijing*). The name *Cercis* comes from the Greek *kerkis* ("a rod"), the name of a kind of poplar with similar heart-shaped leaves and (presumably) a tall, straight trunk.

THE REDBUD, OR *CERCIS SILIQUASTRUM*, ENDED UP WITH THE NAME JUDAS TREE.

Redbuds are small trees that grow on the edges of woody clearings. They have large heart-shaped leaves. The flowers that appear in spring, before the leaves emerge, are like tiny sweet peas, usually purplish-red but sometimes white. In some legends they used to be white until Judas shamed the tree, and they became red. They cover the branches and even grow out of the bare trunk. Then they fall, like drops of blood on the ground. This has enhanced this tree's undeserved reputation associated with sin and blood. Even the most ancient redbuds, often tilted onto the ground and propped up with dying branches, will produce these extraordinary flowers out of their gnarled bark. It makes one wish to associate this tree with the miracle of rebirth, rather than its usual sinister connection.

REDWOOD

I n October 1769 a Spanish
expedition sailing along
the coast of California saw
a grove of huge trees, which they called *palo
colorado*, "wood colored red." Redwoods have thick spongy bark, sometimes a
foot thick, which is a lovely cinnamon red. This bark is resistant to fire and
insects and protects them so well that their only real natural threat is lightning.
Thus they can grow for thousands of years and reach an enormous size.

The California coastal redwood is *Sequoia sempervirens* and the giant redwood, found farther inland, is *Sequoiadendron giganteum*. Closely related to
them both is the dawn redwood, *Metasequoia glyptostroboides*. These three
specimens are all that now remain of what was once, in prehistory, a huge
family of conifers.

The Scottish botanist Archibald Menzies (*see* Monkey-puzzle) saw coastal
redwoods in 1794, but he did not take specimens back to Britain. The first

coastal redwood to be planted abroad was in St. Petersburg in 1840. They were introduced to Britain three years later. The Western world didn't know about the giant redwoods until 1852 when an employee of the Union Water Company, Augustus T. Dowd, was hunting a grizzly bear in the Sierra foothills and followed it high up into the mountains. He came across a grove of these incredible trees and immediately went back to his base camp. He fetched a group of skeptical miners, who had accused him of being drunk and imagining the trees, to see the grove for themselves.

Mr. Dowd attended a meeting of the newly formed California Academy of Science, which had been established by Albert Kellogg (for whom the Californian black oak, *Quercus kelloggii*, is named). Dowd told the group, which included William Lobb, a plant collector from England whom Kellogg had invited to attend the meeting, about his discovery. Lobb, losing no time, rushed to find the trees, and took seeds and two saplings back to England where they immediately caused a sensation. There the tree was named *Wellingtonia giganteum* in honor of the Duke of Wellington and his victory at Waterloo. The poet Tennyson's son described "the great event of the year 1864" when Giuseppe Garibaldi visited Tennyson's father and there was "a planting of a Wellingtonia by the great Italian." In England the redwood tree is still widely planted and still called a Wellingtonia or *Sequoia wellingtonia*.

In America, too, news of these great trees spread. Albert Kellogg wanted to name the tree *Washingtonia giganteum* but was overruled, and it was given the name *Sequoiadendron* because of its kinship to the coastal redwoods, which had been already named sequoias. These days the giant redwoods are thought to be a genus of their own. The *dendron* part of their name is from the Greek "tree," and *Sequoia* is for Sequoah, or Sikwayi, the son of a Cherokee chief's daughter. This remarkable man also had an English name, which was George Guess (or Gist), and supposedly his father was a white trader (some say a soldier). Anyway Sikwayi never adopted the ways of the white world, and he spoke only Cherokee. But he did realize the usefulness of reading and writing, and he made the first written alphabet for his people. From then on, Native Americans were not forced to choose between learning English and being illiterate.

Illiterate or not, the Native Americans had lived alongside and looked after these giant trees much better than the Westerners who "discovered" them. The native people had used the redwood timber, but only from fallen trees, for canoes and other building projects. Native Americans quite often started fires to clear the brush, but redwoods benefited from this because their cones need fire to open and release the seeds. Bark and foliage were used medicinally by Indians, but most of all, the trees were revered.

Once news of these amazing trees got out, the response of Europeans and Americans was sadly different. "Nature lovers" came from all over to see them. One of the largest trees was immediately felled to make a dance floor of its cut trunk. Tourists could marvel at its girth while they danced across the stump. The stripped bark was taken intact to San Francisco, where it was made into a room capable of seating forty adults and a piano, or 140 children "without inconvenience." The main trunk became a bowling alley, to give visitors something else to do while admiring the trees.

THE WESTERN WORLD DIDN'T KNOW ABOUT THE GIANT REDWOODS UNTIL 1852.

Redwoods and their relatives once covered the North American continent but did not survive the Ice Age, remaining only in certain separate pockets in California. The coastal redwoods grow near the Pacific Ocean and depend on maritime fogs, which condense on their leaves to provide about a third of the water they need.

Dawn redwoods once grew in North America, too. Until the 1940s they were thought to be totally extinct. At that time a Japanese paleobotanist, Shigeru Miki, realized that the fossils he had been studying were related to the California sequoias, and he named the fossil tree *Metasequoia*, meaning "like a redwood." Not long afterward, Zhan Wang, a professor from Peking University, was held up by an attack of malaria near Modoaxi in central China. The principal of a local agricultural college asked Professor Zhan to identify a strange local tree planted around the rice fields. The biggest had a shrine in front of it. They were known to local people as "water firs." The professor recognized that this tree was the fossil tree named by Miki, and indeed it turned out to be a "living fossil." There was worldwide excitement and before the "bamboo curtain" fell, Asian and Western botanists collaborated to propagate these trees, which existed only in this one area of China.

The dawn redwood is similar to the Chinese swamp cypress, *Glyptostrobus pensilis*. *Glyptostrobus* means "carved cone" (describing the Chinese water cypress's marked cones). *Pensilis* means "hanging." Both swamp cypresses and dawn redwoods are deciduous conifers. The name dawn was bestowed by a Californian professor to note that this tree goes back to the "dawn of history," as do all redwoods.

Dawn redwoods grow fast and are planted in American gardens and parks where, if all goes well, they may grow for thousands of years. Meanwhile, some of the oldest and biggest redwoods have been named for other heroes, like the immense General Sherman. We can drive our cars though the arched trunks of these huge trees and name them for victorious generals. But we can only hope that they endure to tell their silent story. We know not who will be here to see them, and to listen.

ROWAN

The rowan's brilliant red fruits, bright as arterial blood, have from prehistory associated this tree with the magic of life. Some say that the name rowan has the same etymological root as *rune*, a magical sign. Others say that the Old Norse name *raun* is connected with the word for "red," or means "northern." This hardy small tree is abundant in northern countries, often growing on bleak moors and tundra.

In 1551 the Reverend William Turner, the author of several popular religious books, published the earliest English *Herball*, calling the tree a "rountree." In the highlands of Scotland, where rowans are plentiful, its name was *caorann*. In both Scotland and Ireland cutting the sacred rowan tree was forbidden except for certain purposes. In Scotland the wood could be used for funeral pyres and for threshing tools and the berries made an alcoholic drink. Rowan wood was used for spinning wheels by the Irish. The Germans believed that butter paddles made from rowan prevented the butter from going rancid.

The botanical name for the European rowan is *Sorbus aucuparia*. *Sorbus* was the ancient Latin name for the service tree (*Sorbus domestica*), sometimes called the Sorb-tree, with bright edible fruits called *serves* in the sixteenth century. *Aucuparia* is from *avis*, "a bird," and *capere* "to catch." The berries are attractive to birds, and bird catchers would trap small birds in hair nooses baited with rowan berries.

Although the berries can be eaten by humans they are very tart until cooked or "bletted." John Lindley, a distinguished British botanist, secretary to the Horticultural Society and founder of the *Gardeners' Chronicle*, adopted the word for this process from the French *devenir blet* (translated literally as "become sleepy"). In his 1828 *Introduction to Botany*, Lindley described how fruits, after ripening, "undergo a new kind of alteration; their flesh either rots or blets." Fruits that, like rowanberries, are best consumed bletted include persimmons and medlars.

Another name for the rowan is mountain ash, because of the ashlike pinnate (feathery) leaves and because it grows on high slopes. It isn't an ash but rather a member of the rose family. Once it was thought to be a kind of pear, and the white flowers are similar to pear blossoms. Some ancient writers advised that pears could be grafted onto rowans. They can be, but the result isn't very productive.

Another old name for the rowan was the quicken-tree, from "quick" meaning "life giving." Sprigs of rowan might be taken on board ships or hung on door posts as protection against misfortune and evil spirits. Sometimes rowans were called wiggan-trees, probably meaning wicca (or witch) trees. According to an old saying, "Rowan tree and red threed, / Put the witches to their speed."

The nineteenth-century horticultural writer Henry Phillips described the rowan in his *Sylva Florifera* (1823), noting that most churchyards included rowan trees, planted to prevent the dead from rising out of their graves. He also described these trees encouraging a different kind of magic: "The mountain-ash, which our northern friends so religiously planted to keep off enchantment and sorceries, is most carefully propagated by our more southern neighbours as one of the principal charms by which they entice the belles of Paris into the public gardens, where they are at liberty to use all the spells and witcheries which they are mistresses of." More probably they were planted in the gardens because they are so very ornamental.

MOST CHURCH-YARDS INCLUDED ROWAN TREES, PLANTED TO PREVENT THE DEAD FROM RISING OUT OF THEIR GRAVES.

The European rowan has naturalized in North America and by 1741 Peter Kalm described it in his *Travels* as "pretty common in the woods hereabouts." There is an American mountain ash, *S. americana*, which is more shrublike, and an Asian *Sorbus*, which is also small. The rowan tree can reach sixty feet tall and creates its magic in some of the most barren parts of the northern world.

RUBBER

I t's funny that one of the most useful substances in our lives should first have been recognized as a toy. Christopher Columbus described American Indians playing with balls that bounced "incredibly" when lightly dropped onto the ground.

Prehistoric South American Indians had discovered that the substance they called caoutchouc, exuded by the rubber tree, could be heated and used to make waterproof bowls and shoes. In Europe caoutchouc was regarded as a curiosity until 1770, when Joseph Priestly (the same man who discovered oxygen) described small cubes of it being sold to erase or "rub out" pencil marks on paper. These cubes were called (and in Britain still are) "rubbers." So the tree was named.

The botanical name of the rubber tree is *Hevea brasiliensis*, after a Brazilian town, and it is sometimes called the Para rubber tree (after another Brazilian town). When the bark of these trees is slashed, latex, or "milky" juice, flows out of the wound. Latex, a protective strategy, is not the same as sap, which nourishes the tree. The rubber tree is related to the spurges, which also produce latex.

Hevea is not the only source of rubber, and it is not the ornamental "rubber tree," with huge glossy leaves, often found in hotel vestibules and doctors' offices. That tree is *Ficus elastica* ("elastic fig"), sometimes called the India rubber tree. Notable for its large size and high aerial roots, it is a native of Malaysia. It, too, yields rubber but less economically, because the whole tree has to be felled, rather than tapped like the *Hevea*, to procure the latex. Another very brittle rubberlike material is gutta-percha, from the sapodilla tree. It is not as good as rubber for most purposes, except for underwater cables because, unlike rubber, it is highly resistant to salt water. The Spanish name sapodilla comes from the Nahuatl, *tzapotl*.

SOUTH AMERICAN INDIANS HAD DISCOVERED THAT THE SUBSTANCE THEY CALLED CAOUTCHOUC, EXUDED BY THE RUBBER TREE, COULD BE HEATED AND USED TO MAKE WATERPROOF BOWLS AND SHOES.

By the middle of the nineteenth century para rubber from Brazil was in great demand. In 1820 rubber hoses replaced leather ones, for watering huge Victorian parks and gardens. In 1823 Charles Mackintosh patented a waterproof coat, which still bears his name. Galoshes (from *gallica solea*, the Latin for "Gaulish shoe") and Wellington boots (named for the Duke of Wellington's high boots) could now be made of waterproof rubber. Rubber gaskets replaced leather ones.

A turning point for rubber was in 1839, when Charles Goodyear discovered by accident that rubber could be "vulcanized" by heating it mixed it with sulfur, thereby losing its stickiness. Until then, rubber goods were tacky when warm and rigid when cold. Goodyear (in spite of our familiarity with his name) didn't patent his invention successfully and never made a fortune from it—although others did.

The rubber collected from wild trees in Brazil was not enough to supply the increasing demand, and new sources were sought. In 1866 Henry Alexander Wickham was sent to Brazil to collect *Hevea* seeds and bring them back to Kew Gardens. He obtained his seeds and packed them in baskets between layers of banana leaves to keep them moist. Rubber seeds are oily but dry out fast. Wickham hired the ship *Amazonas* to rush the seeds back to London while they were still viable. Perhaps to add glory to his achievement, he exaggerated the subterfuge he used to export his cargo: "If the authorities guessed the purpose of what I had on board," he wrote, "we should be detained . . . if not interdicted altogether." But there seems to have been little trouble from the authorities concerned, and when the rubber seeds were planted in Kew more than a thousand seedlings flourished. Rubber plants were exported to Sri Lanka and Malaysia, to found a huge, exploitive rubber empire for Britain.

The rich oil content of rubber seeds makes them a favorite food of rodents. Some rubber collectors thought that certain snakes had a pact with the rubber tree. The snakes were said to lie in wait, curled around the base of the trunk, and snatch up the rodents as they came to get the seeds, so feeding themselves and saving at least some of the seeds for the future trees.

Today some of the functions of rubber have been taken over by plastics, but by no means all. Very few people, if any, do not need to use rubber tires, one way or another, on cars, buses, airplanes, and bicycles. In these days of low maintenance, however, many of those handsome rubber plants seen in waiting rooms are probably made of plastic. With their healthy, shiny leaves they are indistinguishable from the real thing, unless you were to scratch the bark.

SAGUARO

Early explorers of America saw and described cacti, unique to the New World. By the beginning of the seventeenth century, John Gerard's *Herball* mentioned two "gummy thistles," one of which was called a *Cereus*: "There is not among the strange and admirable plants of the world any one that gives more cause of marvell." *Cereus* comes from the Latin for a "wax taper."

The name cactus comes from the Greek *kaktos*, meaning a "prickly plant." When Linnaeus came to name the cacti, he mentioned twenty-two species, some of which we no longer classify as cacti. It was not until the century after him that enough cacti were seen and known for botanists to begin sorting them out. Dr. George Engelmann, a German botanist whose own name was given to a mountain, a daisy, and several trees (*see* Spruce) first described to Western botanists the Mexican *suwarro*. He called it the *Cereus giganteus*.

In Engelmann's time most cacti were called cereus, not least among them being the famous night-blooming cereus, which was raised in many a Victorian parlor. This plant (like the saguaro) only opens its flowers at night. In an age less equipped than ours with home entertainments, the blooming of the cereus, which only flowers once a year, was an occasion for a social gathering of neighbors. It's rather touching to think of our forebears, the frock-coated gentlemen and petticoated ladies and probably a few excited children allowed to "stay up," waiting and watching for the huge white blooms to slowly unfurl. They would be wilted by morning, and the show would be over for another year.

The saguaro's waxy flowers are pollinated by night creatures, including bats. They, too, fade the next day and the greenish fruits, the size of a goose egg, slowly develop. Papago Indians depended on these fruits before their staple beans and corn were ready. The pulp is bright red and the seeds are shining black. Desert animals also eat both the seeds and fruit.

Few of the many seeds germinate and those that do need shade, or they will soon die. Sometimes they grow under the shade of a mesquite tree. They grow very, very slowly, reaching only a quarter of an inch high in the first 2 years and only four inches after 20 years. They won't flower until they are 60 years old. If all goes well they might live 250 years.

This desert tree cactus isn't strictly a "tree," and indeed cacti have no close relatives in the plant world. Most saguaros grow in Arizona (whose state plant they are), but they were formerly more widespread, although relatively recent to evolve as adaptations to a desert climate.

Although they grow taller than many trees (up to sixty feet) saguaros don't have a woody trunk but have a framework of supportive rods within their fleshy exterior. The wood of this framework was used by humans for building, as it is strong and light. The soft outside of the saguaro grows in spiny ridges, which can expand or contract according to how much water is available. The spines protect the fleshy outside and also cool the interior when breezes blow around them. A saguaro can swell to several times its usual size and its upward-pointing branches slowly bend downward with the weight of stored water. When a saguaro is "filled" with water it can do without more for several years.

The armlike branches caused early Spaniards to describe the region where saguaros grow as a "land of marching giants," and they have never lost their mystique for us. Few Hollywood cowboy movies lack a saguaro or two in the background and (until protected) they were often carted away to die in collectors' conservatories.

When, in 1848, Engelmann named the saguaro, still only twenty-five or so different cacti were known. By the next century many more could be classified. This, in the 1920s, gave Britten and Rose, two members of the Desert Laboratory of the Carnegie Institute near Tucson, Arizona, an opportunity to reclassify and rename Engelmann's *Cereus giganteus*. They called it *Carnegiea giganteus*, in honor of Andrew Carnegie.

Andrew Carnegie, born in Scotland, came to America as a young boy. He started work as a "bobbin boy" in a cotton factory and ended his life as a multimillionaire steel magnate. In 1889 he wrote the *Gospel of Wealth* in which he stated that rich men should distribute their surplus wealth for the general good. Carnegie lived by his word, becoming famous as the greatest of philanthropists. The Carnegie Institute was just one of his many endowments.

In spite of the Desert Laboratory and all those who study to protect saguaros they seem to be in decline. Pollution, change of climate, and human expansion into their habitat may be some of the reasons they are threatened. Clearly we need a few more philanthropists and earth-loving multimillionaires (not to mention our own selves) to help rescue these and other coinhabitants of our world, so that we may still "marvell" at their strange and awesome beauty.

SANDALWOOD

In the earliest civilizations recorded, the prosperous wore sandals (the poor went barefoot). But although sandals were often wooden soles strapped to the feet, their name is not connected with the sandalwood tree, also used from ancient times, but for its aromatic wood, not for footwear.

The name for the footwear comes from a Persian word for a light slipper (called in Greek a *sandalon*). The name of the tree, sandalwood, comes from the Sanskrit word *chandana*, meaning "fragrant," and the wood was used for incense. The main source of sandalwood was (and still is) the *Santalum album*. The Greek name for the tree was *Santalon*, and *album* means "white"). This tree originated in India and the Island of Timor, but was traded to other countries, particularly China, early on. The wood was used in Hindu and Buddhist worship, not only as incense but also for building temples, perfuming worshippers, and embalming corpses. Sandalwood retains its scent indefinitely. It was also used for fans and for boxes that repelled insects.

The fragrant sandalwood oil comes not from the bark but only the inner heartwood and roots of the tree. In India, a sandalwood tree was felled and left until white ants had eaten away the outer wood, leaving the fragrant core to be harvested. The sandalwood tree is about twenty to thirty feet tall and is a hemiparasite. It's capable of photosynthesis through its leaves but also depends on host trees or plants to obtain some essential nutrients. From its roots grow tendrils (called haustoria), like the tentacles of an octopus, which attach to the roots of hosts, including bamboo and acacias. The essential oil of sandalwood is only found in trees over twenty-five years old. Harvesting too many trees without replacing them will, of course, reduce the supply.

FROM ITS ROOTS GROW TENDRILS (CALLED HAUSTORIA), LIKE THE TENTACLES OF AN OCTOPUS, WHICH ATTACH TO THE ROOTS OF HOSTS, INCLUDING BAMBOO AND ACACIAS.

In the mid-nineteenth century a new source of aromatic sandalwood, the *S. spicatum*, was discovered on some islands off the northwest coast of Australia. The natives there didn't use sandalwood themselves and were happy to trade the wood for iron and tobacco. The chief market was China, where this sandalwood was exchanged for most of the tea drunk in Britain and Australia.

It was a dangerous trade for the "sandalwooders," who often knew nothing of the people they encountered, with disastrous results. There were massacres of natives and massacres of sailors on the trading vessels. The Europeans could not appreciate a gift basket of human flesh; the "savages" resented brutal reprisals when they helped themselves to the possessions of these strange white men. Nor could the natives understand why the traders wanted sandalwood anyway: "They would not believe it was used for burning . . . [and] came at last to the conclusion that we ground it into Powder and used it for food, and no explanation could dissuade them" wrote Captain Andrew Cheyne in 1852.

The fragile relationship came to an end when the British started growing tea in India and Ceylon, eliminating the need to trade it for sandalwood.

Sandalwood was always a luxury and, accordingly, expensive. In his poem *Cargoes*, John Masefield described ". . . apes and peacocks, / Sandalwood, cedarwood, and sweet white wine" being rowed across mysterious Eastern seas. He contrasts this luxurious cargo with that of a "Dirty British coaster with a salt-caked smoke-stack / Butting through the Channel in the mad March days." This cargo is of lead, iron-ware, and "cheap tin trays." If you lived in remote fragrant groves of sandalwood trees, an iron nail might be a luxury. If you lived in a world of clanking metals, the sweet scent of sandalwood might have brought heaven a little nearer.

SASSAFRAS

Spanish physician Nicolás Monardes gave an early description of the sassafras tree in his *Joyfull Newes out of the New Founde World*, which was "Englished" in 1577 by John Frampton. When European explorers first saw the trees (in Florida), "Thei thought that thei had been Trees of Sinamon, and in part thei were not deceived, for that the rinde of this Tree hath as swete a smell, as the Sinamon hath, and it doth imitate it in coulour and sharpnesse of taste," he wrote.

Explorers of the New World hoped to find the Eastern spices growing there. As we know, they found other trees instead, some equally valuable. The sassafras *is* in the same laurel family as the cinnamon tree, but it came to be used in very different ways. Monardes told how the Spaniards discovered the properties of the tree when they "did beginne to waxe sick" and an infusion of its wood cured them miraculously.

The Indian name for the tree, wrote Monardes, was *pauame*, but the Europeans called it sassafras or *sassafragia*. If this was so, they may have been naming it from *saxifrage*, or "stone breaker," because it was believed to break "stones" in the urinary tract. Some etymologists, however, say that "sassafras" simply comes from an Indian name sounding the same, and they ignore Monardes's *pauame*. The tree's botanical name is *Sassafras albidum*, "whitish" (for the underside of the leaves).

The leaves, bark, and root of the sassafras are all fragrant, but each has a different smell, ranging from lemony to medicinal. The small greenish flowers are also fragrant. The tree was sometimes called the universal plant, because it was believed to cure so many ailments, particularly syphilis, or pox, which appeared in Europe at about the same time as the sassafras. Because it came from the New World it was (sixteenth-century physicians thought) a cure specifically provided by God for what was thought of as an American disease.

Although Gerard in his 1597 *Herball* said he had seen a "little [sassafras] tree, which grew in the garden of *Mr. Wilmot* at Bow," the wood more often than the trees themselves was brought to Europe. Indeed for a while sassafras wood was the second largest commodity (after tobacco) to be exported from Virginia to Britain. In 1603 a Bristol Company was formed solely to trade in sassafras wood. Two ships set out loaded with goods to trade with the natives, including "hats of divers colours." But so much sassafras wood was available no one could monopolize the trade to make much of a fortune. At the same time another New World tree, the lignum vitae or "wood of life," was discovered in South America and also attributed with marvelous curative properties against syphilis. In spite of his praise for the sassafras, Monardes thought that the lignum vitae, or *Guaiacum* (from a native word) *officinale*, was "the most antient and powerfull antidote that is yet known" against the "Poxe." He devoted several pages to curing syphilis with guaiacum wood, concluding that "it is certain that it healeth most perfectly . . . except the sicke man doe returne to tumble in the same bosome."

Even so, sassafras was used medicinally for centuries. In 1722 a concoction of sassafras mixed with opium was advertised as "Godfrey's Cordial," and we are not surprised that it made users feel better. In addition, sassafras tea was drunk on both sides of the Atlantic, especially as a spring purge. It was used in *filé*, an ingredient of southern dishes, and it provided the main ingredient of root beer until the FDA unsportingly fed large quantities of it to rats and declared it carcinogenic.

The sassafras tree flourishes in woods all over the eastern United States. It is second to no tree for the brilliance of its fall foliage. Even the acerbic Fanny Trollope (mother of Anthony), who in 1827 traveled, grumbling, around America, could praise the sassafras. She called Jefferson "an unprincipled tyrant." She called American women "the least attractive" in the world. She called the government "disorderly at the expense of the orderly." But the sassafras tree, she said, was beautiful in every way: "The leaves grow in tufts, and every tuft contains . . . five or six different forms. The fruit is singularly beautiful; it resembles a small acorn, and is jet black; the cups and stem looking as if they were made of red coral." Clearly Mrs. Trollope thought such a tree was too good for the "uncouth" Americans she described. "I cannot imagine," she concluded, "why it [the sassafras] has not been naturalized in England."

THEY MAY HAVE BEEN NAMING IT FROM *SAXIFRAGE*, OR "STONE BREAKER," BECAUSE IT WAS BELIEVED TO BREAK "STONES" IN THE URINARY TRACT.

SPRUCE

Firs and spruces are closely related, and indeed the botanical name of the common Norway spruce is *Picea abies*, which means "spruce fir." The two trees are easily confused. Tree experts can (one presumes) tell conifers apart, but for the rest of us mnemonic devices are helpful: the needles of *s*pruces are generally *s*quarish (beginning with the letter "s"), and those of *f*irs are *f*lat (beginning with the letter "f").

The needles of spruce grow from a projection called a pulvinus (Latin for "cushion"), and where the needles come off the twig, a rough bumpy surface is left. When fir needles come off they leave scars, but the bark remains smooth. The cones of spruces (and other conifers except firs) are pendulous. The female spruce cones hang down from the ends of the branches.

Christmas trees are traditionally called firs, as in Hans Christian Andersen's "little fir-tree," left neglected in the attic after the festivities were over. The trees in the trash collection after *our* celebrations might well be little spruce trees (although balsam firs and Douglas "firs" are also popular). Spruce trees, especially when young, tend to grow symmetrically with a typical Christmas tree shape. Their stiff branches, with needles surrounding the twigs like bottle brushes, support lights and ornaments well, but they aren't generally as fragrant as firs.

Spruces do produce resin and in fact their botanical name *Picea* comes from the Latin *pix*, or "pitch," and was used from ancient times to caulk boats. Spruce resin was once popular, both in Europe and America, to chew. In North America the resin of black and red spruce was chewed by Native Americans and by settlers until the nineteenth century, and called spruce gum. After Texas became an American state, a new kind of chewing gum was introduced by Mexican refugees. It was *chictli*, from the sap of the Mexican sapodilla tree. By the end of the century peppermint-flavored chicle gum had replaced spruce gum (and paraffin gum, which had also been chewed). In 1910 chicle pellets were coated with white candy, and Chiclets became popular. Even in Alaska, the new gum outsold the habitual "chew" of whale blubber. Nowadays, if we chew, we chew flavored plastics.

We still get "spruced up" for parties.

Beer can be made from spruce trees by boiling spruce needles and twigs with molasses and then allowing the mixture to ferment. After drinking it, wrote Henry David Thoreau, a man might "see green" and dream he heard "the wind sough" in the trees.

The common name spruce means "from Prussia." In his 1670 *Sylva, or A Discourse of Forest-Trees*, John Evelyn wrote that "for masts, etc. those [trees] of Prussia, which we call Spruce . . . are the best." "Spruce" also meant "smart," because of the curt dandies "appareleyled after the fashion of Prusia or Spruce," explained Edward Hall in his *Chronicle* of 1542. The finest leather (probably tanned with spruce bark) was called Prussian or spruce leather. It could be, too, that the trees' neat, smart appearance added to the adoption of "spruce" for their name, and we still get "spruced up" for parties.

Spruces grow in cooler climates, and often don't mind damp soil. The Norway spruce, Europe's tallest tree, does well in North America, too, and is widely planted in parks and gardens. Native American spruces include the red, black, and white spruces. The Sitka spruce is named for the town of Sitka, the capital of Alaska until 1906. This spruce is widely planted in Europe, often in straight gridlike lines to renew bare hillsides. Spruces and other conifers are often planted in this uncomfortable way, especially if they are going to be "harvested" for pulp or lumber.

The Colorado spruce, *Picea pungens* (or "sharp," for its pointed needles), is often found in gardens in its blue form and is known as the blue spruce. There is also a blue, or glaucous, form of the Engelmann spruce. The soft needles of the Engelmann spruce point forward along the branches and the tree smells of camphor. It is named for George Engelmann, a nineteenth-century doctor who was also a keen botanist and collector. He came to St. Louis from Germany in 1832 and is credited with discovering the yucca moth's unique role in pollinating the yucca plant (*see* Joshua Tree).

Engelmann also compiled a herbarium in which the pressed grape leaves, he found, contained galls of the *phylloxera* aphid. The discovery of these galls was an important link for nineteenth-century French botanists searching for the source of what was destroying French vines and the wine industry. American vines had introduced the *phylloxera* aphid to Europe where the vines were not resistant to it. French vines were subsequently grafted onto American stock, with some success, but the phylloxera plague changed European wines forever. Some wine lovers fear there will never be wine as good as that before the plague. One hopes they are not forced to drink spruce beer instead. Most of those who try spruce beer say (in spite of Thoreau) that it tastes a bit like turpentine.

STEWARTIA

The stewartia that is in most North American gardens is a small pyramid-shaped tree covered with camellia-like blossoms in summers. Its bark peels off in patches, making it exceptionally beautiful in winter as well

The name stewartia is after John Stuart, Earl of Bute. The name Stewart was originally the name of a Scottish family, a branch of which inherited the throne of Scotland in 1371. During the sixteenth century, French influence on Scotland led to the use of the spelling Stuart (and Steuart), since there is no letter "w" in the French alphabet (the letter is used only in borrowed words). Bute's ancestors most probably were originally stewards, responsible for administering the royal household in Scotland. The names Stewart, Stuart, and Steward continued to be used. The tree we grow in our gardens and know by the first of these names is, however, the Japanese stewartia, or *Stewartia pseudo-camellia*. *Camellia* describes the white flowers, and stewartias, like camellias, are related to the tree *Camillia sinensis*, from which tea comes (*see* Tea).

The Japanese stewartia wasn't brought west until the nineteenth century, but the American stewartia was discovered in 1742, and sent to Britain by John Clayton (for whom *Claytonia*, or "spring beauty," which carpets our eastern woods is named). Mark Catesby (*see* Catalpa) received the tree, planted it, admired its flowers, and named it: "I am obliged to my good friend Mr. *Clayton*," he wrote, "who sent it me from *Virginia* . . . the right honourable and ingenious Earl of *Bute* will, I hope, excuse my calling this new genus of plants after his name." Catesby actually called the tree a Steuartia, but Linnaeus understood the name to be Stewartia, which (by the rules of nomenclature) remained.

The Virginia stewartia is *S. malacodendron* (meaning "soft tree"). It is sometimes called the mallow tree or silky camellia. It was enthusiastically introduced into British gardens but was only marginally hardy there and never became widespread. The mountain stewartia is *S. ovata* (for the "egg-shaped" leaves). The Japanese stewartia, once introduced, became a popular tree both in America and Britain.

Sometimes those for whom plants are named are very soon forgotten. But the Earl of Bute remained an important figure. This "ingenious" earl, as Catesby described him, "knows Dr. Linnaeus's method extremely well," no doubt thus encouraging Linnaeus to confirm the name (even if he did misspell it). John Stuart was head of the Scottish island of Bute, inheriting the earldom when he was ten years old. He was educated at Eton College, then lived and botanized on the island of Bute, until in 1746 he came to London to make his way in society. There he met Frederick, Prince of Wales, son of George II. Apparently a sudden downpour at the races caused Frederick and his consort, Princess Augusta, to invite the Earl to share their carriage. The

Earl was known for his good looks and immense charm (and was said to have had "the most elegant legs in London"). Bute soon became fast friends with the royal couple, and helped them design Frederick's garden, which eventually became Kew Gardens.

When Frederick died the Earl remained a friend of Augusta. They continued to plan the garden together, and it was generally supposed that she was his mistress. Her son, aged twelve, was besotted with his mother's admirer. When the prince became King George III, Bute's influence was considerable, and he was even appointed prime minster from 1792 to 1793. He was particularly hated for taxing cider and was so unpopular he had to resign.

STEWARTIAS, LIKE CAMELLIAS, ARE RELATED TO THE TREE FROM WHICH TEA COMES.

Botanically he left his name and a twelve-volume treatise of *Botanical Tables*, plus his part in founding Kew Gardens. There was another tree named for him, the *Butea* or *Dhak* tree, from Indian and Southeast Asia, sometimes called flame of the forest. The yellow dye it yields is called butein. Bute died a botanist's death trying to reach a plant growing on the cliffs at Highcliffe in Hampshire. The cliffs crumbled; he fell and never recovered from his injuries.

A century later, Thomas Hogg was sent by President Lincoln as the U.S. marshal to Japan. He shipped a Japanese stewartia to his family nursery in New York City and this beautiful little tree has graced our gardens ever since. But Hogg didn't always do quite as well for us: He also sent home the invasive kudzu vine.

STRAWBERRY TREE

The commonly named strawberry tree is also called a madrone in America and an arbutus in Europe. The arbutus grows in warmer regions of Europe. It is found in Ireland, too, where it may have come via Brittany. Irish legend says that Bresal, an Irish monk who had lived in Spain teaching choral music there, missed the warm climate when he returned home. Arbutus trees miraculously sprang up in Killarney to comfort him and have been there ever since. Bresal, who became abbot of Iona, died in 801 AD.

The fruits do look like strawberries but aren't as tasty. In 1548 the herbalist William Turner described this tree with "fruite like a strawberry, wherefore it may be called in English strawberry tree." The tree's botanical name is *Arbutus unedo*. *Arbutus* was its Latin name. *Unedo* traditionally comes from the abbreviated Latin for "I eat one," suggesting that having eaten *one* of the fruits no one would want another! Even though they aren't particularly good, the fruits were eaten by those called, in John Gerard's *Herball*, "the poorer sort of people."

The Spanish name for the tree is *madroño*, which means a "round tassel" (for the shape of the fruits). In Spain the fruits were used to make wine. So when Spanish missionary monk Father Juan Crespi saw strawberry trees on the Pacific coast of North America, he recognized them immediately as relatives of the Spanish *madroño*. Crespi was part of an expedition to find the legendary Bay of Monterey and establish Jesuit settlements there. After traveling for months the expedition successfully planted a cross at Monterey and set up a mission in the Carmel valley. In his diary Crespi noted that he saw "many madroños, though with smaller fruit than the Spanish trees." That's where our name, madrone, originated.

The botanical name of the American strawberry tree, *Arbutus menziesii*, is for Archibald Menzies, who collected specimens of this and other plants on Captain Vancouver's 1791 expedition to the Pacific Northwest. According to Menzies, Vancouver interfered with the care of his plants and mostly they all became "dead stumps" (*see* Monkey-puzzle). The first specimens of the madrone to reach Britain were sent back by David Douglas in 1827. Douglas noted the "peculiar smooth bark of reddish brown" and reminded himself in his diary to "put up a treble supple of its seeds, being evergreen it is the more desirable."

The strawberry tree is very beautiful. It's almost always in leaf, the older leaves turning scarlet as the new fresh green leaves emerge. The bark is layered, and the brown outer layer peels back to reveal the bright green underbark. The flowers are like creamy white vases, and you can see from them that the tree is related to heather. The fruits ripen slowly until they dangle from the branches like mature strawberries.

A lovely wildflower also in the heather family is the trailing arbutus. But strawberry trees *aren't* related to the trailing strawberry plant that gave them their name. Nor do the strawberries we eat get their name from the straw that is often put around them to protect them from damp (the name predates the custom), but their Anglo-Saxon name *streaw berige* refers to a berry that strews, or spreads, itself across the ground.

New World strawberry trees, which also occur in Arizona and Texas, can be seventy-five feet high, but European strawberry trees are considered shrubs in Britain. They are popular in gardens wherever they will survive. We know that Henrietta Maria, wife of the executed Charles I, grew one in her garden. When her property was disposed of and inventoried, the plants included a "very fayre tree called the Irish arbutus . . . very lovely to look upon." It was valued at thirty shilling, a good sum at the time.

Another name for the European strawberry tree is Cain-apple, because the fruits were like the drops of blood shed by Cain's murdered brother, Abel. Although not botanically related, the strawberry fruits we eat were also associated with blood, and many Renaissance paintings depict strawberry plants in Nativity scenes, to predict the drops of Christ's blood in the future and reassert, with their three leaves, the Holy Trinity.

ANOTHER NAME FOR THE EUROPEAN STRAWBERRY TREE IS CAIN-APPLE, BECAUSE THE FRUITS WERE LIKE THE DROPS OF BLOOD SHED BY CAIN'S MURDERED BROTHER, ABEL.

Another way that strawberry fruits and the fruits of the strawberry tree are related is that they are both lovely to look at. Only the former, though, is also lovely to eat.

SUMAC

T his tree is like a weed in this country," wrote the
eighteenth-century Swedish explorer Peter Kalm, in his
Travels in North America. Kalm was a pupil of Carl Lin-
naeus's, sent to America by him to find any plants useful to import to Sweden.
Kalm found no use for the sumac, remarking that "the Swedes here have no
particular name for it, and therefore make use of the English name."

Despite his opinion, there *were* uses for this tree. American Indians smoked
the leaves of the smooth sumac, *Rhus glabra*, and they made medicines from
it. The seed cones of the staghorn sumac, *R. typhina*, are still used by beekeepers in their smokers to calm the bees at honey-gathering time, perhaps because
they are (like the sumac leaves smoked by the Indians) somewhat hallucino-

genic. *Typhina* probably refers to the pithy or "reedlike" wood, which isn't good for much, or it may come from a belief that the sumac could be used to cure typhoid fever.

The staghorn sumac's branches are covered with soft down, similar to a stag's horns before the "velvet" has been rubbed off them during the mating season. The smooth sumac doesn't have these hairy-antlered branches, hence the name *glabra*, meaning "hairless."

Peter Kalm described "boys of Philadelphia" eating sumac berries, "there being no danger of falling ill after the repast; but they are very sour." These edible sumac berries, which can also make a kind of lemonade, are red. They are very different from the white berries of the poison sumac, or *Toxidendron vernix* ("poison varnish tree"). Poison sumac is not as widespread as the smooth or staghorn sumacs and grows mostly in swampy ground. It is (like all sumacs) a relative of poison ivy, and its sap can cause a bad allergic rash. "It appears," wrote Kalm, "that though a person be secure against the power of this poison for a while, yet in the course of time he may be affected by it just as much as people of weaker constitution." Kalm wrote this with personal feeling. At first he thought he was immune to sumac allergy. After experimentally rubbing himself with the sap, he found this not to be so and wrote that he did not have "any desire" to repeat the experiment. Anyone who has suffered from sumac or poison ivy rash will surely sympathize with him.

The sap of the American poison sumac contains a kind of varnish, but this isn't used much, if at all. The Asian *T. vernicifluum* ("flowing with varnish") has, however, been used for its varnishlike sap for centuries. It, too, is toxic and on July 2, 1869, the French missionary explorer Abbé Armand David (*see* Handkerchief Tree) wrote that he had finally seen a grove of varnish trees growing on the banks of a Chinese river. He described how some people "cannot endure being near it, or even seeing it or hearing it mentioned without breaking into ulcers of the skin and large swelling here and there in the body." Evidently psychological rashes were not unknown in nineteenth-century China.

By Abbé David's time, using the sap of the varnish tree, as they are still called, was a technique already centuries old. The bark was tapped and the sap collected in mollusk shells. It was heated and filtered, then applied in thin layers to whatever was to be lacquered. The color of the lacquer could be varied by adding dye or even gold dust. Sometimes hundreds of layers of varnish were applied to get the right effect, and each layer had to be dried for two to three weeks in a damp atmosphere. Lacquered objects can resist high heat and were used as cooking vessels, as well as exquisite bowls and carvings.

THE SEED CONES OF THE STAGHORN SUMAC, *R. TYPHINA*, ARE STILL USED BY BEEKEEPERS IN THEIR SMOKERS TO CALM THE BEES AT HONEY-GATHERING TIME.

The classical name for the tree was *rhus*, but the name sumac is also ancient, probably coming from the Syriac, *summaq*, meaning "red." The Mediterranean *R. coriaria* was a source of red dye.

All sumacs are related to cashew nuts, in the Anacardiaceae family, so called for the heart-shaped fruits. The cashew nut has poisonous qualities like some sumacs. Between the nut and the shell is a highly caustic layer. If this hasn't been cleaned off, or the cashew nuts have not been properly roasted, they can give the unwary cocktail nut consumer a rash quite as nasty as that of poison sumac.

SWEETGUM

I n 1516 Hernando Cortés met with the Aztec emperor Montezuma. Bernal Diaz, who accompanied Cortés, described how after feasting (*see* Cacao) the guests were offered pipes to smoke, containing "an herb called tobacco," mixed with American liquidambar. Both ingredients were new to the Europeans. After the Ice Age the natural habitat of *Liquidambar*, or the sweetgum tree, was isolated to Asia and America.

Oriental liquidambar (not from this tree) had been used as far back as Old Testament times, but like other exotic substances, it was costly. So when the Spanish physician Nicolás Monardes wrote *Joyfull News out of the New Founde World* (*see* Sassafras), he enthusiastically described American liquidambar, and the "certaine trees verie greate and faire" that yielded this precious gum.

"Liquid Amber," claimed Monardes, "taketh awaie the paines of any manner of griefe." No wonder it was sought after.

The American sweetgum's botanical name is *Liquidambar* ("liquid amber") *styraciflua*. The second part of *styraciflua* comes from *fluere*, the Latin for "flow," and the first part refers to the gum called storax that was used in the ancient world for perfumes and incense. Storax came from an unrelated tree, native to the Middle East, the *Styrax officinale*. Storax was probably the substance God told Moses to burn at the altar. The perfumed gum was extracted by pressing the inner bark of the tree in horsehair bags and then soaking the residue in hot water until the storax floated to the surface. It was more available and cheaper than frankincense (*see* Frankincense). In Gerard's revised *Herball*, the styrax tree was described as only "producing his gummy liquor in full perfection of sweetnesse" in hot countries. So it was certainly (rather charming) hearsay that described the gum looking like icicles "that hang from the eaves of houses in Winter."

Storax was gradually replaced by the imported gum of the *Liquidambar orientalis*, from China. It was widely used in incense and medicine. Scenting the air was thought to change any dangerous components of it, and in the sixteenth century perfumed gloves held protectively in front of the face were believed to shield wearers from the plague. Mondardes said that liquid-amber "doe dresse Gloves therewith for the common people."

In the sixteenth century perfumed gloves held protectively in front of the face were believed to shield wearers from the plague.

Peter Kalm (*see* Alder) wrote about the sweetgum tree: it grew best in damp places but was "unfit for making canoes because it imbibes the water." Sweetgum wood does warp easily. Kalm noted that the farther north the trees grew, the less gum they produced. In the North the yield was "too small to pay for the labor of collecting it."

Nowadays sweetgums are usually planted in gardens in Europe as well as elsewhere for the brilliance of their star-shaped leaves in autumn. Sometimes they are called alligator trees because the formation of the bark on the young twigs is in finny ridges. The fruits are prickly balls, which hang on long stems. Peter Kalm described them: "The seeds are contained in round, dentated cones, which drop in autumn. It is therefore not particularly pleasant to dance bare-foot under these trees." One can't help wondering under what circumstances he discovered this.

SYCAMORE

Oriental plane trees, brought home to Britain by returning crusaders, were often called sycamores. The name sycamore is said to come from the use of the plane tree leaves in medieval religious mystery plays. The leaves of the biblical sycamore fig tree (from *shikmim* in Hebrew) were thought to have been Adam and Eve's first garments. When the large lobed leaves of the plane tree were used on stage instead of unobtainable fig leaves, the tree took the name sycamore from the *F. sycomorus*. In America, plane trees are still called sycamores, but not in Britain.

Huge plane trees with their large hand-shaped leaves and dappled bark were loved and venerated far back in time. The oriental plane, *Platanus orientalis*, grew in gardens and around tombs in ancient Egypt, Greece, and Persia. The Greeks and Romans planted groves and avenues of plane trees where, under their dense shade, they could walk and talk. John Gerard's *Herball* (*see* Banana) quoted Pliny as writing that plane trees were sometimes watered with wine rather than water, which was "very comfortable to the rootes." The Latin name *Platanus* (from the Greek *platy-*, "broad, wide") is for their flat, broad leaves, or possibly the wide-spreading branches of these trees. The bark of all plane trees is not elastic enough to grow with the tree and, instead of splitting as the trunk expands under it, flakes off in patches, leaving that distinctive dappled pattern.

The oriental plane, called the chenar, was planted in Persian and in Islamic gardens where its shade was highly valued. Muslim poets said that in Islamic gardens the plane tree's broad leaves, fluttering like prayerful hands, led the other trees in praising God.

A famous oriental plane tree was one the Greek historian Herodotus described catching the attention of the Persian emperor Xerxes on his way to invade Greece around 480 BC. Xerxes admired this tree so greatly he halted his huge army so he could enjoy it, and he collected up gold ornaments from his followers to hang from its branches. He appointed a guardian to take care of the tree (and presumably its gold ornaments) after the army moved on. John Evelyn (*see* Ash) elaborated on Herodotus's story, writing that Xerxes called the tree "his Mistris, his Minion, his Goddesse, and when he was forc'd to part from it, he caus'd the figure of it to be stampt on a Medail of Gold, which he continually wore about him." Just a short while after this touching arboreal incident Herodotus described the tree-hugging general ordering that a young man be cut in half and that the Persian army march between the two halves of the body. At least we know that he loved trees.

When pioneers came to America they found New World sycamores (*Platanus occidentalis*). They also called them buttonwoods on account of the button-like hanging seed balls, which often stay on the tree all winter before breaking and dispersing. The size of these trees was often astonishing. Old buttonwoods are usually hollow but keep on growing. Settlers sometimes used the trees' hollow interiors as rooms for themselves or stables for their livestock.

Buttonwoods, which grow quickly, were planted in new cities and towns. Peter Kalm, a pupil of Linnaeus's, described walking through eighteenth-century New York City, which, he wrote, "seemed like a garden." The buttonwood trees planted along the streets were "very plentiful," and gave "an agreeable shade in summer." In July 1793 Thomas Jefferson wrote to his daughter Martha from Philadelphia, "I never before knew the full value of trees. My house is entirely embossomed in high plane-trees . . . and under them I breakfast, dine, write, read and receive my company." He added, "What would I not give" that the trees planted around his house at Monticello were as large. Many householders have shared such a wish.

The American sycamore, or American plane, *P. occidentalis*, was probably taken back to Britain at the end of the seventeenth century by John Tradescant the Younger. He, with his father, had a museum and garden at Lambeth, London, and there were also Eastern plane trees growing in that garden. Traditionally the oriental and the new Western plane trees growing there hybridized to produce the famous London plane. An immense early specimen survived at Magdalen College, Oxford, providing material for debates on whether it came before Tradescant's. The first London planes in Britain date from around that time, but some botanists think the hybridization occurred in Spain. The London plane's recent botanical name was *P. hispanica* ("Spanish") for this reason, but now seems to be *P.* × *acerifolia* ("maple leaved"). Thus do botanists keep us on our toes!

The London plane tree, hardier than either of its forbears, is tolerant of air pollution. So it is planted in cities worldwide, including New York City where, sadly, we are no longer reminded of "a garden." Unlike many hybrids, the seeds of the London plane are viable. The seed balls hang in pairs, not singly like the "buttons" of the Western sycamore. The oriental plane has several seed balls hanging together.

Confusingly, the name sycamore is not only applied to American plane trees. Sometime in the fifteenth or sixteenth century the plane-leaved maple, *Acer pseudoplatanus* ("false plane maple"), was introduced to Britain. Its leaves are somewhat similar to the plane tree

SETTLERS SOMETIMES USED THE TREES' HOLLOW INTERIORS AS ROOMS FOR THEMSELVES OR STABLES FOR THEIR LIVESTOCK.

leaves. In 1803 Thomas Jefferson's chargé d'affaires in London, Christopher Gore, brought the "sycamore maple" back home to Massachusetts. In Britain a sycamore means a sycamore maple. Sycamore maples are prolific reseeders. Their seeds are winged, not shaped like balls, and their foliage is often slippery from honeydew insects, which they attract. They aren't preferred hardwood trees on either side of the Atlantic. The poet Robert Louis Stevenson wished his readers

> A bin of wine, a spice of wit,
> A house with lawns enclosing it,
> A living river by the door,
> A nightingale in the sycamore!

In Britain this would mean the sycamore maple. Most of us would prefer a nightingale in a plane tree—even if it doesn't rhyme.

TAMARISK

When Abraham was a sprightly hundred-year-old, his wife, Sarah (also a senior citizen), finally conceived and gave birth to Isaac. In those days longevity seems to have been more common than psychology and there must have been a bit of sibling jealousy in Hagar's son, Ishmael. When he witnessed all the fuss over his little half brother during the party to celebrate Isaac's weaning, Ishmael "mocked" the baby (we are not told exactly how). Sarah was so upset that she persuaded Abraham to leave Ishmael and his mother in the desert with only a bottle of water and a bit of bread. The water ran out and Hagar left her little boy under a tamarisk tree to die. But an angel appeared, showed her a hidden well, and mother and child survived.

The tamarisk tree grows well in sandy desert, putting down deep roots to find water, and in Hagar's story most probably the tree used the same source of water that the angel revealed. Tamarisks have very small leaves, which don't lose water but do release salt, so they can grow in barren, briny places. But although its foliage is economical, the pink flowers are abundant. It is a very pretty tree indeed.

Tamarisks grow all over the Middle East and southern Europe as well as in Asia. Nomadic Arabs valued them not only for shade but for the manna that dropped from the leaves. This is caused by insects perforating the leaves, which then lose sap (and shouldn't be confused with honeydew that is exuded by insects [*see* Sycamore]). Tamarisk sap can be collected and made into sweet cakes. The biblical manna that tasted like "wafer made with honey," which the Jews found when they wandered in the desert after leaving Egypt, may have been these very cakes (though there are other possibilities). The Hebrew *man hu*, meaning "what is this?" gave us the translation "manna."

Tamarisks were valued for their medicinal properties, too. The first tamarisk (*Tamarix gallica*) was said to have been brought to Britain by Bishop Edmund Grindal, who had been exiled during the reign of "Bloody" Queen Mary. In 1558 he returned to serve under Queen Elizabeth and brought tamarisks home, because "many people hath received great health from this plant," wrote Richard Hakluyt, who published three books on plant "discoveries" at the end of the sixteenth century. Parts of the tree were supposed to be particularly good at curing maladies of the "spleene" and sufferers could even be helped if they drank from a cup made from tamarisk wood.

There are about fifty species of tamarisk, the most common being the *T. gallica*, once called *T. nilotica* ("Nile") or *T. mannifera* ("manna"). Soon after their introduction tamarisks were planted all over England to stabilize banks and waterways, becoming naturalized in many coastal areas. Fishermen in Cornwall made lobster pots from the willowy branches. The Chinese tamarisk (*T. chinensis*) is also called a red willow or, more poetically, the hear-prayer willow.

Tamarisks were brought to America in the early 1800s, both as ornamentals and to control erosion of banks and dykes. Although camels are said to browse contentedly on tamarisks, most wild creatures can't eat them. Where there aren't any camels to control them and water is plentiful, tamarisks compete with other plants and can drain water tables.

The origin of this tree's name has elicited several scholarly suggestions. The simplest is that it is the ancient Latin name for the tree, *tamarix*. Some say that name came from the Spanish river Tamaris (or Tambra) where many tamarisks grew. Others say it is from the Sanskrit *tamas*, "darkness," on account of the dark bark. One thing sure is that tamarisks are not related to the similar sounding tamarack (*see* Larch) or to the leguminous tamarind (whose name comes from *tamr hindi*, ("Indian date"). Herbalist Nicholas Culpeper called the tamarisk a "gallant Saturnine herb." In America it is sometimes called a salt cedar, but it isn't a cedar.

Tamarisks grow so abundantly on beaches in America it's hard to remember they aren't native trees. In these places they are more like shrubs than trees, while in hot countries a full-grown tamarisk can be a substantial tree, good for shade and timber. In his poem "Christmas in India," Rudyard Kipling uses the tamarisk tree as a symbol of homesickness, as he watches, from dawn until dusk, the sky "behind the tamarisks." The hot, foreign day passes slowly,

> And at Home they're making merry 'neath the white and scarlet
>   berry—
> What part have India's exiles in their mirth?
>
> . . . .
>
> They will drink our healths at dinner—those who tell us how they
>   love us,
> And forget us till another year be gone!

The beauty of the tamarisks, outlined against the tropical skies, seems not to help at all.

TEA

According to a Chinese saying,

The first cup moistens my lips,
The second breaks my loneliness,
The third seeks my empty stomach,
The fourth makes me perspire,
The fifth is purifying,
The sixth beckons the immortals,
The seventh . . . I cannot drink.

Because we so love tea, we rarely allow it to become a tree. If left alone tea trees can reach sixty feet high with a girth of three feet, but most tea is selected and grown as a shrub, about three feet high, so the shining evergreen leaves can easily be picked and harvested.

Our former botanical name for tea was *Thea sinensis*, but since it's related to the camellia, its botanical name is now *Camellia sinensis* ("from China").

The camellia is a shrub, *C. japonica*, named for Georg Joseph Kamel, a Moravian missionary who botanized in the Philippines. Linnaeus first called tea *T. viridis* (for "green" tea) and *T. bohea* (a Western name for a mountainous area in Manchuria called the Wuji where "black" tea was thought to grow). Until the nineteenth century it was thought that green and black teas came from different plants and different places. The difference is that green tea leaves are not fermented before being dried, but black tea leaves are. Oolong tea is from partially fermented leaves.

Tea was drunk in China for centuries, first as a medicine and then for pleasure, going so far back that it's not known how the plant originally got there. But in spite of the name *sinensis*, it may well be native to India, where it grows wild. In 1843 Robert Fortune was sent to China to find areas where green and black tea grew and (secretly) to collect tea plants to be planted by the British in India, thereby breaking the Chinese monopoly on tea. At that time "all the tea in China" meant all the tea known. After planting tea taken from China, the British were astonished to find tea growing wild in Assam. In India it had not been used as a beverage although it became popular there (very popular) later on.

The legendary originator of tea drinking was the Bodhidharma (or Daruma), who was traditionally a blue-eyed Indian monk who took Buddhism to China in the sixth century. He was determined to meditate for nine years without sleep. When he found himself dozing off, the story says, he cut off his eyelids in a fury and flung them onto the ground—whereupon two tea plants sprang up. He, and his followers, thereafter could sip tea to keep awake when meditating. In the eighth century Zen monks went from China to Japan, taking tea drinking as well as their religion with them.

The Chinese name *chai*, or *t'e*, and the Malaysian *te* became "tea" or "tay" in English. Sometimes it was called char, as in a nice "cuppa char." Tea wasn't known in the West until the sixteenth century, which was about the time the "teahouse" ritual was established in Japan. This was the ultimate ceremony of preparing and serving a cup of tea, and included architecture of its own (known as *chaseki*). The teahouse was always set in a specially designed garden that allowed tea drinkers, as they progressed slowly toward the house, to stop at designated places along the pathway, thereby approximating the experience of shedding their worldy cares.

FOR THIS TEA, TINY FIRST-LEAF BUDS WERE PICKED AND PLACED IN A BASKET THAT WAS WORN OVER THE BREASTS OF A YOUNG WOMAN, WHOSE BODY WARMTH MATURED THE LEAVES.

The names of tea are many, some, like Assam or Darjeeling, being for places, some descriptive. Of the latter, the Chinese "Fragrance of a Young Girl" is the most exotic. For this tea, tiny first-leaf buds were picked and placed in a basket that was worn over the breasts of a young woman, whose body warmth matured the leaves. Pekoe is made from the leaves around the bud tips, its name coming from *pek* ("white") and *ho* "feathery"). Russian Caravan tea came to Russia on camel caravans from Mongolia. The Mongols themselves took their leaves cooked in a thick broth dressed with fermented yak butter.

In the seventeenth century Europe suddenly discovered the pleasure of drinking tea. In 1661 Samuel Pepys described "tea (a China drink) of which I had never drank before." The new beverage was introduced by the wife of Charles II, Catherine of Braganza, whose dowry included Bombay. The British East India Company began trading there for tea. Charles II taxed tea, thus encouraging smuggling as the brew grew more popular. Peter Stuyvesant took tea to New Holland, and settlers in America drank it enthusiastically until George III tried to tax it there. After the Boston Tea Party of 1773 it was considered "unpatriotic" to drink tea, and coffee was the preferred drink of Americans. In Britain tea grew ever more popular, giving a name to a meal and the "tea break." By the 1960s British workers were legally allowed two tea breaks every day.

The "tea tree" or "ti tree" products so popular these days aren't from *Camellia sinensis* but a totally different tree, *Melaleuca alternifolia*, a small tree native to Australia. It has dark (*mel-*) leaves and a pale (*leuc-*) trunk and was used medicinally by Australian aborigines. Captain Cook gave it the name tea tree when he boiled the leaves and drank the beverage, a usage not recommended today. But the aboriginal one of using it as a lotion was recently fashionable here too. Some claimed it had antibacterial properties and was good for shampooing irritated scalps. In Papuan New Guinea the bark of the *Melaleuca* was used effectively to stuff and preserve the *severed* scalps of enemies.

TREE OF HEAVEN

The tree of heaven was brought from France in 1784 by William Hamilton, and planted at Woodlands, his Pennsylvania garden (*see* Ginkgo). Seeds of the tree had been sent to France from China in 1751, by Pierre d'Incarville, a Jesuit missionary. D'Incarville had been one of the few Europeans accepted at the imperial court. After he had made the formidable emperor Ch'ien-lung laugh, by giving him a sensitive plant (*see* Acacia) that collapsed when touched, d'Incarville was granted permission to botanize in the countryside around Peking. He collected seeds of the tree of heaven and sent them home to France. The seeds traveled with a Russian caravan and took months to arrive. Nevertheless they germinated in the Jardin du Roi in Paris and thrived. Soon there were enough specimens to supply collectors in France, England, and America, where the exotic tree of heaven was enthusiastically received.

This doesn't surprise us. The tree of heaven is one of the hardiest plants imaginable. It resists drought, cold, and pollution. It can sprout where no other tree would grow: in vacant lots, between railway lines, and out of tiny cracks in concrete pavements. It's an immigrant inhabitant of neglected inner cities and forgotten tenements. It makes shade where apartments have no air conditioning and children play on scorching sidewalks. It's impossible to feel neutral about this tree. You either love it for its ability to provide life where other trees die, or you hate it as a devilish weed that can't be controlled. No one could have predicted that Hamilton's cherished import could have penetrated so many lost corners of America.

Early on the tree of heaven was used as a street tree, but city planters soon discovered that the flowers of the male tree smell terrible. That's why Father d'Incarville had called the tree *frêne puant*, or "stinking ash." It has pinnate ashlike leaves that can be a foot long. The bark is pale gray, and yellow flowers bloom in springtime. A mature tree of heaven can reach over eighty feet high. Its botanical name, *Ailanthus altissima*, means it is "very tall." The first part of the botanical name, *Ailanthus*, comes from the Moluccan (Spice Islands) name *ai lanit*, or "sky tree."

A mature tree of heaven is a handsome sight, and if these trees were rare, they might be more treasured. Andrew Downing, in his *Landscape Gardening and Rural Architecture* (1841) wrote that the "Ailanthus is a picturesque tree, well adapted to produce a good effect on the lawn, either singly or grouped." But by 1859 Henry Withrop Sargent, who, after Downing had drowned, edited a later edition of the book, added a footnote that "public opinion has very much changed about this tree, since the early editions of this book."

In the meantime, whole orchards of ailanthus were planted across the United States in an attempt to start an American silk industry (*see* Mulberry). The Arrindy silkworm feeds on ailanthus leaves (as well as on the castor oil plant) and its silk, known as pongee silk, is coarser than silk from the mulberry silkworm. Like all silk, it requires cheap labor to make it cost-efficient, so the industry failed in America. Pongee silk is made in India.

The ailanthus tree is closely related to the quassia tree, *Quassia amara*, of the West Indies. The quassia's bitter bark (*amara*) is still used as a natural insecticide and was once a popular febrifuge and vermifuge. In Suriname a pupil of Linnaeus, Daniel Rolander, came across a freed black slave, Graman Quassi, who was using the bark of the tree to treat fevers. Rolander persuaded Quassi to sell him some bark and brought it back to Linnaeus. Linnaeus heard the story and named the tree *Quassia amara*. Rolander was less successful when he sent Linnaeus cochineal insects. The insects were in a jar along with the cactus plant they fed on. No one cautioned the gardener not to wash off the cactus when it arrived, so by the time Linnaeus got to the jar the insects were gone. Linnaeus wrote that his disappointment caused "the most dreadful fits of migraine" he had ever felt. He could perhaps have tried an infusion of quassia bark to cure his migraine — but we don't know if he did.

THE FIRST PART OF THE BOTANICAL NAME, *AILANTHUS,* COMES FROM THE MOLUCCAN (SPICE ISLANDS) NAME *AI LANIT,* OR "SKY TREE."

TULIP TREE

Some of the finest specimens of this magnificent tree are to be found not in their native land of eastern North America but in great gardens elsewhere. When first discovered in the New World, tulip poplars were exported abroad as ornamental trees by European "collectors," sent by the rich from Europe in search of plants and trees to embellish their estates.

The Tradescants, John the Elder and John the Younger, were both collectors (of just about anything). John the Elder, employed by the Earl of Cecil, went as far as Russia searching for "curiosities" and new plants (*see* Larch). When he died in 1638, his son inherited the Tradescant garden in Lambeth, London.

John the Younger made three plant-collecting expeditions to Virginia. It was he who brought back the tulip tree and planted a specimen in his garden. We know this because the plants in the Lambeth garden were listed on a blank page of the family copy of John Parkinson's *Paradisi in Sole Paradisus Terrestris*, published in 1629.

Peter Collinson (*see* Horse Chestnut) also made plant lists in his gardening books. In his copy of John Evelyn's *Sylva, or A Discourse of Forest-Trees* (1664), there is a note that a tulip poplar grew in the garden of Lord Petre (Bartram's patron). John Evelyn himself wrote, "They have a *Poplar* in *Virginia* of a very peculiar shap'd leaf, as if the point of it were cut off, which grows very well with the *curious* amongst us to a considerable stature. I conceive it was first brought over by John *Tradescant* under the name of Tulip-tree, but is not that I find taken notice of in any of our *Herbals*; I wish there were more of them."

He was right. More tulip poplars was then, and still is, better. These are the tallest deciduous trees of North America. They can reach well over a hundred feet high with towering columnar trunks and quite unique leaves and flowers. They are a kind of magnolia, once widespread but now left only in northeastern America, with one relative in China very similar to them.

The flowers, like magnolias or "tulips," have a beautiful yellow and orange base tinted with green above. They are only produced after the tree is about ten years old and quite high, perhaps originally to protect them from tall prehistoric browsers. Humans more often see the flowers on the ground beneath the trees than high up where they bloom, facing upward. There is only a short period when they can be pollinated (by insects), after which the light-colored stigmas darken and the flowers drop while still intact and beautiful. They can be picked up, floated in a bowl of water like small perfect water lilies, and last for days.

The "poplar" part of the tree's name is partly because of the pale wood and partly because of the loosely attached leaves, which flutter in the breeze. In both these ways they resemble poplars—to which they are not related. The wood was used by Native Americans to make huge canoes out of whole trunks, which were hollowed out by burning away the centers. The tree was sometimes called a canoe wood tree by settlers. The Indian name was *rakiock*. In later times tulip poplar wood was valued for making hat forms, since it doesn't absorb steam used to shape the hats.

A common name for the tulip poplar was old woman's smock, because the strange leaves are shaped a bit like a dress for a paper doll.

The Swedish traveler Peter Kalm wrote that a common name for the tulip poplar was old woman's smock because the strange leaves are shaped a bit like a dress for a paper doll. The tree has an unusual way of protecting its new leaves, with a two-sided sheath around them. When the leaf is ready to open, the sides of this sheath part, allowing the folded leaf to emerge but remaining on each side of it until it's a bit stronger, rather like a clam shell.

The tulip poplar was used medicinally but without spectacular results. Peter Kalm reported that taking an infusion of the bark "sometimes" helped cure ague (malaria). But he also wrote that he knew of an old woman who had been cured of this disease by putting "some spider's web inside a baked apple which she ate." Some people, he added, "used no medicines at all, and let the disease be until it passed away of itself." Tulip tree flowers, he added, "have no smell to delight the nose." This is a common trait of prehistoric plants.

By the mid-eighteenth century, several elegant European gardens had mature tulip trees growing in them. When John Bartram sent Peter Collinson fifteen hundred tulip tree seed cones he was told, unsurprisingly, that he "need not collect any more." The first tulip tree to flower in Britain was said to be one in Parson's Green, the garden of Lord Peterborough, who didn't see the flowers himself because, since he opposed King James II, he was spending time in Holland. Another tree, in Lord Pembroke's garden at Wilton, had five hundred flowers on it in 1720, presumably counted by someone.

Linnaeus bestowed on the tree the lovely name *Liriodendron tulipifera*, meaning "lily tree bearing tulips." The Chinese tree is *L. chinense*. In China it is sometimes called a goosefoot (*ezhangqiu*) or manadarin's jacket (*maguamu*), both names for the shape of the leaves.

By the mid-nineteenth century Americans were planting tulip trees in their gardens, too. Andrew Jackson Downing, whose partner helped design Central Park, recommended them on lawns and along avenues. In his 1865 book on landscaping (*see* Poplar), he wrote that there was a tulip tree "in almost every gentleman's park on the Continent of Europe, so highly is it esteemed." But, he added, "We hope that the specimens yet standing here and there [in America] . . . may be sacredly preserved from the barbarous infliction of the axe." He concluded, and we must surely agree, that whoever has once seen a mature tulip tree "can never forget it."

TUPELO

Carl Linnaeus named many plants and creatures for mythological individuals. This was because he wanted to substitute the very long descriptive names prior to his time with easily remembered personal names. It's harder for us, less familiar with classical mythology, to connect with some of the names he bestowed. Because he understood that the tupelo, or sourgum, grew on swampy ground, Linnaeus named the tree *Nyssa*, after a water nymph, foster mother of Dionysius, god of wine.

Hera was more than once driven to furious jealousy when her husband fell for a young woman. When she discovered that Semele was carrying Zeus's child, Hera was determined to destroy the beautiful mortal. Disguised as a sweet old lady Hera suggested that Semele ask Zeus to reveal himself to his lover in the form of the god he was. Semele did ask Zeus, and he complied, but the searing brightness of his heavenly presence burned her to ashes. Semele's unborn baby was saved and given to the water nymph Nyssa (or Nysa) to bring up in her secret cave. Dionysus grew up to spread the delicious discovery of wine around the world, and Nyssa was rewarded for her services by being transformed into a heavenly body.

The tupelo tree is native to the eastern United States, and was brought to Europe in the eighteenth century. The name tupelo is said to be the Anglicization of the Creek Indian *eto*, "tree," and *opelwr*, "swamp." The *Nyssa sylvatica* ("of woods") grows on drier ground, but the *N. aquatica* (probably the tree first described to Linnaeus) grows in swampy areas, where it tolerates low oxygen. The bulbous lower trunk stabilizes the tree in soft ground. Tupelo trees can grow to sixty feet but don't live long. Their tops break off and the trunks rot and become hollow. They were also called beegums because the hollow trunks were used to house bees. Their flowers make very good honey.

> THE NAME TUPELO IS SAID TO BE THE ANGLICIZATION OF THE CREEK INDIAN *ETO*, "TREE," AND *OPELWR*, "SWAMP."

The name sourgum (also blackgum) is really a misnomer, because tupelos produce no gum. The fruits, however, are sour and the leaves dark. Male and female trees produce their own flowers. The shiny oval leaves turn brilliant red, yellow, and purple in fall. The sourgum is not related to the sourwood, which is a kind of heather, and also has brilliant autumn foliage. Less hardy than sourgums, the sourwood's botanical name *Oxydendron* comes from the Greek *oxys* ("sour"). It is also called the sorrel tree.

Although tupelo trees are supposedly common in the eastern United States, they rarely grow in gardens, and not many people know them. More people do know that Tupelo is the town in Mississippi where, in 1935, Elvis Presley was born. Of course he, like Nyssa herself, became a blazing star.

WALNUT

J ust as there is no such thing as a "French" marigold or an "Irish" potato, "English" walnuts are not English. The name walnut most probably comes from the Anglo-Saxon *walh-knuta*, or *welshe*, meaning a "foreign" nut, specifically a "nut from Wales" (which it isn't). To those who spoke Germanic languages, "Welsh" was synonymous with "foreign," and the German for walnut was *welsche Nuss*.

Scholars don't agree as to when so-called English walnuts came to England. We know that the Greeks and Romans valued them. The pathetic remains of a feast, with walnuts on the table ready for a never-to-be-eaten dessert, were found in the volcanic lava of Pompeii. The Greek name for them was *karya*. Carya was a Laconian princess with whom Dionysus fell in love. When her elder sisters threatened to tell their father, Dionysus changed them into stones and Carya into a walnut tree. Another possible origin of the Greek name was from the Greek *kara*, "head," for the shape of the nut, rather than for the princess. Theophrastus, a Greek philosopher and naturalist (and pupil of Aristotle), called the walnut *Karyon basiliken*, meaning it was a "kingly nut."

The Romans probably got walnuts from the Greeks, and they were mentioned in 116 BC by the Roman writer Varro. Pliny said they came from Persia and called them Persian nuts. When the Romans named the walnut, they called it *Jovis glans*, or "Jove's nut." In the Golden Age of mythology the gods ate walnuts while ordinary mortals ate acorns. *Jovis glans* became *Juglans*, which is still the botanical name for walnuts. There are many species of *Juglans* worldwide, including in both North and South America. The English walnut is meatier and has a thinner shell than other walnuts, but the tree doesn't do well in cold climates.

The walnut was eaten more in Mediterranean countries than in Britain, where it was most valued medicinally. Because walnuts are formed remarkably like human heads, with a skull-like shell and brainlike interior, the doctrine of signatures (*see* Osage Orange) interpreted this as meaning that God had created walnuts to indicate they were a cure for head injuries and ailments. In 1657 William Cole wrote in *Adam and Eve* that a crushed walnut laid "upon the Crown of the Head . . . comforts the brain and head mightily."

Mithridates of Pontus, an expert on poisoning, was said to have taken a daily concoction of powdered walnuts (mixed with figs, rue salt, and juniper berries) as a prophylactic against being himself poisoned. Plutarch wrote that when Mithridates was overthrown, the Roman general Pompey found the recipe for this antidote (along with "a series of wanton letters" to the king's concubines). In spite of the walnuts, Mithradites met a violent end in 63 BC, and, Plutarch tells us, the victorious Pompey didn't keep any of the concubines but sent them back to "their parents and relatives." However, he did keep the walnut recipe, which can still be found in Nicholas Culpeper's 1653 herbal, *The English Physician*.

When Europeans came to America they found walnuts as well as the closely related hickories and pecans. The botanical name for hickories and pecans is *Carya*. "Hickory" comes from *pohickery*: American Indians powdered the nuts and put them in water to make hickory milk, or *pawcohiccora*. "Pignut" hickories aren't good eating, except by hogs. Butternuts are a good (and buttery) kind of walnut, but they are small and hard to crack. Their bark is gray, or "ashy," which is why they are called *Juglans cinerea*. This bark makes good dye, and Confederate troops were sometimes called butternuts because their uniforms were dyed with it.

EARLY FARMERS BELIEVED THEY COULD IDENTIFY THE MOST PRODUCTIVE LAND BY THE SIZE OF THE BLACK WALNUTS GROWING THERE.

European settlers valued the black walnut more for its wood than its nuts, which again are hard to crack. Black walnut trees, *J. nigra*, can grow huge. Early farmers believed they could identify the most productive land by the size of the black walnuts growing there. Growing crops in proximity to black walnuts can be unsuccessful, since the roots of this tree contain *juglone*, a substance known as a phytotoxin, which inhibits some plants from growing well. Vegetable gardens don't flourish near black walnut trees.

Early Americans felled the walnut trees before they started to farm, and they used the beautiful black wood for all kinds of carpentry. Walnut wood, once cured, is very stable, and it was particularly prized for making gunstocks, as it doesn't warp and spoil the alignment so necessary for an accurate aim. Before World War I the German kaiser stockpiled American black walnut wood for equipping his army with guns.

The wood of English walnuts is beautiful, too, and much prized for furniture. Emperor Frederick III was once said to have held a banquet on a walnut wood table twenty-five feet wide. Such trees are history tales now. In Jane Austen's *Sense and Sensibility*, John Dashwood tells Elinor that "the old walnut-trees are all to come down" to make room for his wife's new greenhouse. "It will be a very fine object from many parts of the park" he says. No wonder his horrified sister "could only smile."

In England not only did they cut down walnut trees, they beat them. An unpleasant old English proverb asserted, "A woman, a dog, and a walnut tree / The more you beat 'em the better they be." Modern thinking doesn't believe women, dogs, or walnuts should be beaten. There seems no explanation for why a castigated walnut should be thought to flourish, though some have surmised that the beating might have dislodged insects or stimulated sap to run. Others think it was to get rid of witches, who traditionally inhabited walnut trees. However, according to John Evelyn's *Sylva, or A Discourse of Forest-Trees*, "in Germany no young Farmer whatsoever is permitted to Marry a Wife, till he bring proof that he hath planted, and is Father of such a stated number of Walnut-trees . . . for the extraordinary benefit which this Tree affords the Inhabitants."

English walnuts do well in California and are farmed there to meet the demand for the delicious nuts. Nowadays California farmers harvest walnuts by grasping the tree trunk with giant calipers that shake the tree violently to make the nuts fall. From the tree's point of view, it sounds as nasty as being beaten.

WELWITSCHIA

The *Welwitschia mirabilis* is called *mirabilis* because it's a "marvelous" tree. It only grows in southwestern Africa, mostly in the Namib Desert, so few of us will ever see one. Even if we did see a welwitschia we might not know it was a tree, because most of the trunk is underground, with barely a few feet of it sticking above the surface. From the stump emerges a shredded mop of huge leaves.

Welwitschias have been compared to vegetable octopuses, spreading tangled tentacles across the hot sand. Sometimes a welwitschia is the only living thing in a desolate, shimmering world, and it hardly looks alive itself but more like a bundle of leaves left by the wind. The leaves can be over six feet long, but the most extraordinary thing about them (just one of the extraordinary things about this tree) is that there are actually only *two* leaves, which are the only ones the tree ever produces. They never stop growing, but they become shredded into leathery strips by the desert winds and sand and look like many more leaves than just two.

Welwitschias grow where rainfall is about an inch in a year, with no rain at all some years. Their underground trunk, which is like a huge ten-foot-long turnip with a tapered end, is mainly a storage vessel for water—although it does have a woody interior and real bark. But much of the tree's water comes from the air. When dew condenses at dawn it runs down the ribbony leaves and into the roots. Atlantic fogs frequently roll over these deserts, and their moisture is also caught by the leaves. The strange conelike red flowers are pollinated by insects, and the seeds are spread by the wind. It isn't surprising to learn that this mysterious tree originated in prehistoric times and that it can live for two thousand years.

The first European to discover the welwitschia was Frederick Welwitsch, who was director of the Lisbon Botanic gardens in his adopted country of Portugal. The Portuguese government paid him to collect plants in Africa, where he explored and collected for seven years. He supplemented his income by sending exotic specimens, including cork acorns, to Sir Joseph Hooker at Kew Gardens in London. In 1860 he sent Sir Joseph a letter describing the strange plant he had found. A little later Thomas Baines sent Hooker a sketch of the welwitschia tree. Baines, a house painter who had gone to South Africa in search of adventure, joined the British army as a military artist and then became a botanical artist.

THE LEAVES CAN BE OVER SIX FEET LONG.

The tree already had an African name, which was *otji-tumbo*, meaning "Mr. Big." Welwitsch, when he described the tree, suggested it be named *tumbo*. At a meeting of the Linnaean Society, however, a jingoistic decision declared that this name was "a word with no precise application; like mumbo or jumbo." Baines's name was proposed, and the name *Welwitschia bainesii* was used for a while. Hooker himself authored a monograph on the tree, which he presented to the Linnaean Society, pointing out, he wrote, "a heap of the most curious facts regarding a single plant that has been brought to light."

Like many botanical names given to exotic foreign plants by Western botanists, *Welwitschia* doesn't do much to describe this strange tree. Certainly no more than *tumbo*! Welwitsch, although no doubt worthy of commemoration, leaves us with the name of a man we haven't heard of, to describe a tree we won't see. The Africaans name for welwitschia, *tweeblaarkanniedood*, may be as unpronounceable as our name, but at least it's descriptive. It means "two leaves that cannot die."

WILLOW

Weeping willows were not introduced to Britain until the eighteenth century, but long before, the willow trees native to Britain were associated with loss and mourning:

In such a night stood Dido with a willow in her hand
Upon the wild sea banks, and wav'd her love
To come again to Carthage

This was a reminder to the audience of Shakespeare's *Merchant of Venice* that Dido was sad in love and doomed to die.

The weeping willow was sadder still. Linnaeus named this tree, with its pendulous branches, *Salix babylonica*, commemorating the "willows" in the Bible. The Jews, exiled to Babylon, "wept when we remembered Zion [and] we hanged our harps upon the willows in the midst thereof." The weight of the heavy hanging harps supposedly pulled down the willow branches, which remained pendulant ever after. Scholars later spoiled the story by deciding that those biblical trees were most likely poplars and not willows at all, and it seems that weeping willows originated in China, not in Babylon. By then they were named, though, and Babylonian willows have wept ever since.

The exiled Napoléon spent his last years seated under a weeping willow on St. Helena, very likely weeping occasionally himself. When he died, a weeping willow was planted on his grave until his remains were moved from St. Helena to Paris. The willow tree from the site was made into snuff boxes, which were sold at the Great Exhibition in London in 1840.

Traders brought weeping willows to Europe from the Middle East sometime around the end of the seventeenth century. A romantic story about the weeping willow's introduction to England is that the poet Alexander Pope was given a gift of figs from Turkey in a basket that he took apart, planting the withies (woven willow twigs) in his garden to see if they might grow. Whether or not the story is true, there was a weeping willow in Pope's garden. When Samuel Johnson, an American clergyman, visited Pope's house in 1754 he took cuttings of the weeping willow back to America, where they soon spread. George Washington planted weeping willows in his garden at Mount Vernon.

Withies were used way back to make baskets and weave fences. A single withy, or whithe, gets its name from the Old English *withig* meaning "willow." A "willy" is also a basketlike machine for cleaning cotton. The botanical name

Willow

Salix was from the tree's Latin name. Some suggest that since the Latin *salire* means "to leap," it describes willows growing so fast they seem to "leap." The Gaelic *seileach* has a watery association (including *sail*, meaning "saliva"), and willows like damp places, often growing on stream banks.

The stems of osier willows, too, are good for baskets, especially as the natural color of their bark is sometimes yellow or red. They are popular ornamental shrubs these days, but in the past they were planted in "Sally gardens" (from their Latin name, *salix*) so their withies would be readily available for baskets, bindings, and fences. Between the clustering flexible branches were secret places that could shelter young lovers. "Down by the salley gardens my love and I did meet / She passed the salley gardens with little snow-white feet," wrote William Butler Yeats, nostalgic for a long-ago love.

Willows, or "salix" trees, contain salicylic acid, and it was long known that an infusion of willow bark could help aches and pains. In the past it was thought that since rheumatic pains came from dampness, the moisture-loving willows were created by God to cure rheumatism and other complaints. An eighteenth-century Oxfordshire clergyman, Reverened Edward Stone, gave his parishioners willow tea to cure their ague. "Many natural maladies carry their cures along with them," he wrote, and the tea did alleviate pain. But willow tea contains salicylic acid, which can damage the stomach.

A NINTH-CENTURY CHINESE GARDENER, JI-CHENG, WROTE, "A CURVING BAY OF WILLOWS IN THE MOONLIGHT CLEANSES THE SOUL."

Over a century later, in 1897, Felix Hoffman of the Bayer Company in Dusseldorf found that acetylsalicylic acid *isolated* from willow bark helped his arthritic father without irritating his stomach. The new drug was called aspirin (a name that actually came from spirea, or meadowsweet, which also contains salicylic acid). Aspirin still surprises us with newly found curative properties.

Willow wood was used in England to make springy bats for playing cricket. The charcoal from willow wood is supposed to make the best gunpowder. War aside, most often willows are part of poetry and love. A seventeenth-century Chinese gardener, Ji-Cheng, wrote, "A curving bay of willows in the moonlight cleanses the soul." Dancing girls, sway "like willows." In China willow trees were planted outside the women's part of houses. Willow trees are dioecious, meaning they are either male or female (*see* Holly). Male willows, including the most common *S. caprea* ("goat willow") give us "pussy willows" to celebrate spring for us and to propagate themselves.

Perhaps the most famous willow is that on the willow pattern plates designed in the eighteenth century in Staffordshire, England, when things Chinese were popular. The design is based on the Chinese legend of a rich man's daughter, Koong Shee, who loved her father's secretary, Chang, and refused to marry the man her father had chosen for her. On the plates, the angry father chases the lovers who are trying to escape across a bridge over which hangs a weeping willow. They make it across the bridge to an island and hide in a little house. The father and the rejected suitor catch up and burn down the house where the lovers are sleeping. Koong Shee and Chang perish, but their souls rise again and are shown as two birds flying in the sky above the willow tree.

We are reminded that just as a new live tree can sprout from seemingly dried out willow branches, so could the souls of the two lovers rise from the ashes and fly away, free as birds.

WOLLEMI PINE (AND OTHERS)

Wollemi National Park northwest of Sydney, Australia, is said to have got its name from an Aboriginal word *wollumnii*, meaning "look around you." This is just what David Noble was doing when on September 10, 1994, he and two friends stumbled across a stand of Wollemi pines.

It was as if they had come across a group of browsing dinosaurs. Noble and his companions had never seen a tree like it before. It had a strange bark, like "bubbling chocolate," and in some ways it looked more like a giant fern than a tree. They took a few leafy twigs back to Sydney's Royal Botanical garden. At first botanists thought the new tree might be related to the Chinese plum yew (*see* Yew). Even the local aborigines were unfamiliar with it. After extensive searches only two tiny groves were found, not far off from each other, growing in the deep clefts and gorges of Wollemi National Park. From the beginning their location was kept a secret, for this tree was clearly unique and quite new to science.

THEY HAD SURVIVED AND EVEN REPRODUCED WITHOUT ANY GENETIC DIVERSITY.

As more was discovered about the Wollemi pines, excitement grew. They were found to be identical to fossils of trees that had been widespread before the shape of the continents and the climate had changed, millions of years ago. It seemed impossible, but these few hundred trees were survivors of a prehistoric world. All the trees were found to be genetically identical. They had survived and even reproduced without any genetic diversity. Not only dendrologists but the rest of the scientific world as well were astonished. Diversity, it had been assumed, was essential to survival.

Today, in a startling demonstration of prehistory meeting the modern world, Wollemi pines can be "viewed" and even purchased on the Internet. They have been propagated from cuttings and from collected seeds and grow better in gentler conditions than those in which Noble and his friends found them, clinging to cliff sides and deprived of light. When conditions had been right for them, these trees had thickly covered the southern continent of Gondwana (which included modern Australia, Africa, South American, Antarctica, and India). That was about thirty million years ago.

They were given the scientific name *Wollemia nobilis*, partly for David Noble and partly for their distinguished ancestry. They turned out to be a completely new genus but related to other trees in the Araucariaceae family. Araucarias grow in Australia, New Guinea, Norfolk Island, and South America, reenforcing the idea that they once covered a single continent. The Australian araucarias never made the same horticultural hit as the monkey-puzzles in Europe, because they are less hardy.

The hoop pine is so called for its bark forming horizontal rings or hoops around the trunk. Its botanical name is *Araucaria cunninghamii* after a Scottish botanist Allen Cunningham, who explored New Zealand and Australia. He was offered the position of "colonial botanist" but turned it down in favor of his younger brother Richard. Richard didn't live long. He left a botanizing party to go exploring on his own, became lost in the bush, and finally wandered into an Aborigine camp. The Aboriginal natives were terrified by his delirious behavior and killed him. Allen then accepted the post he had turned down but died shortly afterward of tuberculosis.

The bunya pine, *A. bidwillia*, is for John Carne Bidwell, commissioner of Crown lands. He, too, got lost in the bush and died there.

The Norfolk Island pine, *A. heterophylla* ("different leaved"), is most often seen in American supermarkets, sold as a perfect little indoor Christmas tree. It won't survive cold temperatures and if you keep it for too many Christmases you may have to make a hole in your ceiling. In the wild it can reach two hundred feet high. Norfolk Island is a volcanic island about a thousand miles northeast of Sydney. In the eighteenth and nineteenth centuries the island served as a penal colony for Australia (once a penal colony itself).

The Kauri pine, *Agathis australis*, of New Zealand is believed by the Maori people to possess a spirit of its own and to be related to humans. Before felling a Kauri tree the Maoris hold solemn ceremonies and offer prayers to the tree. Some of these huge trees are believed to be two thousand years old, deserving, it surely seems, to be venerated.

YEW

Lovers of yews (but not lovers of taxes) are sometimes called taxophiles. The botanical name of the yew is *Taxus*, probably connected with "toxic." The Greek word for the poison used for smearing lethal arrows was *toxicon* and most often these arrows were poisoned with yew. Indeed, in one of the celestial squabblings so common between the Greek gods, Artemis used yew to get even with Niobe, who had rashly boasted that she was more fecund than Artemis's mother, Leto. Arrows soaked in yew poison successfully dispatched Niobe's seven children.

Yew branches were used to make bows as they were both strong and very flexible, and the Greek *toxon* means "bow." The typical yew bow was about five feet long. In Chaucer's *Canterbury Tales* the archer is called "yewmanly." In 1415, at Agincourt, Henry V's archers were able to decisively defeat the much larger heavily armored French army by shooting them with arrows from afar. One of the reasons muskets were later used in war was not simply because they were better but because good yew bows became scarcer as slow-growing yew trees were used up and not replaced. For distance and accuracy a good bowman could outshine a musketeer, and for the time it took to fire one musket ball a bowman could let off six deadly arrows.

The yew was sacred to Hecate, queen of the underworld, and in postclassical times the poison was thought to be used by witches. Shakespeare's witches in *Macbeth* made a poetic but lethal brew, including "Gall of goat and slips of Yew / Sliver'd in the moon's eclipse." Yews were often planted in churchyards and many scholars think that they were ancient sacred trees planted *before* the Christian churches were built and that the churches took over the holy site of the tree. Because they grew among gravestones, some thought that the spirit of the dead might come up through their roots into the tree itself. Wrote Tennyson in *In Memoriam*:

> Old yew, which graspest at the stones
> That name the underlying dead,
> Thy fibers net the dreamless head,
> Thy roots are wrapped about the bones.

There was a tradition, dating from the Greek writer Dioscorides's time, that whoever fell asleep under the shade of a yew would die. Sixteenth-century herbalist John Gerard wrote that this wasn't true, and he and "divers of my schoolfellows" had often slept under yew trees "without any hurt at all and that not at one time but many times." Even so, yews were considered gloomy, dangerous trees.

All parts of yews are poisonous except the bright red (sometimes yellow) *aril*, or fleshy cup, surrounding the seed. Perhaps unsurprising to American gardeners, deer seem to eat yew with impunity (as they do rhododendron and laurel, which are toxic to most creatures). Still, we plant lots of yews in our gardens and curse the deer.

> WHOEVER FELL ASLEEP UNDER THE SHADE OF A YEW WOULD DIE.

The European yew is *Taxus baccata*, meaning "having berries." It isn't as hardy as the Japanese yew, *T. cuspidata* ("with stiff points"), which was introduced in the mid-nineteenth century by Dr. Robert Hall, who also introduced the pestiferous Japanese honeysuckle. Both European and Japanese yews have been hybridized hundreds of times, achieving many variations of foliage and form. Fastigiate yews (with branches tapering toward a pointed top) descend from just one tapering tree, spotted and dug up by an Irish farmer of County Fermanagh in 1780.

The yew native to the Pacific Northwest of the United States is the *T. brevifolia* ("short leaved"). Although Native Americans used it for bows and medicine, modern loggers considered it a "weed tree" until in the 1960s a substance in the bark, taxol, was discovered to be a powerful anticancer drug. The Pacific yew was "harvested" for its bark, and it seemed that supply could not keep up with demand, since each patient needed the bark of ten two-hundred-year-old trees for one treatment. Environmentalists predicted the trees would soon be extinct. Others argued that it was heartless to deny effective medical treatment to desperate cancer patients. Bristol Myers-Squibb had a monopoly on collecting the bark, which had to be stripped off the trees, and there were bitter arguments, until taxol was found to be available in yew leaves, too, and eventually could be made synthetically. Yews grow large so slowly it is hard to replace mature trees. If left alone, they continue to grow for thousands of years.

There are other handsome trees similar to and once classified as yews, notably the California nutmeg, or *Torreya californica*, named for John Torrey whose father was a prison official. One of the inmates, Amos Eaton, imprisoned for fraud, taught young John Torrey to love botany—evidently visiting regulations were less strict than now. Both Torrey and Eaton were important American botanists. When Torrey died in 1873 a sprig of *Torreya* (similar to yew foliage) was placed on his coffin, following an ancient custom of placing yew leaves in graves with the dead. This tree is no relation to the spice nutmeg, although its fruits do look a bit similar. The plum yew, *Cephalotaxus* (from the Greek *kephale*, "a head"), whose flowers are born in "heads," has similar fruit. This tree is sometimes called a cowtail pine for its tasseled foliage.

In Japan the yew tree is called *ichii*, or "tree of God." The yew's common name seems to be connected with the German *ewig*, "eternal." Large old yews are rare, but there are probably more yew *shrubs* in the world than ever before. Almost all landscaping includes them and they can be clipped, eaten by deer, or neglected, and still they will survive. If left alone, they would become trees, although that might take a very long time. Maybe the neat suburban gardens they populate as shrubs and hedges might one day become eternal forests, and our houses mere memories.

FURTHER READING

Bartram, John. *The Correspondence of John Bartram*. Edited by Edmund and Dorothy Smith Berkeley (University Press of Florida, 1992).

Bartram, William. *Travels of William Bartram*. Edited by Mark VanDoren (Dover, 1928).

Blunt, Wilfrid. *The Compleat Naturalist: A Life of Linnaeus* (Collins, 1971).

Campbell-Culver, Maggie. *The Origins of Plants* (Headline Book Publishing, 2001).

Dalby, Andrew. *Dangerous Tastes* (British Museum Press, 2000).

Dampier, William. *New Voyage around the World, 1697* (Dover, 1968).

———. *Voyage to New Holland, 1699* (Sutton, 1981).

David, Abbé Armand. *Abbé David's Diary*. Translated by Helen M. Fox (Harvard University Press, 1949).

Duval, Marguerite. *The King's Garden*. Translated by Annette Tomarken and Claudine Cowen (University Press of Virginia, 1982.)

Ellacombe, Henry N. *The Plant-Lore and Garden-Craft of Shakespeare* (Edward Arnold, 1896).

Gothein, Marie Luise. A History of Garden Art (2 vols.) (Hacker Art Books, 1979).

Hageneder, Fred. *The Meaning of Trees* (Chronicle Books, 2005).

Harris, Marjorie. *Botanica North America* (Harper Resource, 2003).

Haughton, Claire Shaver. *Green Immigrants* (Harcourt Brace Jovanovich, 1978).

Jefferson, Thomas. *Thomas Jefferson's Garden Book*. Annotated by Edwin Morris Betts (American Philosophical Society, 1944).

Ji Cheng. *The Craft of Gardens*. Translated by Alison Hardie (Yale University Press, 1988).

Kalm, Peter. *Peter Kalm's Travels in North America*. Edited by Adolph B. Benson. (Dover, 1964).

Lewington, Anna, and Edward Parker. *Ancient Trees* (Collins and Brown, 1999).

Mabey, Richard. *Flora Britannica* (Chatto and Windus, 1997).

Martin, Laura C. *The Folklore of Trees and Shrubs* (Globe Pequot Press, 1992).

Moldenke, Harold N., and L. Alma. *Plants of the Bible* (Dover, 1952).

Musgrave, Toby, and Will Musgrave. *An Empire of Plants* (Cassell, 2000).

Pakenham, Thomas. *Meetings with Remarkable Trees* (Random House, 1996).

Paterson, Wilma. *A Fountain of Gardens* (Overlook Press, 1992).

Peattie, Donald Culross. *A Natural History of Trees* (2 vols.) (Bonanza Books, 1963).

Phythian, J. Ernest. *Trees in Nature, Myth and Art* (Methuen, 1907).

Plotnik, Arthur. *The Urban Tree Book* (Three Rivers Press, 2000).

Rackham Oliver. *The Last Forest* (Dent, 1989).

Roberts, Jonathan. *The Origins of Fruit and Vegetables* (Universe Publishing, 2001).

Rupp, Rebecca. *Red Oaks and Black Birches* (Storey Communications, 1990).

Sponberg, Stephen A. *A Reunion of Trees* (Harvard University Press, 1990).

Stuart, David. *Dangerous Garden* (Francis Lincoln, 2004).

Thacker, Christopher. *The History of Gardens* (University of California Press, 1979).

Tudge, Colin. *The Secret Life of Trees* (Allen Lane, 2005).

Valder, Peter. *The Garden Plants of China* (Weidenfeld and Nicolson, 1999).

Vitale, Alice Thomas. *Leaves in Myth, Magic and Medicine* (Stewart, Tabori and Chang, 1997).

White, Gilbert. *The Natural Selborne* (MacMillan, 1911).

Whone, Herbert. *Touch Wood* (Smith Settle, 1990).

INDEX

Index

Index

Index

Index

Index